The Chinese Birdcage

Heleen Mees

The Chinese Birdcage

How China's Rise Almost Toppled the West

Heleen Mees
Brooklyn, USA

ISBN 978-1-137-58888-3   ISBN 978-1-137-58886-9 (eBook)
DOI 10.1057/978-1-137-58886-9

Library of Congress Control Number: 2016949262

© The Editor(s) (if applicable) and The Author(s) 2016
This work is subject to copyright. All rights are solely and exclusively licensed by the Publisher, whether the whole or part of the material is concerned, specifically the rights of translation, reprinting, reuse of illustrations, recitation, broadcasting, reproduction on microfilms or in any other physical way, and transmission or information storage and retrieval, electronic adaptation, computer software, or by similar or dissimilar methodology now known or hereafter developed.
The use of general descriptive names, registered names, trademarks, service marks, etc. in this publication does not imply, even in the absence of a specific statement, that such names are exempt from the relevant protective laws and regulations and therefore free for general use.
The publisher, the authors and the editors are safe to assume that the advice and information in this book are believed to be true and accurate at the date of publication. Neither the publisher nor the authors or the editors give a warranty, express or implied, with respect to the material contained herein or for any errors or omissions that may have been made.

Cover illustration: © Tamara Kulikova / Alamy Stock Photo

Printed on acid-free paper

This Palgrave Macmillan imprint is published by Springer Nature
The registered company is Nature America Inc. New York

To understand the origins of the global financial crisis, one should not read Michael Lewis' *The Big Short* but Arthur Lewis' *Economic Development with Unlimited Supplies of Labor* instead.

Contents

1 The Chinese Birdcage — 1

2 Western Triumphalism — 11

3 China as the World's Factory — 21

4 Housing Bubbles Across the Western Hemisphere — 33

5 The Global Financial Crisis — 55

6 The Economic Fallout — 75

7 Unlimited Supplies of Labor — 89

8 China's Economic Development — 99

9 Corporate Cash Piles and Falling Interest Rates — 115

10 The Shortfall in Demand	133
11 Piketty Reconsidered	163
12 What Lies Ahead?	175
Index	191

List of Figures

Fig. 4.1	Loose-fitting monetary policy	36
Fig. 4.2	Household debt as share of disposable income versus house price 2000–2007	42
Fig. 4.3	Global income growth from 1988 to 2008	46
Fig. 7.1	Capitalist surplus with unlimited labor supplies	93
Fig. 7.2	Capitalist surplus with unlimited labor supplies	94
Fig. 10.1	Adjusted labor income shares in developed economies, Germany, the USA and Japan, 1970–2010. The adjusted labor income share makes an adjustment for the self-employed	134
Fig. 10.2	Labor share of non-farm business in the USA	138
Fig. 10.3	Construction employment versus house price 2000–2007	159
Fig. 10.4	Manufacturing employment versus house price 2000–2007	159
Fig. 10.5	Exports versus house price 2000–2007	160
Fig. 10.6	Unit labor costs versus house price 2000–2007	160

Introduction

The festivities for the celebration of the 25th anniversary of the fall of the Berlin Wall in 2014 were markedly subdued. The countries in the West were still reeling from the havoc caused by the global financial crisis. The single European currency, which was meant to seal the European unification, had come under such severe strain that it might just as well collapse. Around the globe, populists both on the left as well as the right scored resounding victories, shattering the political center and rendering some nations virtually ungovernable. Instead of forging ever expanding political unions, national borders were increasingly being questioned—not for being cast too narrow but for being cast too wide or being too porous.

The contrast with a quarter century before could not have been greater. The night that the Berlin Wall was brought down, in December 1989, people were dancing in the streets. Western triumphalism over the dawn of a new era knew no boundaries. The belief in free market capitalism was so high that the then American president, Bill Clinton, told his Chinese counterpart Jiang Zemin in 1997 that trade between the two countries would lead to a spirit of freedom—read democracy in China—as inevitable as the fall of the Berlin Wall. That's also the reason China was put on a fast track to becoming a member of the World Trade Organization.

While the West was smarting over the bursting of the dot-com bubble, and, more critically, over the attacks on the World Trade Center and the

Pentagon, in December 2001, China quietly became a member of the World Trade Organization. China's economy grew so briskly that 25 years after the fall of the Berlin Wall, which also marked the 25th anniversary of the bloody suppression of the student protests at Tiananmen Square, China passed the United States as the world's leading economic power.[1]

Although trade with China exploded after the trade barriers were taken down, it did not transform China into a democratic paradise, as President Clinton had assumed. Present-day China has little resemblance to the communist bulwark it was under Mao Zedong, where every private initiative was quenched. However, the suppression of dissenting voices under the leadership of Xi Jinping leaves no misunderstanding that China is far from a free society. People in China are free to compete, start enterprises, and become billionaires. They are free to challenge the authority of the Communist Party of China privately but not so much publicly. The state-run media are under increasing pressure to toe the Communist Party's line and act as its mouthpiece.

Instead of transforming China into a liberal democracy, as Francis Fukuyama had prophesized in *The End of History and the Last Man* (1992), China's entry into the World Trade Organization sort of wrecked rich countries' economies and subverted Western democracies. So what went wrong? Does not Econ 101 teach us that international trade is a win-win situation for all countries involved? Even if in the short term, some people will gain and others will suffer, economic orthodoxy has it that the gains of the winners from free trade, correctly measured, work out to exceed the losses of the losers. While, strictly speaking, trade with China did follow standard economic theory, things at large did not quite turn out that way. China proved too big a chunk for the world economy to simply digest.

With China's accession to the World Trade Organization, almost a billion workers were added to the global economy. Many of these workers not so long ago lived off a dollar a day. So it was foremost very cheap labor. Just when China made its (re)appearance on the global stage, the spread of low-cost computing and the Internet broke down the old geographic boundaries between labor markets. Not only manufacturing jobs became thus susceptible to outsourcing but service jobs as well. Within no time, China became the world's factory, and India, thanks to its people's fluency in English, became the world's back office.

---

[1] China poised to pass US as world's leading economic power this year, *The Financial Times*, April 30, 2014.

Western companies moved production facilities and offices to China and India or outsourced work to companies in those countries. Think not only of the iPhones and iPads that are made in China by Foxconn but also of espresso machines, barbecue grills, sneakers, apparel, and Christmas decoration. For multinational companies like Apple, the situation was ideal. Apple was able to pay its workers Third-World wages while selling its products at First-World prices. No wonder that corporate profits skyrocketed.

Nobel laureate Arthur Lewis described this dynamic eloquently in his 1954 essay "Economic Development with Unlimited Supplies of Labor." The implication of unlimited supplies of labor is that the capitalist sector can hire ever more workers without the need to raise wages. All that employers have to pay is a subsistence wage that keeps the workers alive. Under these conditions, any gains in labor productivity do not translate into higher wages, as the mainstream economic theory has it, but in higher profits instead. Lewis wrote his model for an emerging economy and a closed economy for that matter, however, in a globalized world, the effects of unlimited supplies of labor spill over to advanced economies as well.

Because of China's entry into the global economy, the new labor-market-clearing real wage was lowered. In the USA, labor's share of national income decreased between 1980 and 2013 with 9 percentage points, while over that same period, profits as a share of income increased by roughly the same amount. That happened not only in the USA but in virtually every advanced economy, like Germany, the UK, and Japan. Of course, labor's decline did not hit all workers equally hard. The pain was disproportionately felt by workers at the lower and middle ranks of the labor market, those who are deemed the losers of globalization. No wonder these workers now revolt.

Arthur Lewis' model assumes that the higher return on capital, the so-called capitalist surplus, is reinvested in the economy and that the increase in the capital stock, in turn, leads to the creation of new jobs. The process thus becomes self-sustaining and leads in emerging economies to modernization and economic development. That is indeed what happened in China, where both the corporate sector as well as the government invests heavily in roads, public transportation, and real estate. While China's investment-led growth model has come under fierce criticism from Western economists, it entirely makes sense as long as China is still endowed with unlimited supplies of labor.

But that's not what happened in rich countries. American multinationals, just like their European counterparts, have been hoarding billions of dollars and euros in cash. Publicly listed companies in Europe, the Middle East, and Africa in 2014 had amassed $1.3 trillion in cash reserves, a 50 percent increase compared to 2007, and just shy of the $1.5 trillion in corporate cash piles held by US non-financial companies. And do not take piles of cash too literally. It is not that the corporate cash is stashed away in bank vaults. It is mostly invested in low-risk securities like US Treasuries instead.

Amid the huge demand for US Treasuries and other government bonds, not only from big Western multinationals but also from China and oil-exporting countries, long-term interest rates reached new lows by the mid-2000s, fuelling housing bubbles in virtually every country in the Western hemisphere. Many households took out second mortgages and spent the cash handouts on consumer goods, thus masking the fall in real wages. We know all too well what happened next. Once the housing bubbles began to lose steam in the summer of 2007, the mortgage losses mounted, starting with subprime mortgages but soon affecting prime mortgages just as well.

Within a matter of months, governments had to shore up systematically important banks as the entire financial system teetered on the verge of collapse. Households have been nursing their financial wounds ever since. But while labor's share continued to fall in the aftermath of the global financial crisis, corporate profits soared to new record highs. Multinationals are holding onto more cash now than before the global financial crisis struck.

According to Unilever chief executive Paul Polman, companies are not investing because consumers are not spending. The same goes for other companies, as research by Olivier Blanchard and Larry Summers shows. Blanchard and Summers concluded in a 1994 empirical study that fundamentals (i.e., consumer demand) rather than the cost of capital drive corporate investment. Hence, the lack of demand creates the lack of potential supply. This is precisely the inverse of Say's Law, which holds that supply creates its own demand.

The shortfall of consumer demand is not only the result of the financial crisis and the housing bubbles that burst, forcing households to cut spending in order to shore up their balance sheets. The lack of demand is just as much the result of the fall of labor's share of national income. So it is not just a cyclical problem, as Keynesians tend to argue, but a structural problem as well. China and India offer little solace in terms of consumer demand. Both countries are still characterized by a rather schizophrenic demand for high-end consumer products on the one hand, such as Ferraris and Hermès Birkin bags, and basic commodities like food and energy on the other hand. There is not a solid Chinese or Indian middle class yet with corresponding consumption patterns to compensate for the lackluster consumer demand in advanced economies, even though the Chinese middle class is expanding rapidly.

Larry Summers has warned against a prolonged period of economic stagnation, or secular stagnation. Consumers have too little money to spend while big companies do not know where to stash their cash. What is more obvious than to increase the corporate income tax and use the revenues to bolster labor, that is, transferring income from the capitalist sector to labor? Not simply by way of cash handouts but in a way that reinforces labor's position, including education, universal health care, child care and paid sick leave.

Even if China eventually runs out of its surplus of workers, and the International Monetary Fund reckons that will happen somewhere between 2020 and 2025, rich countries are still not out of the woods. China is quickly moving up the technology ladder. If China manages to close the innovation gap, trade with China will yield net economic losses for advanced economies. Westerners tend to think of China as a giant sweatshop. In reality, the country is at the forefront of medicine, hi-tech and computing. China has the world's fastest supercomputer, Chinese scientists have developed the lightest material ever known and China is also at the forefront of human genome mapping.

It is a fallacy to think that a country that is not governed by way of a liberal democracy cannot be a beacon of innovation and intellectual progress, as Bill Clinton tried to impress on Jiang Zemin back in 1998. The planner's hand has served the Middle Kingdom well, judging by the hundreds of millions of Chinese that have been lifted out of extreme poverty in the past three decades. Not without reason, China's rise has been deemed a growth miracle. And for all the gloom about China's economic prospects, it is too early to tell that the miracle has run its course yet.

The design of this book is as follows. Chapter 1 describes the economic transformation under the leadership of Deng Xiaoping that started in 1978. It juxtaposes the economic reforms in former East Bloc countries and China and shows how resistance in China's bureaucratic apparatus to reform was overcome. Chapter 2 shows how in the West, the free market doctrine became ubiquitous after the election of Margaret Thatcher and Ronald Reagan. In the euphoria after the fall of the Berlin Wall, free market economics was deemed a cure-all, not only economically but also politically.

In Chapter 3, we show how China, after its accession to the World Trade Organization, quickly became the world's factory. China's growing exports came with piles of foreign exchange reserves that were predominantly invested in US Treasuries and agency bonds. Chapter 4 discusses the housing bubbles across the Western hemisphere in the early 2000s, the rise in household debt associated with that, the income inequality within and between countries, and the electoral success of populist politicians.

Chapters 5 and 6 are devoted to the global financial crisis and the economic fallout. Chapter 7 lays out Arthur Lewis' framework for economic development with unlimited supplies of labor, and Chapter 8 describes China's economic development against the backdrop of Arthur Lewis' framework. Chapter 9 discusses the global imbalances and rising corporate stockpiles that contributed to low interest rates, which fuelled housing bubbles across the Western hemisphere. Chapter 10 looks at the use of the capitalist surplus and the shortfall of demand flowing from labor's declining share of national income, arguing that the shortfall is structural rather than cyclical.

Chapter 11 puts Thomas Piketty's finding that the rate of return on capital historically has always exceeded the rate of economic growth, giving rise to ever expanding dynastic wealth, in a new context. It argues that the relative labor shortages following World War I and World War II and the Russian Revolution in 1917 emboldened workers and eroded the returns of the capitalists. Since 1980, the process has gone into reverse. Chapter 11 also shines a light on the prospects of labor amid the rise of the robots. Chapter 12 discusses what lies ahead for rich countries and China.

Heleen Mees
Brooklyn, USA

CHAPTER 1

The Chinese Birdcage

BIRDS IN A CAGE

Zhao Ziyang was premier under Deng Xiaoping when the student protests broke out in 1989 in Tiananmen Square. Zhao was a reformist leader and the architect of the model for transforming the socialist system via gradual economic reform. He successfully introduced the Special Economic Zones in China's coastal provinces to attract foreign investment. Because Zhao showed too much understanding and sympathy for the students at Tiananmen Square, he was purged from office in June 1989 and placed under house arrest in Beijing until his death in early 2005. In 2009, Zhao's secret diaries were published in English. In *Prisoner of the State* (2009), he describes how the hardliners in the Chinese politburo envisioned a birdcage economy, in which the centrally planned economy was the cage and the birds were the market economy. The basic idea is that dealing with the economy is like raising birds: you cannot hold the birds too tightly, or else, they will suffocate, nor can you let them free since they will fly away, so the best way is to raise them in a cage.

REFORM AND OPENING UP

In 1978, after the ruinous reign of Mao Zedong and the ousting of the Gang of Four Maoist faction, income per capita in China amounted to just over half of income per capita in India.[1] It was less than a tenth of income per capita in Poland, and only a fortieth or 2.5 percent of that in the USA. Not surprisingly, there was widespread support among the elite in China for the economic reforms that would ultimately turn the world's most populous nation into an economic superpower. As the preeminent leader of China, Deng Xiaoping, whose official titles included Chairman of the Central Advisory Commission of the Communist Party of China, led the push for economic reform. Deng's closest collaborators during the initial stage of economic reforms were Zhao Ziyang, who in 1980 became premier, and Hu Yaobang, who in 1981 became party chairman.

Under the leadership of Deng Xiaoping, China opened up to the outside world. Egalitarianism, so viciously propagated under Mao Zedong and the Gang of Four, became all of a sudden obsolete. Mao had advocated an ideal of classless, equal development, in which no individual or segment of society was to advance at the expense of another.[2] While Mao had seen himself as the great leveler, the Communist Party now expressly encouraged Chinese citizens to seek personal wealth. "HAVE NO FEAR OF BECOMING PROSPEROUS" read one of the many headlines to that effect in a Chinese newspaper in the early 1980s. The Communist Party organized campaigns to celebrate the so-called ten-thousand-yuan households, that is, households earning more than 30 times the national average.

In a historic interview with Mike Wallace on CBS *60 Minutes* in September 1986, Deng laid out his view on communism. In the words of Deng, the communist society is based on material abundance, not on pauperism. In the eyes of Deng, to get rich was no sin. After all, only when material abundance is realized, the principle of a communist society—that is, "from each according to his ability, to each according to his needs"—could be applied.[3] During the interview, Deng emphasized the need to develop "productive forces" first, which would allow China to keep increasing the material wealth of society, steadily improve the life of the people, and that way, create the material conditions for a communist society. No longer were state-owned enterprises glorified and private

---

[1] GDP per capita in 1980 measured in Purchasing Power Parity (PPP), International Monetary Fund.

[2] Orville Schell, *To Get Rich Is Glorious*, Pantheon Books, New York, 1984.

[3] It seems that Deng Xiaoping never actually said "To get rich is glorious," although Wallace's questions suggest that he did and Deng doesn't deny it.

businesses excoriated. As Deng famously proclaimed, "it doesn't matter whether the cat is black or white, as long as it catches mice."

The Third Plenum of the Central Committee in December 1978 in Beijing laid out the groundwork for the economic transformation of China, known as *gaige kaifang* or "reform and opening up." The transformation was carried out in two stages. The first stage, in the late 1970s and early 1980s, involved the freeing up from the collective control of the agriculture sector, the opening up of the country to foreign investment, and giving entrepreneurs the opportunity to start businesses. Under the so-called household responsibility system, rural land was divided into private plots. Until then, all work was done collectively with commonly owned tools. Individual peasants were just pawns in the collective system with no responsibility of their own.[4] After the reform and opening up, households were able to keep the revenue after paying a share to the state, effectively restoring the link between effort and reward.[5]

The Communist Party was very deliberate about how to introduce capitalism to the people. Special Economic Zones for foreign investment were introduced in the southern coastal region near the cities Shanghai and Guangdong, purportedly because the Chinese in the south possessed a more entrepreneurial spirit than the Chinese in the north did. These Special Economic Zones successfully tested the market economy and new institutions and became role models for the rest of the country to follow. The boom in trade and export-related production in the Special Economic Zones shifted the leading edge of Chinese growth southward. A dual price system was introduced, in which state-owned industries were allowed to sell any production above the plan quota, and private businesses were allowed to operate for the first time since the communist takeover in 1949.[6]

The economic reforms not only transformed the streetscape in big cities like Beijing but in the countryside as well. Orville Schell cites the anthropologist Jack Potter: "When I first visited the Zengbu brigade there [in Guangdong province], in 1979, there was virtually nothing in the market. When I came back in 1981, things had started to pick up. But when I returned in 1983 I couldn't believe what I saw. There were hundreds of people selling things. There were tanks of live fish, and piles of fruits and

---

[4] Schell (1984).
[5] Loren Brandt and Thomas G. Rawski, "China's Great Transformation," in Brandt, Loren; Rawski, G. Thomas, *China's Great Transformation*, Cambridge University Press, 2008.
[6] Brandt and Rawski (2008).

vegetables heaped up everywhere. You could buy Coca-Cola, Budweiser beer, and foreign cigarettes at private shops. The prosperity was impressive." When Schell in 1984 had the chance to visit a rural market town in the southern province Guangdong himself, the private enterprises he saw there made the free markets of Beijing and other northern cities seem like a sideshow.[7]

The second stage of reform, in the late 1980s and 1990s, involved the privatization and outsourcing of much state-owned enterprises and the removal of price controls, protectionist policies, and regulations. An important element was decentralization, which created room for provincial leaders to experiment with privatization and ways to increase economic growth. The economic reform program initially brought about bouts of inflation, which reputedly contributed to the 1989 student revolts.

Party chairman Hu Yaobang died in April 1989. The day before his funeral, some 100,000 students marched on to Tiananmen Square. What began as a spontaneous public mourning for Hu evolved into nationwide protests supporting political reform and demanding an end to corruption, ultimately leading to the Tiananmen Square protests of 1989. Following the government's bloody suppression of the 1989 protests, Zhao Ziyang, who had succeeded Hu in 1987 as the party's top leader, was placed under house arrest. He was not seen in public anymore until his death in 2005. In the eyes of the Communist Party's elders, Zhao had shown too much sympathy for the students in Tiananmen Square.

Despite the political upheavals, Deng remained firmly committed to economic liberalization. During his Southern Tour in 1992, Deng Xiaoping famously proclaimed: "Let some people get rich first." Deng, who had officially retired just a few months before, embarked on his Southern Tour to crush the resistance of the left wing of the Communist Party against further economic reforms.[8] The Southern Tour is seen as the source of Deng's exhortation "Let some people get rich first," but Deng had said the same before in his interview with Mike Wallace for CBS's *60 Minutes* in September 1986, and before that, it had already been published in Deng Xiaoping's *Selected Works* in 1983.

---

[7] Schell (1984).

[8] Deng officially retired in 1992 but he remained China's preeminent leader until his death in February 1997.

Private businesses grew, and with them, the incentive for a lot of money to change hands. Progressive advocates such as the dissident Bao Tong argued that Deng Xiaoping with those words knowingly ushered in an era of rampant corruption in China.[9] According to Bao, Deng must have understood very well that certain groups, that is, the party elite, would be best positioned to take advantage of the new opportunities. Other Chinese intellectuals, however, have argued that Deng's exhortation was necessary because China's entrepreneurial class, with memories of the Cultural Revolution still fresh, loathed getting rich. Back then, anyone who attempted to make money was at risk of being labeled a counterrevolutionary and sentenced to a labor camp.

A more likely explanation is that Deng Xiaoping realized early on that it would be impossible to elevate the more than 1 billion Chinese simultaneously from poverty—as Mao Zedong had set out to do but had miserably failed at. Therefore, it was imperative to let some people get rich first so the others could follow.

After Deng's resignation in 1992 and his death in 1997, a new generation of pro-reform political leaders took the helm of the Communist Party. Jiang Zemin and Zhu Rongji continued the path of economic liberalization laid out by Deng. Between 1995 and 2005, close to 100,000 firms with ¥11.4 trillion ($1.8 trillion) worth of assets were privatized, comprising two-thirds of China's state-owned enterprises and state assets, making China's privatization the largest in the world.[10] The state-owned enterprises' share of industrial output and total industrial employment declined from 50 percent and 60 percent, respectively, in 1998 to 27 percent and 20 percent, respectively, in 2010.[11]

Two cities were the breeding ground for the policy of privatization, Zhucheng, near Beijing, and Shunde, in Guangdong province. In 1993, they started to privatize many of their companies.[12] These were the first attempts to change the state's relationship with its enterprises. At first,

---

[9] "How Deng Xiaoping Helped Create a Corrupt China," *The New York Times*, June 3, 2015.

[10] Gan, J., (2009), "Privatization in China: Experiences and Lessons," *China's Emerging Financial Markets: Challenges and Opportunities* (J. Barth, J. Tatom, and G. Yago, 2008 eds.), The Milken Institute Series on Financial Innovation and Economic Growth.

[11] Sarah Tong & Huang Yanjie, China's State-owned Enterprises in the Post-Crisis Era: Development and Dilemma, 694 EAI Background Brief 7, National University of Singapore, 2012.

[12] "Capitalism confined," *The Economist*, September 3, 2011.

Shunde and Zhucheng turned their firms over to employees. In 1997, again before a broader shift in national policy, the two began selling companies directly to existing managements. Early signs of success led to new rules on the ownership of companies in 1995. In 1997, the State Council approved a big shift of ownership from the central government to municipalities with the explicit goal of expediting privatizations.

These changes laid the groundwork for the dramatic privatization efforts in the late 1990s of Zhu Rongji, the then prime minister, that led to the remaking of China's economy. However, in spite of undertaking the largest privatization in the world, China was, in 2015, still home to 150,000 state groups, which control $17 trillion in assets and employ more than 35 million people.[13] As these state-owned enterprises produce returns far lower than their private peers, their privatization is often seen as key to revitalizing the economy.

Shock Therapy Versus Gradualism

As the Eastern Bloc crumbled following the fall of the Berlin Wall in 1989, many of the post-communist states underwent so-called shock therapy to transition from a centrally planned to a market economy. Shock therapy, which is also dubbed the Big Bang approach, includes the sudden release of price and currency controls, withdrawal of state subsidies, trade liberalization within a country, and usually also large-scale privatization of previously public-owned assets. Proponents of shock therapy argue that speed is of the essence because the establishment of democracy creates a "window of opportunity." The proponents of shock therapy suggest that during this "honeymoon period," governments will adopt reforms as fast as possible.

The results of shock therapy in the post-communist states have been equivocal at best. Some countries that used shock therapy (such as Poland and the Czech Republic) did well, but others (such as Russia and Bulgaria) did not fare well at all. While Russian per capita income was 65 percent higher than that in Poland in the early 1990s, it took Poland only five years to surpass Russia. In 1990, average income in Bulgaria exceeded average income in Poland, but these days, Bulgaria veers more toward China with an average income that is 35 percent below average income in

---

[13] "China cautiously embraces privatization of state-owned enterprises," *The Financial Times*, September 25, 2015.

Poland.[14] Russia's fire sale of state assets far below the actual market value of the assets under pressure from the USA, the International Monetary Fund, and World Bank, created a powerful class of Russian oligarchs who hid billions of dollars in private Swiss bank accounts rather than investing in the Russian economy.[15]

The bottom-up approach of the reforms promoted by Deng, in contrast to the top-down approach of the *perestroika* in the former Soviet Union, is considered an important factor contributing to the success of China's economic transition.[16] The gradualism of Deng's approach is probably of even greater significance. The argument for gradualism is that an appropriate sequencing of reforms provides successes to build upon, thus creating platforms for further reforms.

In China, the successful de-collectivization of the agricultural sector generated the support that was needed for further reforms. Thanks to the introduction of the household responsibility system, farmers could claim the fruits of any extra effort they did for themselves. The output in the agricultural sector quickly expanded, leading to higher energy levels in a population that earlier had suffered from chronic under-nutrition. Farm labor productivity increased so rapidly that millions of villagers began looking for outside employment.[17]

Not only did the Deng administration carry out the economic transition in stages, stretching out over more than two decades, as mentioned before, Deng also ordained that the party should allow "some people and some regions" to become prosperous first. As Deng explained in his interview with Mike Wallace: "To get rich in a socialist society means prosperity for the entire people. We permit some people and some regions to become prosperous first, for the purpose of achieving common prosperity faster." Deng Xiaoping thus created the conditions for economic growth that could feed on itself and become self-sustaining, much like Arthur Lewis envisaged in his essay *Economic Development with Unlimited Supplies of Labor* (1954).

The gradual transitioning of the Chinese economy from a Soviet-style planned economy to a socialist market economy resulted in a 90 percent

---

[14] GDP per capita measured in PPP, International Monetary Fund.

[15] Joseph Stiglitz, *Globalization and Its Discontents*, Penguin, 2003.

[16] Susan L. Shirk, *The Political Logic of Economic Reform in China*, University of California, Berkeley, 1993.

[17] Brandt and Rawski (2008).

decrease in the share of people living in deep poverty between 1990 and 2010, that is, living off less than $1.25 a day.[18] This result is in sharp contrast to the economic shock therapy that the USA, the International Monetary Fund, and the World Bank advocated for former Eastern Bloc countries. The shock therapy led in some instances to a more than tenfold increase in the poverty rate in countries like Bulgaria.[19] The old communist system, which had provided most people in the former Eastern Bloc with a reasonable standard of living and certainty, had all of a sudden vanished without much else to take its place.

Reform in a Centrally Planned Economy

China's strategy of economic reform without political reform has been surprisingly successful—surprisingly, as liberal economists tend to think of communist political institutions as hostile to innovation and not conducive to economic growth. Although Deng Xiaoping never articulated his political strategy of economic reform, his actions show that he chose to retain the traditional communist political institutions and bureaucracy.[20] He did, however, lay out a political reform agenda to replace the personality-driven, patriarchal rule under Mao Zedong with a system governed by rules, clear lines of authority, and collective decision-making institutions.

Deng decided to keep the traditional communist institutions largely intact, and the bureaucrats that had previously served under Mao were now tasked with the implementation of the economic reform policies. Thanks in no small part to the success of the household responsibility system, which rapidly raised farm labor productivity and nutrition levels, bureaucratic support for economic reforms increased exponentially over the years. The notion that communist bureaucracies are so obstinately attached to central planning that they block any attempts to change proved false.[21]

China's political system of gradualism also allowed widespread experimentation and regional variation within broad guidelines set by the central leadership. This experimentation encouraged local officials to develop strategies whose success might attract high-level attention and also allowed

[18] Poverty & Equity Databank, World Bank.
[19] *Id.*
[20] Shirk (1993).
[21] *Id.*

national leaders to "play to the provinces" by assembling coalitions of like-minded officials to demonstrate the merits of their preferred policy options and to lobby for nationwide implementation of those policies.[22] China's political economy proved to be highly innovative in finding policies and institutions to master the complex challenges of large-scale economic change while avoiding systemic breakdown.

The political contest for the party's leadership motivated the contenders, including Deng Xiaoping, Hu Yaobang, and Zhao Ziyang, to propose innovative solutions to China's problems. Many of the early reforms—such as the freeing up from collective control of the agricultural sector, the implementation of free trade zones, the introduction of a dual price system, and the decentralization of fiscal revenues to local governments—originated from these political contenders. In their own way, the contests injected a certain degree of meritocracy in the Chinese government. In the decades that followed the start of reform and opening up, China made tremendous progress toward a market economy. It did not, however, commit to democratic rule or give up on the centrally planned economy.

[22] Brandt and Rawski (2008).

CHAPTER 2

Western Triumphalism

The Thatcher/Reagan Revolution

Margaret Thatcher and Ronald Reagan won the elections in 1979 and 1980 on a platform of lower taxes, smaller government, deregulation, and ending the power of trade unions. The oil crises of the 1970s had ushered in years of stagflation—a combination of high inflation and high unemployment—in much of Europe and the USA. In the UK, the labor strikes during the winter of 1978/79, organized by trade unions that were not satisfied with a pay rise of 5 percent, proved fertile ground for the neoliberal policies of the 1980s. What the trade union strikes did for Margaret Thatcher, the 14 months-long Iranian hostage crisis did for Ronald Reagan—it handed him a resounding victory in the general election.

Just like Thatcher, Reagan won on a platform of lower taxes, smaller government, deregulation, and ending the power of trade unions. They were quite successful at the latter. Membership of trade unions has since been cut in half both in the UK as well as in the USA. Their brand of neoliberalism became highly influential throughout the 1980s as it quickly established itself as the Washington consensus.[1] Through the edicts issued by the International Monetary Fund and the World Bank, often as preconditions for financial aid to crisis-stricken countries, Margaret Thatcher's and Ronald Reagan's economic ideology affected the lives of hundreds of millions of people in Africa, Asia, and South America.

---

[1] John Williamson coined the term "Washington consensus" in 1989.

The Washington consensus sums up the ten policy recommendations applied by the major economic policy institutes in Washington D.C., such as the International Monetary Fund, the World Bank, and the US Treasury Department. While it is commonly understood that the Washington consensus is aimed at developing countries, advanced economies took the medicine themselves too. The policy prescriptions read much like the ten commandments.

The first commandment regards fiscal discipline, which entails strict criteria for limiting budget deficits. One could argue that the Washington consensus was the mother of the euro convergence criteria, agreed upon in the Treaty of Maastricht in 1992. Aspirant members had to meet those criteria to be able to join the single currency. For advanced economies, a budget deficit of 3 percent and a government debt to GDP ratio of 60 percent is considered not excessive. However, there have been plenty of economists arguing that the convergence criteria, especially the debt criterion, are much more stringent than those required to ensure public sector solvency.[2]

The second commandment, which sets priorities for spending, may be the least circumspect. According to the Washington consensus, the expenditures should move away from subsidies and bureaucracy toward pro-growth fields like primary education, primary health care, and infrastructure investment. However, some countries, most notably the USA and Germany, cut public spending on pro-growth fields like infrastructure altogether. The decline in the quality of infrastructure in these two countries led the International Monetary Fund in 2014 to publish a document imploring countries to increase infrastructure spending in the face of flailing economic growth, arguing that such spending would pay for itself.[3]

The third commandment, tax reform, may well be the most heeded policy prescription. The Washington consensus spells out that countries should broaden the tax base and cut marginal tax rates. Many countries did the latter, including in the field of corporate income tax, where countries engaged in consecutive rounds of tax cuts in a competitive race to the bottom. However, they often did so without an offsetting broadening of

---

[2] Willem Buiter, Giancarlo Corsetti, Nouriel Roubini, and Jeffrey Frankel, "Excessive Deficits: Sense and Nonsense in the Treaty of Maastricht," *Economic Policy*, Vol. 8, No. 16, April 1993, pp. 57–100.

[3] World Economic Outlook, "The Time Is Right for an Infrastructure Push," September 2014.

the tax base, not-seldom resulting in a drop in corporate tax revenues even in the face of rising profits. The highest rates of the personal income tax were slashed as well, most notably in the USA and the UK. The tax burden was often shifted to lower income groups or consumption taxes were raised, which disproportionally affected lower-income households as well.

The fourth commandment, which dictates that interest rates ideally be determined by the market, has met considerable criticism from economists, including then chief economist at the World Bank, Stanley Fischer, for being too narrow.[4] Financial liberalization should not only pertain to interest rates, but it must also include the liberalization of credit flows, and it must be supplemented by prudential supervision if it were not to lead almost inexorably to a financial crisis. The latter turned out to be all too true, but most economists learned that lesson only after the global financial crisis.

The fifth commandment concerns "competitive" exchange rates. According to Williamson, that is to be understood as a rate that is not *over*valued, meaning that it is either *under*valued or correctly valued. With the increasing weight in the world economy of emerging economies that peg their currency to the US dollar, and the world's largest currency areas lining up for a currency war, the mood in Washington on competitive exchange rates has undoubtedly soured.

The sixth commandment, trade liberalization by ending quantitative restrictions and adherence to low tariffs, is relatively undisputed inside Washington D.C., but quite controversial outside the US capital. Trade agreements have increasingly come under fire. Even if free trade agreements produce a win-win for each country involved, the gains are generally not evenly distributed. Free trade agreements have exacerbated economic inequality, especially in the more developed trading partner. The trade agreements, therefore, draw fire from trade unions, consumer advocacy groups, and populist politicians alike.

The seventh commandment concerns the liberalization of foreign direct investment by reducing barriers. Foreign direct investment frequently renders the recipient country significant benefits in the form of increased economic growth and increased tax revenues. Greater competition can lead to productivity gains, greater efficiency, and improved corporate governance in the recipient country. Foreign direct investment often results in the transfer of soft skills through training and job creation,

---

[4] John Williamson, "A Short History of the Washington consensus," 2004.

the availability of more advanced technology for the domestic market, and access to research and development resources. Foreign direct investment related to the extraction of natural resources, however, is often associated with excessive levels of pollution and environmental degradation.

The eighth commandment regards the privatization of state enterprises. What originated as a neoliberal idea high on Thatcher's political agenda, gained in the 1980s a broad acceptance. The only point of contention was the privatization of public goods and services, such as education, health care, postal services, and public utilities. It also matters how privatization is carried out. The recent history, notably of Russia, shows that it can be a highly corrupt process that transfers assets to a privileged elite for a fraction of their actual value, creating an entirely new class of oligarchs.

The ninth amendment concerns deregulation. As policymakers in Washington convinced themselves that markets were always right, the argument for deregulation became all the more obvious. The markets would well be able, after all, to put a price tag on any kind of human failure in the form of risk premiums. In the push for deregulation, the USA in 1999 repealed most part of the Glass–Steagall Act of 1933 that had prohibited financial institutions from acting as any combination of an investment bank, a commercial bank, and an insurance brokerage. The Basel Committee in 2004 published Basel II, which was the second of the Basel Accords, lowering the capital requirements for many banks. It also instructed banks to use computer models instead of credit-risk officers to assess borrower's risk profile.

The tenth commandment orders the legal security for property rights, inspired by Hernando de Soto's analysis which argues that a strong market economy requires that the informal sector has the ability to gain property rights at an acceptable cost. In the absence of transparent and enforceable property rights, an elite minority enjoys the economic benefits of the law and globalization, while the majority of entrepreneurs are stuck in poverty. It is Hernando de Soto's reasoning that led Francis Fukuyama to conclude that communism was doomed.

Although the Washington consensus has been subject to intense criticism over the past years, most prominently from Nobel laureate and former World Bank chief economist Joseph Stiglitz, by the end of the 1980s, the neoliberal economic policies touted by Thatcher and Reagan went largely undisputed. Taking the bitter medicine themselves as well, most advanced economies, including the UK and the USA, grew briskly by the end of the 1980s.[5]

In the 1980s, Neoclassical and New Classical economics ruled in academia. Milton Friedman had convinced virtually the entire economics profession that technocrats at central banks had sufficient tools at their disposal to prevent economic depressions, and Robert Lucas was about to receive the Nobel Prize for his rational expectations hypothesis. In Lucas' world, financial markets are efficient, and even the bureaucrats at the helm of central banks are unable to change the course of the economy. Lucas is considered the most influential economist of that era.[6] Keynesianism had all but vanished from economic discourse in the late twentieth century. That is with the exception of a handful of New Keynesian theorists, featuring most prominently Stanley Fischer, who built economic models that assumed, on the one hand, rational expectations, and on the other hand, market failures.

THE FALL OF THE BERLIN WALL

On November 9, 1989, protesters toppled the Berlin Wall that had been erected in 1961 as a physical reflection of the division between East and West Berlin, between Eastern Europe and Western Europe, and between communism and liberal market economy. It was the culmination of events that started with the perestroika in the former Soviet Union under President Mikhail Gorbachev and that arguably created the conditions for the 1989 Revolutions in Eastern Europe.[7] The fall of the Berlin Wall also signaled the beginning of the end of the Cold War that had gripped the world for four decades.

In June 1989, Poland held its first partially free elections in eight decades, with Solidarity winning virtually all seats in parliament at the same time that the Chinese leadership suppressed the student protests, lending credence to Gorbachev's assertion that his policy of nonintervention in Central and Eastern Europe enabled the fall of the Berlin Wall.[8] In August 1989, Hungary gave up the defense of the border with Austria.

---

[5] International Monetary Fund, WEO Database, October 2015.

[6] Paul Krugman, "Why Weren't Alarm Bells Ringing?," *The New York Review of Books*, October 23, 2014.

[7] Katrina vanden Heuvel and Stephen F. Cohen, "Gorbachev on 1989," *The Nation*, November 16, 2009.

[8] *The Nation* (2009).

In the months that followed, many thousands of East Germans tried to flee from Hungary to Austria. When Hungary stopped the flow of East Germans crossing the border with Austria and returned the refugees to Budapest instead, they sought refuge in the West German embassy in the nation's capital. Ultimately, the East German authorities allowed people to leave, provided that they did so by train through East Germany. This led to demonstrations in East Germany itself, spreading throughout East Germany in September 1989.

As the wave of refugees leaving East Germany via then Czechoslovakia and Hungary kept increasing, Berlin's Communist Party decided on November 9, 1989, that refugees could leave directly through crossing points between East Germany and West Germany, including between East and West Berlin. That evening, the spokesman for East Germany announced that its citizens were free to cross the country's borders. East and West Berliners flocked to the wall, drinking beer and champagne and chanting. The momentous events in Berlin were quickly followed by revolutions in Bulgaria, Czechoslovakia, and Romania that very same year, then the reunification of East and West Germany in 1990, and finally, the dissolution of the Soviet Union in 1991.

After the fall of the Berlin Wall, the Washington consensus was applied mechanically to post-communist states, resulting in the radical dismantlement of central planning, the privatization of state assets and the liberalization of prices. Little attention was paid to the rule of law, resulting in large-scale looting, with oligarchs hiding billions of dollars of state treasures in private Swiss bank accounts.[9]

The End of History

In the spring of 1989, a deputy director of the State Department's policy planning staff, Francis Fukuyama, held a lecture at the University of Chicago's John M. Olin Center in which he declared the "unabashed victory" of economic and political liberalism. It was right after Russia held the first competitive, democratic elections in its history but before the fall of the Berlin Wall. That summer, a rendering of Fukuyama's lecture

---

[9] According to Zucman, the fraction of wealth held abroad in Russia is as much as 50 percent (Gabriel Zucman, "Taxing across Borders: Tracking Personal Wealth and Corporate Profits," *Journal of Economic Perspectives*, Volume 28, Number 4, Pages 121–148, 2014).

appeared in *The National Interest*. The fact that in the meantime the student demonstrations at Tiananmen Square in Beijing had been quashed had not changed Fukuyama's view. Rather, according to Fukuyama, the protests should be seen as the beginning of what would inevitably be mounting pressure for change in the political system [of China] as well.

For a short while, Fukuyama's essay "The End of History?" was a truly global hype, making headlines in *Time*, *Newsweek*, and everywhere else.[10] Within weeks, the essay became an absolute bestseller and Fukuyama's photograph appeared in the *Time* that summer. In Washington, a news dealer on Connecticut Avenue reported that the summer issue of *The National Interest* was outselling everything, even pornography.[11]

Three years after the publication of the essay, *The End of History and the Last Man* appeared in book form. The question mark that had graced the original essay's heading had vanished by then. According to its author, evidence of the triumph of the West could, first and foremost, be found in the total exhaustion of viable systematic alternatives to Western liberalism. But it could, in Fukuyama's own words, also be found in the spread of Western consumerism exemplified by color television sets omnipresent throughout China and the clothing stores that opened in recent years in Moscow. More importantly, Fukuyama asserted that political liberalism, albeit more slowly than many had hoped, followed economic liberalism with seeming inevitability.

His argument was simple. Democracy would win out over all other forms of government because the natural desire for peace and wellbeing would set nations on a path to progress from which it was impossible to divert. If a state, even a communist state, wished to enjoy the greatest prosperity possible, it would have to embrace some measure of capitalism. Since wealth creation depends on the protection of private property, the capitalist bend would invariably lead to greater legal protection for individual rights. In the 20th century, the USA and its allies had decisively defeated totalitarianism, or so they thought.

The End of History, and more specifically, the assertion that economic liberalism would inevitably lead to political liberalism, provided consum-

---

[10] Alan Ryan, "Professor Hegel Goes to Washington," *The New York Review of Books*, March 26, 1992.

[11] "What Is Fukuyama Saying? And To Whom Is He Saying It?," *The New York Times* magazine, October 22, 1989.

mate cover for Western politicians who avidly eyed the enormous Chinese market. As long as they publicly denounced China's repressive policies, nothing stood in the way of nurturing close relations with the Chinese leadership. The joint press conference in Washington D.C. that President Clinton and his counterpart Jiang gave in 1997, which lasted well over an hour, provides a perfect example of this type of political triangulation in international relations.[12,13]

After short introductory statements by both presidents, in which Clinton offered Jiang assistance on issues like rule of law, democracy, and religious freedom, the floor was to the journalists.[14] In the fifty minutes that followed, Jiang was quizzed about each and every possible sensitive topic—ranging from the China's handling of the student protests eight years earlier to religious freedom in Tibet, to the jailed Chinese dissidents Wang Dan and Wei Jingsheng, and to the status of Taiwan. President Jiang assured the assembled press that President Clinton had grilled him on those issues as much as they did while subtly dismissing the criticism directed at him as "noise." For the Chinese president, the indignation must have been a small price to pay.[15]

The professed belief in free market capitalism was so strong that President Clinton told President Jiang Zemin that same year that trade between the two countries would lead to a spirit of freedom—read: democracy in China—as inevitable as the fall of the Berlin Wall. It was the perfect pretext to put China on a fast track to becoming a member of the World Trade Organization. After all, doing so would both contribute to the US economy by stimulating international trade, as well as invigorate the democratization process in China. Selling US goods to spread democracy, just as Henry Ford, one of the great American industrialists, once envisioned consumerism as the key to peace. Talking about killing two birds with one stone.

---

[12] Old Executive Office Building. Washington, DC, October 29, 1997.

[13] Triangulation is the term given to the act of a politician presenting his ideology as being above or between the left and right sides.

[14] President Jiang's travel schedule included a visit to Independence Hall and Liberty Bell in Philadelphia, generally regarded as the cradle of American democracy.

[15] In the aftermath of President Jiang's visit both Wang Dan as well as Wei Jingsheng were released and given a free passage to the USA.

China's Accession to the World Trade Organization

In 1997, it was already the fifth time that Jiang and Clinton met, but it was Jiang's first state visit to the USA. The next year, in July 1998, President Clinton went on a state visit to China, the first by a US president in a decade. Defending his trip to China against criticism from US Congress, Clinton argued that by bringing China into the community of nations and the global economy, the USA had a better chance of advancing US interests and democratic values. "Over time, I believe China's leaders must accept freedom's progress because China can only reach its full potential if its people are free to reach theirs," as Clinton put it.[16]

In November 1999, the American and Chinese trade representatives signed a landmark trade agreement that would lower many trade barriers between the two countries, making it easier to export US products to China. The agreement could only take effect if China was both granted permanent normal trade relations status by the US Congress as well as accepted into the World Trade Organization. At the time, the fear was that China might face a sharp rise in unemployment as its inefficient state industries would face increased competition.[17] But while China quickly became one of the fastest growing export markets for US goods and services, US imports from China grew much faster, more than doubling within five years from $51.5 billion in 1996 to $102 billion in 2001.[18]

China proved an eager aspirant member of the World Trade Organization, and the USA was its biggest sponsor. In the second half of the 1990s, China dramatically accelerated its drive to liberalize international trade relations.[19] A significant portion of the tariff reduction and other trade liberalization measures that the Chinese government unilaterally undertook in the late 1990s were essentially part of China's World Trade Organization accession process. In the final negotiations with the USA in 1999, China agreed to an additional set of conditions that were far more stringent than the terms under which other developing

---

[16] Talk at the National Geographic Society, Washington D.C., June 11, 1998.
[17] BBC News, November 24, 1999.
[18] US Census.
[19] Lee Branstetter and Nicholas Lardy, "China's Embrace of Globalization," in *China's Great Economic Transformation*, edited by Loren Brandt, Thomas G. Rawski, Cambridge University Press, 2008.

countries had acceded. In certain respects, China's liberalization commitments exceeded even those of advanced industrial countries.[20]

The additional concessions mandated under the later accession agreement made China's economy the most open of any large developing country. While foreign direct investment into China briefly slowed after the crackdown on the Tiananmen Square protests, the inflows quickly resumed and grew briskly in the 1990s as Japanese, American, and European firms increased their foreign direct investment into China. As Branstetter and Lardy note, Chinese trade and investment developments have generally conformed to patterns of China's comparative advantage, producing those goods and services that it can produce at a lower relative opportunity cost, yielding—in theory—important benefits to both China as well as her trading partners.[21]

What caught the attention in the West, though, was not China's extensive trade liberalization, but its currency exchange regime. The Chinese authorities devalued the official exchange rate in stages, from 1.5 renminbi to the dollar in 1981 to an effectively fixed exchange rate of 8.3 renminbi to the dollar in 1995, where it basically stayed until the summer of 2005. According to the International Monetary Fund, the Chinese currency lost about 70 percent of its value against the dollar in real terms over the period from 1980 and 1995, substantially enhancing the competitiveness of China's exports.[22]

But it was well into the 2000s before anyone took notice. In the late 1990s, when China was put on a fast track to becoming a member of the World Trade Organization, virtually everyone viewed China as the one-billion-people market. Few fathomed that China would prove first and foremost a competitor.

---

[20] Branstetter and Lardy (2008).

[21] The theory of Ricardo implies that comparative advantage, rather than absolute advantage, is responsible for much of international trade.

[22] International Monetary Fund Staff Country Report No. 96/40, People's Republic of China – Recent Economic Developments, 1996.

CHAPTER 3

China as the World's Factory

Manufacturing Powerhouse

On November 10, 2001, less than a month after the attacks on the Twin Tower in New York and the Pentagon in Washington D.C. shook the Western world, the 142 members of the World Trade Organization in Geneva approved China's accession to its body. China would legally become a member 30 days after the World Trade Organization had received formal notice that its parliament had ratified the agreement. The Chinese parliament did not waste any time. Exactly 30 days after the World Trade Organization's ministerial conference gave the green light, on December 10, 2001, China became a full-fledged member of the world's leading trade body.

Within a year of China's accession, the World Bank ran an article in its Transition Newsletter under the headline "China Is Becoming the World's Manufacturing Powerhouse."[1] The article pointedly describes how the Dutch electronics company Philips, when it began in the early 1980s planning for business opportunities in China, adopted what seemed a natural strategy at the time: sell products to a billion Chinese. Instead, China became a place where the company made its products—and then shipped them elsewhere. By 2002, Philips operated 23 factories and produced

---

[1] The World Bank Transition Newsletter, Vol. 13, No. 6, October–November–December 2002.

about $5 billion worth of goods in China each year, nearly two-thirds of which are exported overseas.

In 2000, about $10 billion in Chinese-made merchandise made its way to Wal-Mart store shelves every year, either directly from manufacturers in China or from other suppliers that source their goods in the country. By 2005, that number had sextupled to $ 60 billion. In 2004, 60 percent of Wal-Mart's merchandise was imported, mainly from China, compared with just 6 percent in 1995.[2] Manufacturers ranging from General Electric (GE) to Samsung Electronics to Toshiba, as well as thousands of Chinese companies, found out that it was often more profitable—and almost always, far easier—to use China as an export base than selling goods inside the world's most populous nation. Once viewed as the 1-billion-people market, China had quickly turned into the world's factory floor, redrawing not only the global corporate landscape but the macroeconomic cosmos as well.

Minuscule Wages

It does not take higher math to understand the—perhaps historical—miscalculation the West made. Looking at China's development in a historical context, it is striking how economically backward China was when it started to open up to the world under Deng Xiaoping's leadership. Using the raw national accounts measure of GDP, Huw McKay and Ligang Song (2010) compared the relative output per capita of the USA, Japan, South Korea, and China during their respective high-growth era. In 1870, at the start of its period of rapid industrialization, income per capita in the USA was 75 percent of the frontier's income per capita, that is, the economically most advanced region, at the time represented by Western Europe. That compares with 20 percent for Japan in 1950 and 11 percent for South Korea in 1960. At the start of its high-growth era in 1980, income per capita in China was only 2.1 percent of the frontier's income per capita as represented by the USA.[3] In terms of purchasing power parity, that is, how much goods and services you can buy, living standards in China in 1980 were even slightly worse. Three decades on, in 2010, the Chinese enjoyed a per capita income of only 9

---

[2] Report Wal-Mart Imports from China, Exports Ohio Jobs, 2004.
[3] In terms of purchasing power parity (PPP), living standards in China in 1980 compared even worse with the USA, but only slightly so.

percent of the frontier as represented by the USA, which was still below the position of South Korea at the beginning of South Korea's high-growth era.

With hindsight, the idea that the Chinese people would eagerly buy Western television sets once trade barriers had been removed—as Francis Fukuyama envisioned almost a decade earlier in *The End of History*—is quite absurd.[4] At the time that Fukuyama wrote his bestseller, GDP per capita in China was a dismal 1.5 percent of GDP per capita in the USA, based on formal exchange rates.[5] By 2001, the average Chinese lived off an income of $3,000 per year, measured on a purchasing power parity basis. That is a tenfold increase compared to 1980, but still less than a tenth of what the average American made in 2001. On a formal exchange rate basis, which is a more suitable measure to gauge a Chinese consumer's ability to buy Western products, income per capita in China in 2001 was a paltry 2.7 percent of income per capita in the USA.

Moreover, a typical Chinese household in those days would allocate more than 40 percent of its income to food while over a third of Chinese lived below the international poverty line of $1.25 a day.[6] In 2001, nearly 700 million Chinese still lived on farms and earned, on average, just $285 per year. As the World Bank Transition Newsletter in 2002 dryly noted, these minuscule wages "slowed" China's transition to a consumption-driven economy. The paltry wages resulted in an almost endless stream of inexpensive labor instead. Between 2001 and 2010, nearly 200 million Chinese abandoned the countryside and moved to the coastal provinces to find a better future.[7]

The World Bank Transition Letter described the process of low-cost manufacturing in China as follows. Often a foreign company introduced a new product. Within months, manufacturers, mostly private Chinese companies, lined up to make that same product. Then a fierce competition would start and send prices sliding. It was just a matter of time before the producers began to look for new markets, most of them overseas. Driving all this, according to the article in the World Bank Transition Letter, was a combination of forces, to wit, foreign investment totaling $600 billion

---

[4] According to Orville Schell (1984), many Chinese had television sets by the early 1980s.
[5] International Monetary Fund, WEO Database, October 2015.
[6] Shaohua Chen and Martin Ravallion, "China is Poorer than we Thought, But No Less Successful in the Fight against Poverty," World Bank, Policy Research Working Paper No. 4621, May 2008.
[7] China Statistical Yearbook, multiple years.

in the previous two decades, an appetite for foreign technology, and the nationwide entrepreneurial zeal. What the article notably left out is the role that China's government played in bringing about these seismological economic changes.

The Planners' Hand

As James Kynge eloquently describes in *China Shakes The World* (2006), the Chinese planners knew quite well what they were doing. They had carefully studied the USA's network of interstate highways, which reduced the costs for US manufacturing companies during the first 40 years by more than one trillion dollars. In the late 1990s, following the example of the then global superpower, China started with the construction of its modern highways.

While they virtually started from scratch, by the end of 2004, the total length of modern highways in China reached 34,300 km (21,300 mi), that is almost half of the total highway mileage in the USA. In 2011, China's first-grade highway system surpassed the overall length of the American Interstate Highway System, a milestone that Chinese planners originally had planned to reach around 2025. Even for the numbering of the highways, the Chinese government drew inspiration from American highway system.

But the planners did not leave it at building highways. In *How The City Moved To Mr. Sun* (2011), Daan Roggeveen and Michiel Hulshof show how small towns in China were transformed at breakneck pace into huge metropolises with many millions of inhabitants. Initially, the megacities—that is, cities with more than 10 million people—arose in the coastal areas where the Special Economic Zones were located, such as Shanghai, Guangzhou, and Shenzen. But soon, urbanization also spread to Central and Western China. As Roggeveen and Hulshof note, in size, these megacities rival global cities like Rio de Janeiro, London, and Moscow, but few people in the West have ever heard of them.

According to a report by the Organization for Economic Cooperation and Development, China counted 15 megacities in 2015, the largest being Shanghai with a population of 34 million, the smallest being Harbin, a city northeast of Beijing, with a population of 10.5 million.[8] That is more than twice compared to the United Nations' tally, which puts the number

---

[8] OECD, *Urban Policy Reviews: China 2015*.

of megacities in China at 6.[9] The reason is that the Organization for Economic Cooperation and Development's analysis looks at so-called *functional urban areas*, rather than cities defined by administrative borders, as the United Nations does.

In the West, these newly minted cities are often derided as ghost cities. However, as Wade Shepard shows in *Ghost Cities of China* (2015), these recently urbanized areas only stay depopulated for a few years. Once the government lets businesses move to the area, which according to Shepard will invariably happen, the apartment blocks will fill up too. The ghost cities are often brought to life by opening a campus of a university, extending a metro, and offering benefits, such as free transport, low rents or even a couple of years rent-free. So, few places remain ghost cities for long.[10,11]

Shanghai's Pudong, which currently is home to China's financial center and the *Shanghai Stock Exchange*, is the classic example of an urban construction project deemed ghost-like at first. Milton Friedman even called it a Potemkin city, referring to the fake portable city that Potemkin erected to fool Empress Catherina II during her journey to Crimea in 1787. Pudong, however, quickly became a fully occupied urban center, with a population today of more than 5 million and a GDP per capita of more than $20,000 on a formal exchange rate basis.

Since China started its economic reform plan in 1978, its urban population quadrupled to more than 700 million, mainly due to internal migration. While China's fast economic growth is, on the one hand, driving urbanization, urbanization is also a major factor contributing to that growth. Overall, the major cities in China enjoy high levels of income and productivity, with the biggest cities accounting for the highest levels of labor productivity, according to the Organization for Economic Cooperation and Development. The high growth rates in China's megacities cannot be attributed solely to so-called *catch-up growth*, that is, accelerated growth following a period of low development.

Metropolitan areas in advanced economies also tend to have a higher growth rate than smaller cities and rural areas. According to Ed Glaeser, economic growth rates in large cities tend to be higher because

---

[9] United Nations, *World Urbanization Prospects: The 2014 Revision*, July 2014.

[10] In China, skyscrapers do not coexist with shanty towns, mainly thanks to the hukou (or household registration) system that regulates domestic migrant flows.

[11] By 2015, China had all but eradicated urban poverty (preview of China Household Income Project 2016).

cities magnify humanity's strengths. Cities spur by facilitating face-to-face interaction, they attract talent and sharpen it through competition, they encourage entrepreneurship, and they allow for social and economic mobility. If you accept Glaeser's proposition, then the Chinese government's build-first approach to urbanization, where apartment blocks arise, and businesses and people follow only later, has significantly contributed to China's economic development.

The government did not leave it at building cities either. Government policies have helped nurture domestic capabilities in consumer electronics and other advanced areas that would most likely not have developed in their absence. As a result, China has ended up with an export basket that is significantly more sophisticated than what would generally be expected for a country at its income level.[12] This has been an important determinant of China's rapid growth. What matters for China's future growth is not the volume of exports but whether China will continue to latch on to higher-income products over time.

Foreign direct investment has played a key role in the industry's evolution. They are the most productive of the producers, they are the source of technology, and they dominate exports. China's openness to foreign direct investment and its willingness to create Special Economic Zones where foreign producers could operate with good infrastructure and with minimum hassles must, therefore, receive considerable credit. China not only welcomed foreign companies, it has always done so with the objective of fostering domestic capabilities.

Foreign investors were required to enter into joint ventures with domestic firms in mobile phones and computers. Domestic markets were protected to attract market-seeking investors, in addition to those that looked for cost savings. Weak enforcement of intellectual protection laws enabled domestic producers to reverse engineer and imitate foreign technologies with little fear of prosecution. And, in another sign of China's decentralized approach to reform, localities were given substantial freedoms to fashion their own policies of stimulation and support, which led to the creation of industrial clusters in particular areas of the country.[13]

---

[12] Dani Rodrik, "What's So Special about China's Exports?," NBER Working Paper No. 11947, 2006.

[13] Id.

One Big Factory Floor

Not before long, the Chinese policies began to bear fruit. During the 1980s, under Deng Xiaoping's program of reform and opening up, net foreign direct investment into China initially only rose gingerly, reaching a little under $2 billion in 1990. But from 1990 on, inbound foreign direct investment took off, increasing 37-fold to reach $75 billion in 2007. By 2013, foreign direct investments into China amounted to over $250 billion per year, that is, almost 3 percent of GDP. The total stock of foreign direct investment in China stood at more than $2 trillion by the end of 2012. For comparison, foreign direct investment into the USA stood at $190 billion in 2013, that is, somewhat over 1 percent of GDP.

That is, however, only part of the story. As noted before, once a foreign company introduces a new product, other manufacturers, often Chinese but also Taiwanese companies would rush in to make that same product at lower costs. The company most known is Foxconn, the Taiwanese contract manufacturer that manufactures, among other things, the iPhone. Its largest factory is in Shenzhen, in what is dubbed Foxconn City, employed between 250,000 and 450,000.[14] It includes 15 plants, countless worker dormitories, swimming pools, a fire brigade, its television network Foxconn TV, and a city center with a grocery store, bank, restaurants, bookstore, and hospital. Its workers work up to 12 hours a day for six days each week.

Quanta is another contract manufacturer from Taiwan with a large production facility near Shanghai. It is the biggest manufacturer of notebook computers in the world with customers including Apple, Compaq, Dell, Gateway, Hewlett-Packard, Amazon, Cisco, Fujitsu, and Lenovo. One out of every three laptops in the world is manufactured by Quanta. Eüpa, another mega-factory near Shenzhen that is specialized in consumer electronics, employs 17,000 workers who churn out 15 million irons per year, millions of sandwich grills, microwaves, coffeemakers and blenders.

A Great Wall of Money

The Chinese economy had already been growing briskly in the decades leading up to China's accession to the World Trade Organization.

[14] "Suicides at Foxconn – Light and death," *The Economist*, May 27, 2010.

However, its status as a full member of the World Trade Organization did not hurt. From 2003 to 2008, China registered five consecutive years of double-digit growth, with economic growth reaching more than 14 percent in 2007. The effect of China's accession to the World Trade Organization was most notable, though, in China's current account and gross national savings rate. China's current account surplus increased from under 1.5 percent of GDP in 2001 to over 10 percent in 2007. As China's GDP doubled during those years, the current account surplus measured in US dollars increased more than 20-fold, from a mere $17 billion in 2001 to over $350 billion in 2007.[15] In the years following China's accession to the World Trade Organization, China's gross savings rate, which in the 1990s meandered between 35 and 40 percent of GDP, quickly increased to top 53 percent of GDP in 2008.

Due to its systemic current account surpluses, China rapidly built up a reservoir of foreign exchange reserves.[16] In 1978, foreign exchange reserves stood at under $2 billion, less than half the foreign exchange reserves of India at that time.[17] Initially, the build-up of reserves in China was seen through the lens of the severe financial crises from 1995 to 1999 that affected Mexico, East Asia, Russia, and Brazil. Many emerging economies increased foreign reserves much more rapidly than before. In 1999, China had accumulated a little under $160 billion. By 2007, China's foreign exchange holdings had surged to over $1 trillion, a multiple of its estimated adequate reserve level, that is, the amount of reserves needed for self-insurance against financial crises.[18]

As many foreign investors anticipated an appreciation of the renminbi, substantial hot money flows added to China's foreign reserves, in spite of the strict capital controls that were in place. One way for illicit money flows to make it into the country is for exporters in mainland China to exaggerate the prices of goods sent to Hong Kong to evade China's strict currency controls and bring back cash. According to a July

---

[15] Not adjusted for inflation. International Monetary Fund, WEO Database, October 2015.

[16] Foreign exchange reserves officially only include foreign banknotes, foreign bank deposits, foreign treasury bills, and short- and long-term foreign government securities. However, often gold and SDRs are included as well.

[17] China State Administration of Foreign Exchange (SAFE).

[18] Onno Wijnholds and Lars Søndergaard, "Reserve Accumulation – Objective or By-Product?" European Central Bank Occasional Paper Series No. 73/September 2007.

2008 report of the US Congressional Research Service, estimates of the amount of "hot money" in China vary from $500 billion to $1.75 trillion. Global Financial Integrity, a research firm, in 2014, estimated that more that $400 billion has been brought into China since 2006 outside the official channels.[19]

In addition to that, China was a net recipient of foreign direct investment, which adds to its foreign reserves as well. Between 2000 and 2007, inward net foreign direct investment rose from $38 billion per year to $156 billion per year. Although China's current account surplus as a share of GDP quickly receded after 2007, in absolute terms, it remained the largest in the world because of the sheer size of the Chinese economy. In spite of the global financial crisis, inbound foreign direct investment flows doubled between 2008 and 2014, adding again to China's foreign exchange reserves.

Not only the sheer size of China's foreign exchange reserves but also the fact that the Chinese government controls most of the capital outflows from China was considered conspicuous. The People's Bank of China website gives a tally of China's foreign exchange reserves, but it does not provide any details about the way the foreign reserves are invested. An overview of major foreign holders of US Treasuries shows that in September 2008, China surpassed Japan as the largest foreign creditor of the US government and US government agencies.[20] By 2005, the majority of investors in long-term bond issues by Freddie Mac resided in Asia. Only after the US government takeover of Fannie Mae and Freddie Mac in September 2008, China and Japan lost their appetite for US agencies' bonds.

At the end of March 2009, China reported $1.95 trillion in foreign exchange reserves although its actual foreign portfolio probably stood at about $2.3 trillion. The State Administration of Foreign Exchange (SAFE)—part of the People's Bank of China (PBoC)—managed close to $2.1 trillion in March 2009, $1.95 trillion in official reserves and $184 billion in "other foreign assets." China's state banks and the China Investment Corporation (CIC), China's sovereign wealth fund, together

---

[19] "Hot and hidden," *The Economist*, January 16, 2014.
[20] China also purchases US debt through financial centers like those in the U.K. and Hong Kong. Therefore the monthly data consequently understate China's true purchases of US treasuries.

managed another $200 billion. By US data, Setser and Pandey (2009) concluded that China held at least $1.5 trillion in US assets in March 2009, which means that two-thirds of its assets were US dollar denominated. The lion's share of US dollar assets was held in Treasuries, agency bonds, and corporate bonds.[21] Equities made up less than 10 percent of China's portfolio of US assets.[22]

China's Sovereign Wealth Funds

China's largest sovereign wealth fund, the China Investment Corporation, was established in 2007 and stylized according to the Singapore sovereign wealth fund, Temasek. Untill then, China had invested its foreign exchange reserves mostly in US Treasuries and US government agency bonds. The China Investment Corporation's official mandate is to diversify China's foreign exchange holdings and seek maximum returns for its shareholders within acceptable risk tolerance. Although equity made up less than 10 percent of China's US dollar assets, China's acquisitions of (shares in) foreign companies received most media attention in 2007 and 2008.

The China Investment Corporation and other sovereign wealth funds in the hands of autocratic governments (mostly oil-exporting countries but also China) are looked upon with suspicion because they may have non-commercial motives in their transactions and investment decisions. As agents of the state, these funds may be instruments of foreign policy, adding to the conventional diplomatic and military methods for putting pressure on other states. For this reason, the investment decisions of sovereign wealth funds are not perceived in the same way as the investment decisions of private investment funds that have the sole purpose of profit maximization and other private investors.

In the case of China, suspicion extends to state-owned enterprises because decision-making for important matters regarding a state-owned enterprise is typically in the hands of the Chinese Communist Party.[23] Not only does the Chinese Communist Party control senior executive

---

[21] In a speech to the Peterson Institute for International Economics, Larry Summers in 2004 dubbed China's massive holdings of US Treasuries and agencies' bonds a "financial balance of terror."

[22] In June 2014, China's foreign exchange reserves reached a peak of $4 trillion or a quarter of the world's foreign reserves and a quarter of US GDP (World Bank).

[23] Jiangyu Wang, "The Political Logic of Corporate Governance in China's State-owned Enterprises," Cornell International Law Journal, 631, 2014.

appointments in state-owned enterprises, but the party members in the state-owned enterprises also must comply with the party line, and party organizations can participate in state-owned enterprise decision-making. But even private Chinese companies are looked upon with suspicion. In 2008, Huawei, the Shenzhen-based phone equipment maker, dropped a bid for computer equipment maker 3Com Corp after the USA began investigating whether the deal would give China access to anti-hacking technology used by the US government.[24] Since then, there have been three more similar cases involving Huawei.

In 2007, assets under management of sovereign wealth funds amounted to about $2.5 trillion. It was projected at the time that by 2015, the sovereign wealth funds could collectively manage $12.5 trillion.[25] Because of the global financial crisis, it did not come to pass. Not only did commodity prices take a hit during the financial crisis, affecting most of the largest sovereign wealth funds, the public perception of sovereign wealth funds changed as well. Frowned upon at first as potential instruments of foreign policy, the sovereign wealth funds were suddenly looked upon as potential financial saviors when the financial crisis hit.

To shore up its capital levels, Citigroup in 2007 turned to the Middle East, where sovereign wealth funds had been amassing cash as a result of the boom in oil prices. The world's largest sovereign wealth fund, Abu Dhabi Investment Authority, agreed to invest $7.5 billion in Citigroup. In July 2007, the China Development Bank agreed to buy a 3.1 percent stake in Barclays for about $3 billion. Just three months after its establishment, the China Investment Corporation came to the rescue of Morgan Stanley with a $5 billion bailout. In January 2008, Jim Cramer, a financial analyst for the CNBC news network, summed up the trilemma: "Do we want the communists to own the banks or the terrorists?" He answered it himself: "I'll take any of it, I guess, because we're so desperate."[26]

As of March 2015, sovereign wealth funds worldwide had amassed over $7 trillion, with the ten largest funds accounting for $5.5 trillion. While the China Investment Corporation, with $746 trillion in assets as

---

[24] US regulators since then have blocked Huawei from two other acquisitions in the USA, and forced it to unravel its purchase of a defunct California cloud computing company.
[25] Willem H. Buiter, "Taming Sovereign Wealth Funds in," *The Financial Times*, July 22, 2007.
[26] "Overseas Investors Buy Aggressively in USA.," *The New York Times*, January 20, 2008.

of March 2015, only ranked fourth among the sovereign wealth funds, together with the three other Hong Kong/Chinese sovereign wealth funds, it represents almost $2 trillion in value, outstripping by far Norway's Government Pension Fund Global, worth only $882 billion.[27] These $2 trillion in government-controlled wealth funds come on top of China's official foreign exchange reserves and gold reserves.[28]

---

[27] The others are the Hong Kong's SAFE Investment Company, the Hong Kong Exchange Fund, and the China's National Social Security Fund.

[28] As of the end of June 2015, China's gold reserves were 1,658 tonnes (53.31 million fine troy ounces) according to the PBoC, ranking fifth in the world.

CHAPTER 4

Housing Bubbles Across the Western Hemisphere

Western Hedonism

The fact that China quickly transformed itself into a manufacturing powerhouse and built a massive wall of money largely escaped the attention of the West in the early 2000s. Instead of worrying how to stay competitive in a globalizing world, the USA started the new millennium fretting about how to spend its budget surpluses. In 1998, the US federal government had started to run a budget surplus. In the years that followed, government debt as a share of GDP dropped from almost 70 percent in 1995 to under 60 percent in 2001.

During President Clinton's time in office, the Chairman of the Federal Reserve, Alan Greenspan had always insisted on reducing the deficit and the national debt. But in 2001, after Clinton had left office, Greenspan turned like a leaf on a tree. All of a sudden, Greenspan's primary concern was that the US government might pay off its national debt in full. At the time, there was an almost universal expectation among experts that the US government was dealing with a vast budget surplus of which there seemed to be no end. These experts included, but were not limited to, the Office of Budget and Management, the Congressional Budget Office, and the Federal Reserve.

In Greenspan's view, excessive on-budget surpluses would distort the private system, and the government should try to eliminate that. Greenspan otherwise feared an ever-expanding sovereign wealth fund, handing the government way too much sway over taxpayers' money. As he told Congress: "Continuing to run surpluses beyond the point at which we reach zero or near-zero federal debt brings to center stage the critical longer-term fiscal policy issue of whether the federal government should accumulate large quantities of private assets."

To avoid that horrible dictum, Greenspan argued for tax cuts, implicitly backing the tax cuts that the newly elected President Bush had just proposed. In his memoirs *The Age of Turbulence* (2007), Greenspan recounts that in his testimony before the US Senate Committee in January 2001, he said that tax cuts might work, although he refrained from commenting specifically on President Bush's $1.6 trillion, 10-year tax cut plan. It was as if the floodgates had opened. The budget surpluses that had arisen during the Clinton years melted like snow in the sun once the US Congress had passed President Bush's bill to cut taxes by more than $2 trillion over a period of 10 years.[1]

In the new millennium, the Bush tax cuts quickly became, and continue to be to this day, the primary driver of the federal budget deficit.[2] The Bush tax cuts also significantly contributed to the increasing income inequality in the USA in the 2000s as the Bush tax cuts reduced the top marginal tax rates and the tax on capital gains, helping foremost the very wealthy. The lion share of the Bush tax cuts benefited only the top earners in the USA, with 43 percent going to the 80–99 income percentile and no less than 30 percent going to the top 1 percent earners.[3]

Loose-Fitting Monetary Policy

In the new millennium, the freshly introduced single currency, the euro, drastically reshaped the landscape of central banks. The Frankfurt-based European Central Bank superseded the 11 national central banks in the euro area, which became members of the newly created central bank.[4] After Greece joined in 2001, the euro area counted 12 countries of the European Union.[5] The national central banks remained responsible for

---

[1] In January 2013, US Congress made the Bush tax cuts permanent, while raising taxes on the wealthy by $600 billion.

[2] Center on Budget and Policy Priorities.

[3] Tax Policy Center.

[4] The European Central Bank was formally established on 1 June 1998. However, it did not exercise its full powers until the introduction of the euro on January 1, 1999.

[5] As of 2015, the euro area consists of 19 EU member states and is one of the largest currency areas in the world.

the supervision of financial institutions and the financial sector while the European Central Bank administered the monetary policy of the euro area. Other closely watched central banks at the time were the Bank of England and the Bank of Japan. However, the Federal Reserve was unmistakably the leader of the pack, presiding over the largest currency area and the world's reserve currency, the US dollar.

After the dot-com bubble burst by the end of 2000, the Federal Reserve's rate-setting committee, the so-called Federal Open Market Committee, began to lower the overnight federal funds rate. The federal funds rate is the main monetary policy rate, that is, it is the most important instrument the Federal Open Market Committee has to affect economic growth. It slashed it from 6.5 percent in late 2000 to 1.75 percent in December 2001 and down to 1 percent in June 2003. It then kept the rate at 1 percent for more than a year, even though inflation expectations were well above the Fed's implicit inflation target and the unemployment rate was getting closer to 5 percent, which is considered the natural rate of unemployment.

In July 2001, PIMCO's Paul McCulley correctly predicted that the FOMC would cut interest rates to create a housing bubble so American hedonism could be sustained, even though Greenspan would never admit such a thing.[6] To rationalize its low interest rate policy, the Federal Open Market Committee traded in February 2000 its preferred measure of inflation, the general consumer price index (headline CPI), for the personal consumption expenditures (headline PCE), thus mitigating the impact of rising house prices. Subsequently, in July 2004, the Federal Open Market Committee traded headline PCE for core PCE, thus excluding the impact of energy and food prices, just when these started to climb.[7] It was the perfect pretext for a monetary policy that was "loose fitting," as the British magazine *The Economist* dubbed it, compared to monetary policy during the previous two decades.[8] All the while, the Federal Reserve dismissed warnings about a nationwide housing bubble with then Federal Reserve Chairman Alan Greenspan even denying that it was possible to have such a thing (Fig. 4.1).[9]

[6] Paul Krugman, "Running Out of Bubbles," *The New York Times* May 27, 2005.
[7] Orphanides, Athanasios, and Volcker Wieland, "Economic Projections and Rules of Thumb for Monetary Policy," *Federal Reserve Bank of St. Louis Review*, vol.90 (July/August), pp. 307–24, 2008.
[8] See also John Taylor, "Housing and Monetary Policy," in *Housing, Housing Finance, and Monetary Policy*, Federal Reserve Bank of Kansas City, pp. 463–476, 2007.
[9] Remarks by Chairman Alan Greenspan at America's Community Bankers Annual Convention, Washington, DC, October 19, 2004.

The European Central Bank followed the Federal Reserve's lead at the start of 2001, lowering the European Central Bank's main policy rate, the refinance rate, from 4.75 to 2 percent and kept its main interest rate low for much longer, until the end of 2005. Although this policy stance may have been right for the euro area's largest member, Germany, for peripheral countries like Spain and Ireland, that experienced high inflation and a tight labor market, it was way too loose. The Bank of England was the only one of the larger central banks to start raising its main policy rate, the bank rate as early as November 2003, from 3.5 to 3.75 percent, and kept increasing it every three months by 25 basis points. The Bank of Japan was still trying to stave off deflation with a zero interest rate following the bursting of the bubble in 1994 and was neither a guide to nor a follower of its peers.

By the time the Federal Reserve wanted to put the brakes on the US economy and cool down the housing market, it was too late. Long-term interest rates in the USA remained stubbornly low, even though the Federal Reserve raised the fed funds rate from 1 percent in July 2004 to 5.25 percent in June 2006. On February 16, 2005, Greenspan, in his testimony before the Congressional Committee, said: "The broadly unanticipated behavior of world bond markets remains a conundrum." On June

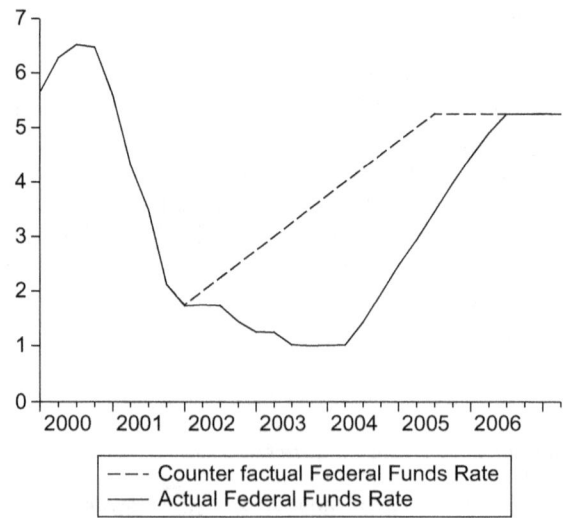

Fig. 4.1 Loose-fitting monetary policy (*Source*: John B. Taylor)

6, 2005, Greenspan elaborated further: "The pronounced decline in US Treasury long-term interest rates over the past year despite a 200-basis-point increase in our fed funds rate is clearly without recent precedent. The unusual behavior of long-term rates first became apparent almost a year ago."[10]

Blaming China

In the Sandridge Lecture for the Virginia Association of Economists in Richmond, Virginia, then Governor Bernanke on March 10, 2005, raised the specter of a global savings glut, noting that a combination of diverse forces has created a significant increase in the global supply of savings—a global saving glut—that helps to explain the relatively low level of long-term real interest rates in the world. Bernanke stressed the reversal in the flows of credit to developing and emerging economies, most notably China—a shift that transformed those economies from borrowers on international capital markets to large net lenders—as the driving force behind the global savings glut.

Emerging economies as a group can increase their current account surpluses only if the industrial countries—read the USA—reduce their current accounts accordingly. According to Bernanke, the requisite shift in the current account balance of the USA was brought about by adjustments in asset prices and exchange rates. Low interest rates and the expansion of US housing wealth, much of it readily available to households through cash-out refinancing and home equity lines of credit, kept the US national savings rate low. In Bernanke's view, the USA was forced into the role of global consumer of last resort. Implicitly, he blamed China for the American housing boom.

At the same time, Bernanke fawned over the depth and sophistication of the country's financial markets, which allowed households easy access to rising housing wealth. The fact that in case the housing boom goes bust, many homeowners would end up "underwater" (with home mortgage loans exceeding the value of the underlying property) apparently did not set off any alarm bells with Bernanke. Nor did Bernanke seem to appreciate the fact that the credit boom through home equity extraction left the financial sector severely exposed to the US housing

---

[10] In a speech to the International Monetary Conference in Beijing (via satellite).

market, vulnerabilities that, in 2008, turned a housing correction into a global financial crisis and deep economic recession.

Not all economists took an equally sanguine view of the global imbalances as Bernanke did. *Financial Times* columnist Martin Wolf and Robert Skidelsky, to name a few, thought the situation to be unsustainable. They pointed out that Americans were living beyond their means, using their houses as ATMs to prop up personal consumption expenditures on a micro level, and running large current account deficits on a macro level. Economists including Paul Krugman predicted a dollar crisis, and only some, notably Nouriel Roubini and Raghuram Rajan, foretold the collapse of the housing market and the financial sector.

In 2007, Niall Ferguson and Moritz Schularick coined the term Chimerica to describe the symbiotic relationship between China and America that was increasingly dominating the world economy.[11] According to Ferguson, Chimerica was a marriage of opposites. Americans consumed, imported and borrowed, using their house as an ATM. The US spending binge boosted exports and savings in China. Not only did the glut of Chinese savings lower the cost of capital, but the glut of Chinese workers reduced the cost of labor. Every asset class on the planet rallied.

While the external account imbalances between China and the USA were amply highlighted in the mid-2000s, few commentators paid attention to the imbalances that arose within the euro area. As a whole, the euro area's external account was virtually in balance, with the current account staying neatly under 1 percent of GDP. The fact that the imbalances between the members of the euro area were at least as large as those between the USA and China was simply overlooked, not only by economic scholars but by organizations like the International Monetary Fund and the Organization for Economic Cooperation and Development as well.

HOUSE PRICES

The new millennium saw a precipitous drop in interest rates in advanced economies. The drop was, first of all, the work of central bankers around the world who in union cut short-term interest rates aggressively after

---

[11] "'Chimerica' and the Rule of Central Bankers," *The Wall Street Journal*, August 27, 2015.

the dot-com bubble went bust in 2000 to stave off a recession. Lower short-term interest rates induced a fall in longer-term yields as well. The simple mathematics of the yield curve governs the relationship between short- and long-term interest rates. Ten-year yields, for example, can be thought of as an average of ten consecutive one-year forward rates. That means that if the Federal Open Market Committee lowers the fed funds rate, yields on longer-term government bonds will drop as well.

Second, the decline in long-term interest rates in the euro area was also the result of the countries' efforts in the previous years to bring public finances under control to meet the so-called convergence criteria for joining the euro area. The criteria entail price stability, a budget deficit below 3 percent of GDP, a government debt to GDP ratio of 60 percent and exchange rate stability. Countries like Spain, Portugal, Ireland, Italy and Greece saw the yield on 10-year government bonds drop from a range of 10 to 18 percent in the mid-1990s to less than 4 percent in 2005.

Third, once central bankers started to raise short-term rates again, long-term yields did not follow suit as they normally had done. In 2004, long-term bond yields remained relatively low, despite the Federal Reserve's campaign to raise interest rates again. Over the entire period, from June 2004 through July 2006, the 10-year Treasury yield increased by about 30 basis points despite a 400-basis-point rise in the funds rate target. The fact that long-term interest rates remained so low added further fuel to the housing bubble. In his Sandridge Lecture, Bernanke blamed China for the stubbornly low long-term interest rates.

Prices of longer-lived assets like houses are determined by discounting the flow of income (or imputed services) by interest rates of the same maturities as the life of the asset. Since the interest on mortgages is often the largest expense for homeowners, the precipitous drop in interest rates was the primary factor driving the housing booms across the Western hemisphere.

Between 2000 and 2007, house prices in most advanced economies rose dramatically. In New Zealand and Australia, house prices rose by 98 and 75 percent, respectively. Spain and France saw house prices increase by, respectively, 90 and 81 percent, and the UK and Ireland saw an increase of 74 and 54 percent. In Sweden, Denmark, Norway, and Finland, house prices increased by 64, 60, 54, and 38 percent. Japan and Germany were the only exceptions to the rule; they experienced house price declines of, respectively, 21 and 12 percent.[12]

[12] OECD.

While the USA is broadly seen as ground zero for the global financial crisis, real house prices in the USA rose on average just over 30 percent between 2000 and 2007, which is rather moderate compared to countries like the UK, Spain, and Ireland, where house prices virtually doubled during that same period. Looking at house prices over a longer period, from 1995 to 2007, the increase in house prices in the USA doesn't come anywhere near the price explosions that occurred in the UK, Spain, and Ireland, where house prices almost tripled during that same period.

Household Debt

Low interest rates not only spurred a housing boom but credit booms as well in virtually all advanced economies. On both sides of the pond, households treated their houses as ATMs. As a result, household debt rose in tandem with house prices. As then Fed Governor Ben Bernanke already pointed out in his Sandridge Lecture, the supposedly "efficient" financial markets made housing wealth readily available to households through cash-out refinancing and home equity lines of credit. Only during the global financial crisis did it became apparent that financial markets were less sophisticated than previously assumed. As Michael Lewis describes in *The Big Short—Inside the Doomsday Machine* (2011), Wall Street banks practically force-fed lesser-off households mortgage debt.

Atif Mian and Amir Sufi blame the run-up in household debt for the financial crisis and the ensuing economic crisis.[13] According to Mian and Sufi, mortgage debt grew more than twice as fast in neighborhoods with low credit scores than in neighborhoods with high credit scores. They argue that the Great Recession was the result of a sharp decline in consumer spending due to the unevenly accumulated household debt in the first six years of the twenty-first century. In Mian and Sufi's view, the economic consequences of the housing bubble going bust were sharply magnified by the way debt in the USA was distributed across different income groups.

---

[13] Atif Mian and Amir Sufi, *House of Debt – How They (and You) Caused the Great Recession, and How We Can Prevent It from Happening Again*, The University of Chicago Press, Chicago, 2014.

While this assessment may be correct for the USA, it overlooks the fact that the housing boom was mostly a global phenomenon. Virtually all OECD countries saw a sharp rise in home values in the early 2000s. Just as the USA, these countries experienced sharp run-ups in household debt, which includes not only mortgage debt but also other forms of consumer credit such as credit card debt and car loans. As it turns out, household debt is strongly correlated with house prices.[14] In an international comparison of the changes in house prices and changes in household debt as a percentage of disposable income between 2000 and 2007, the USA is not an outlier at all when it comes to the build-up of household debt (Fig. 4.2).

Countries that did not engage in a similarly aggressive marketing of mortgage credit to low-income households as the USA did, such as Finland and Norway, experienced equally high, if not, higher run-ups in household debt. Both Norway and Finland are known for their generous welfare state. Income inequality in both countries is much lower than in the USA. The Gini-coefficient using disposable income after taxes and transfers in Norway and Finland is, respectively, 25 and 26, compared to a Gini-coefficient of 41 in the USA.[15] Norway nonetheless went through an economic downturn comparable to the USA while the Finnish economy fared considerably worse.[16]

It also undercuts the argument that the financial crisis and ensuing Great Recession were caused by US government efforts to help low-income families. In *Fault Lines: How Hidden Fractures Still Threaten the World Economy* (2010), Raghuram Rajan argues that American politicians pushed easy housing credit with the help of government units like the Federal Housing Administration and government-sponsored enterprises such as Fannie Mae and Freddie Mac to offset the consequences of rising income inequality. In Rajan's view, this easy credit then fuelled the housing boom. However, countries where governments did not push easy housing credit experienced housing bubbles as well.

---

[14] Calculated using data from OECD.
[15] World Bank.
[16] From December 2007 to January 2011, real GDP growth in Norway was slightly higher (i.e., 0.4 percent) compared to the USA. On a per capita basis, however, real GDP growth in Norway was 2 percent lower compared to the USA.

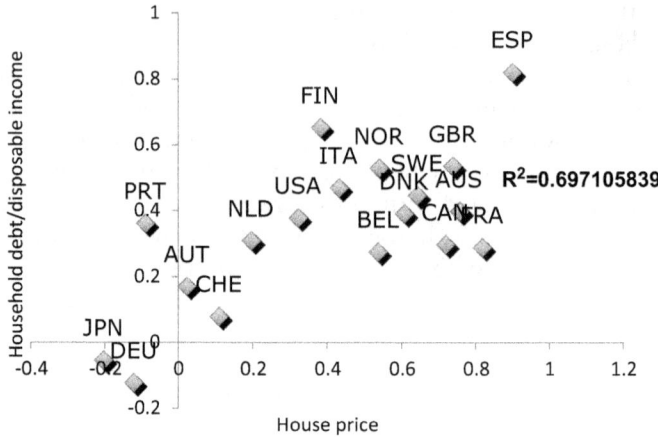

Fig. 4.2 Household debt as share of disposable income versus house price 2000–2007 (*Source*: OECD)

As research by the Federal Reserve Bank of Chicago shows, during the housing boom Fannie Mae and Freddie Mac bought less than 5 percent of the newly originated subprime mortgages while private parties, mostly investment banks bought about 60 percent of the subprime mortgages.[17] The mortgage originator held the rest of the subprime mortgages in portfolio. Only in 2007, when the number of mortgage originations had already fallen by half compared to 2003, the market for subprime mortgages had soured, and private parties had largely rescinded, Fannie Mae and Freddie Mac bought a third of the subprime mortgages that had been originated that year.

Without a subprime mortgage market, the interest rates on prime mortgages would have fallen further. On balance, it may not have made that much of a difference. Neither Norway nor Finland had a government policy in place to push easy housing credit to alleviate income inequality. Their banking sector is relatively well-regulated. Not a single Norwegian or Finnish bank needed a government bailout at the height of the financial

[17] Gene Amromin and Anna L. Paulson, "Default rates on prime and subprime mortgages: differences and similarities," Chicago Federal Reserve, 2010.

crisis. Both countries nevertheless experienced housing booms and run-ups in household debt that surpassed the housing boom and run-up in household debt in the USA.

Lax Lending Standards

Lax lending standards are often blamed for the global financial crisis. The relaxation of lending standards had a quantitative as well as a qualitative component to it. The quantitative component regards lending standards such as the loan-to-income ratio and the loan-to-home-value ratio. The drop in interest rates and the subsequent rise in house prices induced the relaxation of the lending standards. After all, lower interest rates made mortgages more affordable relative to income. As house prices in most countries had been rising for a decade, if not decades, rising home values would bring down the loan-to-home value. As mortgage rates fell by half or more, and house prices more than doubled over the course of a decade, many financial regulators allowed homeowners to take out bigger loans vis-à-vis their income and home value.[18]

Only the most conservative financial regulators restrained themselves, like the German regulators where the loan-to-home-value ratio standard was at a minimum 80 percent. A typical homeowner in Germany faces a down payment of at least 20 percent of the house price and still has to cover taxes and fees of about 10 percent of the house price. Other than in most OECD countries, however, Germany saw house prices declining from 2000 to 2007, so causality may well have run the other way. That is, the drop in house prices may well have led financial regulators in Germany to maintain strict lending standards. In other OECD countries, the tightening of quantitative lending rules in the wake of the financial crisis when house prices were falling may have contributed to the drop in house prices. But again, the causality runs from declining house prices to stricter quantitative lending standards, with a feedback loop to house prices.

The qualitative relaxation of lending rules pertains to the creditworthiness of the borrower, typically the (prospective) homeowner. Home default rates are inversely related to house prices as people are more inclined to hold onto houses and banks are more willing to roll over debt. Because lenders used default figures from this period to assess future risk, they tended to underestimate actual default and liquidity risks. Since default

---

[18] While the relaxation of lending standards may also be a tool of socioeconomic policy, this aspect does not seem to carry much weight in the years leading up to the financial crisis.

risks during the housing boom appeared to be small, lenders started to extend mortgage credit to less creditworthy borrowers. In actuality, while the real default risk increased when house prices entered into bubble territory, real-time indicators including delinquency rates and foreclosure rates suggested otherwise. It shows that lenders should not only take into consideration microeconomic indicators but macroeconomic indicators as well.

Securitization of mortgage debt—that is, the pooling of mortgages so that they can be repackaged into interest-bearing securities—allowed banks to turn traditionally illiquid claims (overwhelmingly in the form of conventional bank loans) into marketable securities. Through securitization, banks can offload part of their credit exposure to the housing market to other investors and diversify their balance sheets, which, in principle, lowers the banks' risk profile. However, as the subprime mortgage crisis has made clear, securitization induces moral hazard. Lenders have scant interest in a thorough screening of borrowers if they lack exposure to default risk, allowing them to sell mortgages to people who either can't afford them or are more likely not to repay them, based on their credit score.

US states that experienced higher levels of securitization did see higher house prices during the boom period prior to 2007 compared to US states with lower levels of securitization. However, international data do not show a clear relationship between securitization of mortgage debt and the accumulation of household debt. Denmark has a vibrant securitization market for mortgage loans, but the accumulation of household debt was not excessive in light of the change in house prices between 2000 and 2007.[19] In Norway, the debt securitization market is virtually non-existent; the country nonetheless witnessed an increase in household debt between 2000 and 2007 that puts it right in line with the USA and Spain.[20]

At the eve of the financial crisis, the securitization market in the USA amounted to $11 trillion outstanding and in Europe to €2 trillion outstanding.[21] If securitization was the trigger, why was both the housing

---

[19] The outcome for Denmark is somewhat flattered because of the denominator effect; in 2000, household debt as a share of disposable income was already among the highest in OECD countries. However, the reverse is true for countries like Spain.

[20] The tax treatment of housing debt may explain the variation in house prices and household debt between countries.

[21] Discussion Paper by Bank of England and European Central Bank, "The case for a better functioning securitization market in the European Union," 2014.

boom as well as the run-up in household debt in the USA relatively muted compared to Europe? If anything, the US banking sector has been spared the worst, as Wall Street banks had offloaded at least 25 percent of their toxic financial assets to banks in Europe before the global financial crisis.[22]

Subprime debt did not cause the run-up in house prices in the USA, which had already started in the late 1990s. It also cannot explain the accumulation of household debt that many countries besides the USA witnessed. The subprime mortgage market in the USA was rather a by-product of rising house prices and the search for yield in a low rate environment.[23] It was the tail instead of the dog. Although there is a two-way interaction between house prices and household debt, most of the evidence suggests a stronger impact from house prices to credit than from credit to house prices.[24]

Rising Income Inequality

In the new millennium, the world was confronted with an anomaly. On the one hand, the world as a whole became more equal than ever. Between 1990 and 2010, the proportion of the world's population living in absolute poverty, which is less than $1.25 a day, was halved from 44 to 23 percent. East Asia registered the most dramatic reduction in absolute poverty, from 78 percent in 1981 to 8 percent in 2011.[25] China alone accounted for most of the decline in extreme poverty over the past three decades. Between 1981 and 2011, 753 million people in China moved above the $1.25-a-day threshold, while the developing world as a whole saw a reduction in poverty of 942 million.

Advanced economies, on the other hand, experienced a sharp increase in income inequality. A chart in *Global Income Inequality by the Numbers: In History and Now -An Overview-* (2012) by Branko Milanović, lead economist at the World Bank Research Department, probably best captures the anomaly. The elephant-like chart shows global income growth from 1988 to 2008 for different income groups in the world. People at

---

[22] Ben Bernanke et al., "International Capital Flows and the Returns to Safe Assets in the USA, 2003–2007," Federal Reserve, 2011.
[23] Christopher J. Mayer et al., "The Rise in Mortgage Defaults," Federal Reserve, 2008.
[24] Santiago Carbó-Valverde et al., "Securitization, Bank Lending and Credit Quality; The Case of Spain," European Central Bank Working Paper Series, No. 1329, April 2011.
[25] World Bank.

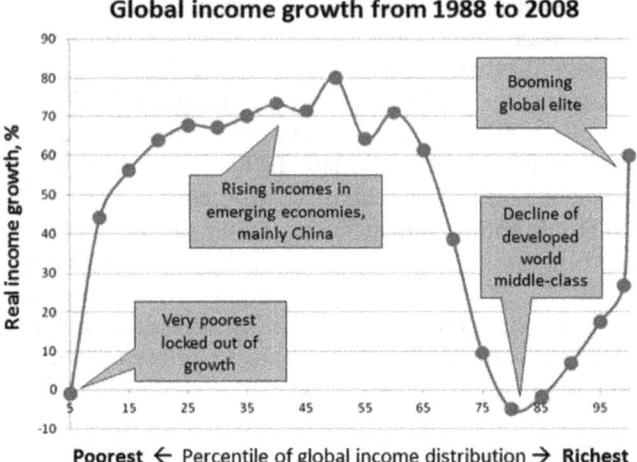

Fig. 4.3 Global income growth from 1988 to 2008 (*Source*: Branko Milanović)

the very bottom of the global income distribution, the poorest 5 percent of the world's population, did not see any improvement in their income situation over those two decades. Or, as the chart pointedly says, the very poorest are locked out of growth. According to Milanović, it is the greatest reshuffle of individual incomes since the Industrial Revolution (Fig. 4.3).

People in the range of the 10–70 percentile, which is almost two-thirds of the world population, saw their incomes on average rise by up to 80 percent, lifting hundreds of millions of people out of poverty. The chart singles out China as the largest source of these income gains. People in the 70–90 percentile of the global income distribution were confronted with a change in fortunes. They either saw their incomes grow only very timidly, or they suffered an outright decline in income. According to the chart's annotation, what we are witnessing is the decline of the developed world's middle class. They are the biggest losers, or, at least, the "non-winners," of globalization.[26]

People in the upper 90–99 percentile were somewhat better off. Their average income rose by less than 20 percent between 1988 and 2008. Only the top 1 percent of the global income distribution, or the global elite as the chart labels them, experienced two truly roaring decades. The top 1 percent saw its income shoot up on average by more than 60 percent

[26] Branko Milanović, 2012.

between 1988 and 2008, which is more than $1 trillion. Because of this booming global elite, absolute income inequality, measured as the absolute dollar gap between the world's richest people and the world's poorest people, increased dramatically between 1988 and 2008. By 2016, the richest 1 percent had more wealth than the rest of the world combined.[27]

INCOME INEQUALITY IN RICH COUNTRIES

In *Capital in the Twenty-First Century* (2014), Thomas Piketty chronicles the rise, fall, and rise again in income inequality in the Western world. According to Piketty, the rate of return on capital (r) has historically almost always exceeded the overall rate of economic growth (g). That is, the rate of return on capital has almost always been higher than the rate of return on labor (l). Piketty attributes this finding to an elasticity of substitution between capital and labor greater than 1. It means that any increase in capital results in a percentage-wise smaller increase in labor, that is, the capitalists get richer while the workers get poorer.

Only during the period running roughly from 1920 to 1980, the rate of return on capital was lower than the overall rate of economic growth, meaning that wages grew faster than profits. During these decades, income and wealth disparities receded. Since the early 1980s, however, income and wealth inequality are back with a vengeance. In the USA, the share of the top decile in total income rose from just below 35 percent in 1980 to 50 percent of national income on the eve of the financial crisis, even surpassing its previous record attained in the midst of the Roaring Twenties.[28] In the UK, the top decile saw its share increase from 28 to 42 percent.

The top 1 percent earners in the USA saw their income rise from 8 percent of national income in 1980 to 18 percent of national income on the eve of the financial crisis, even surpassing its previous record attained in the midst of the Roaring Twenties. In the UK, the top 1 percent's share of total income rose during that same period from 6 to 16 percent, in Canada from 8 to 14 percent and in Australia from 5 to 10 percent. Although the resurgence of income and wealth inequality since the early 1980s is most

---

[27] "Global Wealth Databook 2015," Credit Suisse, 2015.
[28] Piketty defines national (or total) income as domestic output plus net income from abroad.

striking in the USA and the UK, it is apparent in other rich countries, such as Germany and France, as well. In Germany, France, Italy, and Sweden, the top percentile gained about 3 percentage points in the share of total income from 1980 to 2010.[29]

As Saez and Zucman show, the rise of wealth inequality in the USA is almost entirely due to the increase in the top 0.1 percent's wealth share, from 7 percent in 1979 to 22 percent in 2012, a level nearly as high as in 1929. The bottom 90 percent wealth share first increased up to the mid-1980s and then steadily declined. The increase in wealth concentration is due to the surge in top incomes, combined with an increase in saving rate inequality.[30] Evidence from Forbes type of surveys shows soaring wealth at the very top as well. The surge of the 0.1 percent is also visible in the real estate market. While the average home in the USA sells for little over $200,000, in 2015, the priciest apartment in Manhattan was selling for more than $100 million.

In the euro area, the introduction of the euro added an extra twist to the resurgence of income inequality, at least in the core countries. The lower income groups saw their living standards, measured in terms of disposable income, decline both in relative terms as well as in absolute terms. The latter is the result of either a decline in real wages, or more fiscal austerity, or a combination of both. In the Netherlands, a rather typical albeit rather prosperous core country, the 0–10 percentile saw its disposable income decrease between 2000 and 2010 by more than 30 percent, while the 10–20 percentile and 20–30 percentile suffered a decline of almost 20 and almost 10 percent, respectively.[31] The higher income deciles, on the other hand, saw disposable income rise by nearly 30 percent.

In the euro area's periphery, the low income groups did considerably better. In Greece and Spain, people in the bottom decile saw disposable income rise by, respectively, 40 and 30 percent. While the upper income groups in Greece and Spain fared not as well as the lower income groups, they still enjoyed a substantial 20 percent increase in disposable income. Just as with the global imbalances, what played out between the USA and China on a grand scale transpired in Europe on a smaller scale.

---

[29] Thomas Piketty, 2014.

[30] Emmanuel Saez and Gabriel Zucman, "Wealth Inequality in the USA since 1913: Evidence from Capitalized Income Tax Data," NBER Working Paper No. 20625, 2014.

[31] UBS Investment Research, "Who wins with the Euro?," August 17, 2012.

The euro area moved successfully toward greater equality between the member states, witnessed by the rise in income for the bottom deciles in the euro area's periphery. At the same time, income inequality in the euro area's core countries increased significantly.[32] In the words of Milanović, the location component of global inequality (that is the inequality between countries using mean income or "between inequality") became less important while the class component of inequality (that is the inequality within a country or "within inequality") made a comeback.[33]

The distribution of capital is even more skewed than the distribution of labor income is. In any society, the least wealthy half of the population possesses very little (that is no more than 5 percent of total wealth), while the top decile holds about 60 percent of total wealth in Europe and 70 percent in the USA.[34] The top 1 percent possesses 25 percent of total wealth in Europe, compared to 35 percent in the USA. Both sides of the Atlantic experienced a deconcentration of wealth compared to a century ago, but the deconcentration of wealth was more pronounced in Europe than in the USA.

Piketty focuses predominantly on the class component of inequality. On the one hand, he suggests that growing income and wealth inequality is the natural state because the yield on assets historically almost always trumps economic growth. On the other hand, he emphasizes that much of the resurgence of income inequality since 1980 is man-made, that is, the result of policy choices concerning taxation and financial deregulation. Economic theory, he argues, cannot explain why "super managers" in the USA and the UK are rewarded much more handsomely for virtually the same job than anywhere else. Emmanuel Saez and Gabriel Zucman show for the USA that the surge of the top 1 percent is due to the surge of the top 0.1 percent, which owns 22 percent of total wealth.[35]

The rise of the super manager may explain, in part, the income gains the top 1 and top 0.1 percent earners in the USA and the UK made during the period 1980 to 2010. It cannot explain the big gains top earners enjoyed

---

[32] By now, after five years of austerity, most of the gains for the lower income groups in the euro area's periphery in all likelihood have been reversed.

[33] According to Milanović (2012), around 1870, class explained more than 2/3 of global inequality. By 2000, the proportions had exactly flipped: more than 2/3 of global inequality was due to location.

[34] Thomas Piketty, 2014.

[35] Emmanuel Saez and Gabriel Zucman, "Wealth Inequality in the USA since 1913: Evidence from Capitalized Income Tax Data," NBER Working Paper No. 20625, 2014.

in countries like Canada and Australia, which are both major exporters of national resources. To understand what is driving the resurgence of the class component of inequality since the 1980s, we have to enter globalization, and more specifically, China into the equation as well.

The Rise of Populism

In the new millennium, both the USA as well as Europe witnessed a rise in populism. Although the movements on either side of the Atlantic are anti-elitist, populism in the USA has a strong antigovernment strain, while the populist movement in Europe has a virulent anti-immigrant strain. As the increase in populism in Europe coincided with the attacks on the World Trade Center on September 11, 2001, the latter are often seen as the root cause of the rise of populism.

The rise of populism, however, also coincided with China's accession to the World Trade Organization and the introduction of the euro, spurring polarization among the richest quartile of the world population. As the top 1 percent pulled ahead of the developed world's middle class, the developed world was divided into the winners and losers of globalization. As Nobel-laureate Angus Deaton points out, the growing inequality in rich countries means that there is a very angry minority that's left behind that votes for populist candidates or fascist parties, posing a threat to the political stability and economic prosperity.[36]

Populism can be defined as an ideology that considers society to be ultimately separated into two homogeneous and antagonistic groups, "the pure people" and "the corrupt elite," and which argues that politics should be an expression of the *volonté général* (general will) of the people. This means that populism is a particular view of how society is and should be structured, although it addresses only a limited part of the larger political agenda. Populism can be found on both the left and the right. Left-wing populists combine populism with some interpretation of socialism, while right-wing populists combine it with some form of nationalism.

Both in the USA as well as in Europe, the populist movement's impact on political discourse has been considerable since the turn of the century. In the USA, the main political agenda of the right-wing populist movement is a reduction of government spending, opposition to taxation,

---

[36] "Donald Trump Presidency 'Not a Great Idea,' Nobel Laureate Warns," *Bloomberg News*, 2015.

opposition to gun control and adherence to an originalist interpretation of the Constitution. While there has always been a considerable element of nationalism in the ideology of the right-wing populist movement in the USA, it did not share the virulent anti-immigrant strain that characterizes the right-wing populist movement in Europe. That was, at least, true until Donald Trump joined the presidential race in 2015. During the campaign, Trump described illegal Mexican immigrants as rapists and criminals and called for the deportation of all undocumented immigrants, including their US-born children who hold US passports. Trump also repeatedly called for a Muslim ban and blamed China for America's economic woes.

The left-wing populist movement in the USA only gained prominence after the global financial crisis. Its agenda focuses foremost on Wall Street's abuses, income inequality, and free trade pacts. In 2011, the Occupy movement set up camp near Wall Street and gained global attention for its cause. The Occupy movement's slogan—"We are the 99%"—directly refers to the income and wealth inequality in the USA with a concentration of wealth among the top 1 percent earners. In terms of policy, the left-wing populist movement advocates strict regulation of Wall Street, consumer protection, increased taxation on corporations and top earners. It opposes free trade pacts. The unexpectedly strong showing of Senator Bernie Sanders in the 2016 Democratic primaries with his anti-billionaire message shows that the left-wing populist movement is very much alive.

Europe woke up to the populist movement in 1999 when the extreme right-wing Freedom Party of Jörg Haider in Austria won more than 25 percent of the votes and entered a coalition government. The dismay in other countries of the European Union was such that the other fourteen member states decided to a diplomatic freeze of the relations with Austria. But soon the countries that had been most indignant about the Freedom Party's electoral success had to tolerate populist revolts in their midst as well. In France, Belgium, Denmark, and the Netherlands, right-wing populist parties won considerable support, if not a place in government.

While the right-wing populist parties in Europe all have their special characteristics, they share in broad strokes a political agenda that is nationalistic, anti-immigrant, anti-Islam, and anti-European Union. In the USA, anti-immigration sentiments are mostly reserved for illegal immigrants. In Europe, on the other hand, first-generation immigrants with full citizenship and even second-and third-generation immigrants who are natural born citizens do not escape the wrath of the right-wing populists. These sentiments may seem unrelated to China's entry into the World Trade

Organization. However, the voters who are drawn to these parties belong to the income groups that have suffered a considerable loss of disposable income since the turn of the century. It may, therefore, well be that any feelings of discontent about their social status sublimate into an aversion against immigrants, who are in and of themselves a close-to-home manifestation of globalization.

The populist parties of the left only made notable inroads after the crisis in the euro area forced the countries to undergo austerity. They aim to reduce inequality by raising marginal tax rates and limiting bankers' pay. In the euro area's periphery, the left-wing populist parties' political agenda is predominantly anti-austerity, and often also anti-euro and anti-European Union.[37] The landslide victory for the radical party Syriza in Greece, which almost won an absolute majority in January 2015, left leaders of the euro area scrambling to keep the euro area—and by extension, the European Union—from falling apart.

Another strain of populism in Europe, which has been on the rise since the financial crisis but cannot be categorized as either right-wing or left-wing, has been sub-nationalism or splittism. Most notably, in the UK, Spain, Belgium, and Italy, parties that advocate the independence of an entire region have been very successful. In Scotland, an actual referendum was held in September 2014 on the question whether Scotland should be an independent country, with more than 55 percent of the voters voting "no." In November 2015, Catalonia's regional parliament backed a declaration to start a formal secession process from Spain against the will of the central government.

In June 2016, the UK government held a referendum to gauge support for the UK's continued membership of the European Union. Fifty-two percent of voters voted in favor of the UK leaving the European Union. Although the outcome of the Brexit referendum is non-binding, the new UK Prime Minister, Theresa May, announced in July 2016 that 'leave' means 'leave.' Brexit may be the beginning of the unraveling of the whole European Union.

Populist parties' initial successes were in countries with a proportional voting system, that is, in smaller countries. Countries that vote by districts, such as the USA and the UK, where the winner is the person that wins the most votes, generally end up with a two-party system given enough time, that is, one on the left and one on the right. But the outcome of the Brexit referendum and Donald Trump's presidential candidacy show that even

---

[37] The Washington consensus is often blamed for the euro area's rush to austerity.

these countries are not immune to populism. The supporters of Brexit and Donald Trump are mainly concentrated among the white working class. These voters disproportionately feel the adverse effects of globalization and immigration.

A global populist movement emerged at the meeting of the World Trade Organization in Seattle in 1999. The movement then spread around the world in subsequent years, usually gathering to protest against meetings of the International Monetary Fund, the World Bank, and the G8. The movement opposed the neoliberal take on globalization—that is, that free trade and deregulation would bring benefits to developing countries and low-income workers in rich countries alike. The movement's discontent with free-market fundamentalism and the unregulated power of corporations reflected, in part, the criticism articulated later by Joseph Stiglitz in *Globalization and its Discontent* (2004). However, the remedies that the anti-globalization movement sought, such as the dissolution of international corporations, were far more radical than the remedies Stiglitz suggested.

According to Tom Friedman, the global populist movement was a primarily Western-driven phenomenon uniting different forces.[38] Only in name, it represented the interests of workers in the developing world. As the former Mexican Ambassador to the USA, Jesús Reyes Heroles, mused: "In a poor country the alternative to low-paid jobs is not high-paid jobs. It's no jobs at all."[39] The attacks on the World Trade Center in September 2001 and the subsequent outpouring of solidarity with New York and Washington took most of the air out of the anti-globalization movement whose protests had become increasingly violent.[40] In Seattle in 1999, more than 40,000 people turned out to denounce the World Trade Organization. In Washington D.C. in 2002, the turnout was estimated to be less than 2000.

---

[38] Tom Friedman, *The World Is* Flat, 2005.
[39] Johan Norberg, *In Defense of Global Capitalism*, 2001.
[40] In Genoa in July 2001, at the G-8 meeting, a protester died during a showdown with the Italian police.

CHAPTER 5

The Global Financial Crisis

CRACKS IN THE FINANCIAL CEILING

By the mid-2000s, the Chinese economy was growing briskly at a double-digit rate. The US economy was only growing at a lackluster rate in spite of the massive stimulus administered by way of the Bush tax cuts, the rise in government spending and the massive build-up of private sector debt. Only because of rising housing wealth and mounting household debt, the illusion of the *Roaring Aughties* could be sustained. Between 2000 and 2007, the indebtedness of the government, households, and nonfinancial sector combined rose almost 25 percent as a share of the national income. Although the US economy looked healthy on the surface, underneath the surface, a toxic cocktail was brewing.

The US middle class was rapidly falling behind. Not only had the middle class scarcely benefitted from the Bush tax cuts, but competition with China also drove wages and real household income down. In 2005, the weekly pay that the average full-time worker took home was lower than it had been in 2000.[1] Wage stagnation was not an entirely new phenomenon. Except for the second half of the 1990s, real wages have been stagnant since the beginning of the 1980s. Between 1980 and 2008, wages and salaries as a share of GDP fell by 9 percentage points, while over that same period, profits as a share of GDP increased by roughly the same amount. Between China's accession

---

[1] Median Usual Weekly Real Earnings, Federal Reserve Bank of St. Louis.

to the World Trade Organization in 2001 and the start of the global financial crisis, the USA lost a quarter of its 17 million manufacturing jobs. Real median household income dropped by more than 5 percent from $58,000 in 2000 to $55,000 in 2008. After the global financial crisis, real median household income fell by another 5 percent.[2]

Thanks to the minuscule wages in China, China's accession to the World Trade Organization resulted in a drop in prices of all sorts of consumer goods in advanced economies. Products ranging from laptops to espresso machines and from sneakers to bras, all saw prices drop. This is why core inflation, which is consumer prices without food and energy, remained low during the 2000s. It was also the reason for the Federal Reserve and the European Central Bank to keep interest rates low for a very long time. The central banks feared a deflationary spiral, in which consumers postpone spending because they expect prices to fall further, and did not quite realize that China's rise as a manufacturing powerhouse was behind the low core inflation numbers.

After a few years, however, the weight of China's rise was starting to be felt around the globe, most notably in commodity prices. Between 2002 and 2005, the price of oil tripled, albeit to, at the time, still relatively tepid $60 per barrel. Prices of other commodities, like food and metals, began to escalate as well. From 2005, the burgeoning prices of commodities started to outweigh the drop in the prices of consumer goods. Between January 2007 and June 2008, the price of a barrel of oil spiraled from $63 per gallon to $144. The food price index by then had more than doubled as well.[3] Headline inflation, which is the price index for all consumer goods including food and energy, reached 5 percent.

The price surges choked off real wages, erased consumer confidence and depressed retail spending. Between January 2007 and August 2008, the Michigan Index of Consumer Sentiment fell from 93 to 59, the biggest drop in such a short period in the history of the index. Retail spending fell off a cliff as well, falling by 5 percent between July 2007 and August 2008 alone. That was well before the demise of US investment bank Lehman Brothers. During that same period, initial jobless claims started to climb from 300,000 a week in May 2007 to 450,000 a week in August 2008.[4]

[2] Federal Reserve Bank of St. Louis.
[3] Price change between 2000 and 2008, FAO.
[4] 4-week Moving Average of Initial Claims, FRED.

END OF HOUSE MARKET'S BULL RUN

By 2004, an increasing share of newly originated home loans in the USA was either a subprime mortgage or an Alt-A mortgage. Alt-A is a type of mortgage that is considered riskier than a prime mortgage but somewhat less risky than a subprime mortgage because of the mortgagor's credit worthiness. Compared to the early 2000s, the share of risky loans tripled to more than 30 percent of mortgage originations in 2006. As a share of all mortgage loans outstanding, subprime mortgage loans reached a high of about 14 percent in 2007.[5] In 2006 and 2007, the majority of subprime loans were in the form of cash-out loans. However, homeowners used a considerable portion of the equity extracted by way of cash-out loans to repay nonmortgage debt, mostly credit card loans.[6] They were also less likely to default on cash-out loans than on mortgage loans that were used for the purchase of a house.

Even though the subprime mortgage market was just gathering steam, house prices reached their zenith in the fourth quarter of 2005. By the first quarter of 2006, a self-reinforcing drop in house prices had set in. As research by the Federal Reserve Bank of Chicago shows, both for prime as well as for subprime loans, default rates are higher when house prices are falling. This relationship is particularly striking for 2006 loan originations, many of which experienced home price declines over their first 12 months. The relationship between house prices and default rates suggests that the defaults were to a certain extent strategic.[7] This is reinforced by research showing a strong correlation between mortgage defaults and bankruptcy filings, especially among prime borrowers who use bankruptcy to lessen the costs of default.[8]

House prices increased on average 30 percent more in states where mortgages are on a so-called *nonrecourse* basis compared to states where mortgages are on a recourse basis.[9] In the case of nonrecourse mortgage

---

[5] Federal Reserve Bank of Chicago.

[6] Greenspan, Alan, and James Kennedy, "Sources and Uses of Equity Extracted from Homes," Federal Reserve, 2007.

[7] Another explanation is that the housing market affects the general economy and people default on their home loans because they lost their job.

[8] Wenli Li and Michelle J. White, "Mortgage Default, Foreclosures and Bankruptcy in the Context of the Financial Crisis," 2009.

[9] My own calculations using non-trade weighted data from the Federal Housing Finance Agency.

loans, the lender cannot go after the borrower's personal assets for further compensation when the borrower defaults on his mortgage if the foreclosed house does not cover the full value of the loan. In the case of recourse mortgage loans, on the other hand, the borrower has personal liability for the loan. This finding suggests that moral hazard on the part of borrowers contributed to the housing boom in the USA. In the narrative of the global financial crisis, the moral hazard on the part of lenders, that is, the big Wall Street banks, has received a lot of attention. However, there is ample evidence that moral hazard on the part of borrowers played a considerable role in the housing boom and bust as well.

The US mortgage market began to experience increasingly severe problems. The share of mortgage loans that were "seriously delinquent" (90 days or more past due or in the process of foreclosure) averaged 1.7 percent from 1979 to 2006, with a low of about 0.7 percent (in 1979) and a high of about 2.4 percent (in 2002). By the second quarter of 2008, the share of seriously delinquent mortgages had already surged to 4.5 percent. Although default rates among subprime loans were at any time higher than among prime loans, the deterioration in the performance of prime loans happened more rapidly than it did for subprime loans.[10]

The Demise of Bear Stearns

In June 2007, two hedge funds of New York-based investment bank Bear Stearns imploded. At the time, Bear Stearns was the fifth-largest investment bank in the USA. The two highly leveraged hedge funds held more than $20 billion of investments, mostly in collateralized debt obligations (CDO's) backed by subprime mortgages. Because the funds invested in mortgage tranches, they had been able to push the rate of leverage without raising any red flags. However, as more homeowners fell behind on loan payments and foreclosures surged, that investment strategy backfired.

On the morning of June 20, 2007, lenders of the hedge funds tried to sell $2 billion in collateralized debt obligations, in scenes probably reminiscent of those in the movie *Margin Call*. There were no actual margin calls at the two Bear Stearns hedge funds but something that came pretty close—namely, lenders asking to provide additional cash because of the hedge funds' dwindling collateral. As investors reacted lukewarmly to

---

[10] Gene Amromin and Anna L. Paulson, 2010.

the securities on offer, the offer was retracted. Within a matter of weeks, the funds' value was reduced to very little.

What set the failures of the two Bear Stearns hedge funds apart is that they were, in the end, winded-down orderly. The costs were borne by investors, lenders and Bear Stearns itself. When Bear Stearns as such found itself in trouble nine months later, the Federal Reserve chose a different tack. On March 14, 2008, then Treasury Secretary Paulson, New York Federal Reserve Governor Geithner, and Federal Reserve Chairman Ben Bernanke decided against allowing Bear Stearns to fail. Instead, they opted for a lifeline—the first time since the Great Depression that the Federal Reserve used its extraordinary authority to lend to nonbanks.

At first, Bear Stearns was allowed to borrow at the Federal Reserve's primary discount window. Usually, only deposit-taking institutions can access the discount window in case they experience temporary shortages of liquidity. Bear Stearns was not a deposit-taking institution, and therefore, needed JP Morgan to do the borrowing on its behalf. The loan from the Federal Reserve to JP Morgan was nonrecourse, meaning that if Bear Stearns were to default on its loan to JP Morgan, the latter would not have to repay its loan to the Federal Reserve. It was, effectively, a collateralized loan from the Federal Reserve to Bear Stearns on favorable terms.

Section 13-3 of the Federal Reserve Act, which was enacted in 1932, provided the Federal Reserve with broad authority to lend money "in unusual and exigent circumstances" to "any individual, partnership, or corporation" provided that the loan was "secured to the satisfaction of the Federal Reserve Bank." That means that a firm must be solvent and have adequate collateral to lend against. At least five members of the Federal Reserve Board must agree with the credit advance, and the Reserve Bank must show that such credit was not available elsewhere.

It was a remnant of the Great Depression. The Federal Reserve's decision to use Section 13-3 to bailout Bear Stearns, by lending $29 billion to JPMorgan Chase in connection with its purchase of the investment bank, has been harshly criticized. As Willem Buiter in March 2008 noted, Bear Stearns was not a deposit-taking institution, just a private business that misleadingly was labeled a financial *institution*.[11]

---

[11] Willem H. Buiter, "Rescuing the Bear: why and why this way?," *The Financial Times* blog, March 14, 2007.

According to Buiter, the Federal Reserve should only support individual businesses if failing to do so threatens serious negative externalities. He distinguishes four kinds of externalities that justify the Federal Reserve helping individual businesses.

First, externalities in the financial field are often by means of contagion effects, as in the case of the classical bank run by a large number of depositors who withdraw their deposits at the same time out of fear that the bank is insolvent. Second, contagion in financial markets may also occur if buyers of securities leave the market in herds because of escalating risk aversion, fear, or panic, which may or may not be rational. The reason that the Federal Reserve has special liquidity facilities for certain deposit-taking financial institutions is that these institutions are deemed systemically important. For the same systemic financial stability reasons, such institutions are often bailed out when they are not just illiquid but also insolvent. Deposit-taking institutions are deemed to fall into this category because they are an important part of the retail payment mechanism.

Third, other institutions too are deemed systemically important to fail because they play a key role in the wholesale payments, clearing, and settlement system. Fourth, some institutions are provided with liquidity on nonmarket terms or bailed out when they are insolvent because the Federal Reserve fears that their failure would trigger a chain reaction of contagion effects. Fear and panic would spread like fire through the markets and first illiquidity and then insolvency would threaten institutions that would have remained both solvent and liquid but for the failure of this.

Bear Stearns was not a deposit-taking institution. It played no role in the retail payment mechanism and was not systematically important to the proper functioning of the wholesale payments, clearing, and settlement system. Bearn Stearns was not a significant share of the market for any security it held either. It was too small to be of intrinsic systemic significance. Nonetheless, without a decent assessment of its solvency, on February 16, 2008, the Federal Reserve extended a loan of $29 billion in connection with JP Morgan's acquisition of Bear Stearns. JP Morgan acquired Bear Stearns for $2 a share, which it later raised to $10 a share. Less than two months before that fateful weekend, the shares Bear Stearns had traded for over $90 on the New York Stock Exchange. In contrast to Bear Stearns' shareholders, the investment bank's bondholders came out unscathed.

The Slowing of the Music

In the first months of 2007, the difference between the interest rates on short-term US government debt and on interbank loans, that is, the rate at which banks are willing to loan money to each other, started to increase significantly. The comparison between the yield on three-month Treasuries and the three-month LIBOR-rate, better known as the TED-spread, is a gauge of the default risk on interbank loans. In normal times, the TED-spread generally remains within the range of 10 and 50 basis points. In 2007, however, the TED-spread increased significantly, albeit rather jittery, from 31 basis points in January to 241 basis points in August.

It was in that same summer that then Chief Executive of Citigroup, Charles O. Prince, famously was quoted saying: "As long as the music is playing, you've got to get up and dance," adding: "We're still dancing."[12] He was commenting on Citigroup's position as a major provider of leveraged lending. The bank ranked third, behind J.P. Morgan and Bank of America, among book runners for leveraged loans in the USA during the first half of 2007. Leveraged lending is a very profitable business, but a very risky one in case credit dries up. If Charles Prince had been a good listener back then, he would have noticed that the music was already slowing.

While the demise of Bear Stearns may have stood out in those early days, it was not the only sign that the music was slowing. On the other side of the pond, conditions had already started to deteriorate as well. In August 2007, the European Central Bank injected €95 billion into the euro area's banking system to stave off a potential financial crisis. The move by the European Central Bank followed a sharp rise in the interbank rate, which is the rate at which banks are prepared to lend overnight to each other. The liquidity injection was designed to ensure that money markets could continue to function. The cash injection was the biggest in the European Central Bank's history, exceeding the €69 billion that the European Central Bank had provided the day after the terrorist attacks of September 11, 2001.

On October 31, 2007, a financial analyst at Oppenheimer & co., Meredith Whitney, called out Citigroup, back then America's largest bank. According to Whitney, Citigroup had so mismanaged its business that it would have to slash its dividends if it were to survive. Between 2003 and

---

[12] "Citi Chief on Buyouts: 'We're Still Dancing'," *The New York Times*, July 10, 2007.

2005, Citigroup had more than tripled the issuance of collateralized debt obligations to more than $20 billion, thus becoming the biggest player in the collateralized debt obligation market. However, Citigroup's risk models never accounted for the possibility of a national housing downturn nor the prospect that millions of homeowners would default on their mortgages. Meredith Whitney's call on October 31, 2007, caused Citigroup's shares to lose 8 percent the same day. Citigroup's chief executive Prince had to resign only four days later, less than four months after his "We're still dancing" quip.[13]

In February 2008, a month before Bear Stearns' demise, Northern Rock, a medium-sized mortgage bank in the UK, was nationalized. In the years before the nationalization, Northern Rock had been pursuing a very aggressive policy aimed at expanding its market share. In 2007, it had gained 40 percent of gross new mortgage lending and 20 percent of net new mortgage lending in the UK. Only a quarter of its funding came from deposits, the rest through the issuance of asset-backed securities. When the collateralized debt obligations market in the USA started to crumble, sentiment in Europe soured as well and Northern Rock found itself in trouble. Northern Rock's shareholders were wiped out entirely. Again, the bondholders came out unscathed.

In the spring of 2008, something was also brewing in Iceland, and it was not the infamous volcano Eyjafjallajökull that would cripple air travel across Western and northern Europe and strand travelers all around the world two years later. Instead, rumors were spreading about the unsustainability of the financial sector in Iceland. Hedge fund managers were starting to short Iceland and the specter of bank runs on one of its three main banks, Landsbanki, Glitnir, and Kaupthing, was raised. The latter had used the Internet to aggressively market deposit accounts with unseemly high interest rates abroad. Ultimately, Iceland's global banking ambitions turned out to be incompatible with its tiny size and minor-league currency. In the spring of 2008, however, Icelanders were still dancing, albeit on a volcano.

When the Music Stopped

In September 2008, it all started to unravel quickly. Government-sponsored enterprises Fannie Mae and Freddie Mac, which were created in 1938 and 1970 to promote homeownership in the USA, were placed

---

[13] Michael Lewis, *The Big Short*, 2011.

in conservatorship by the US federal government. Fannie Mae and the smaller Freddie Mac (also known as the Federal Home Loan Mortgage Corporation) either owned or guaranteed about half of all residential mortgage loans in the USA. No wonder that they were particularly vulnerable when the housing market deteriorated.

Treasury Secretary Paulson had little choice. Standing by idly while these mortgage giants were faltering was not really an option. China had invested no less than 10 percent of its GDP in these government agencies' bonds. The stakes were too big, too vital to the entire US housing market, and too important to the Chinese government for its debt not to be paid back on time and in full. China was a major holder of US Treasuries as well. China's exposure to US debt in 2008, if you take government agencies' bonds and US Treasuries together, was an approximate $1 trillion, or a quarter of the entire Chinese economy.

Once Fannie Mae and Freddie Mac were placed into conservatorship on September 7, 2008, the US Treasury had unlimited authority to lend money for the purpose of stabilizing Fannie Mae or Freddie Mac, albeit that it was still limited by the amount of debt that the entire federal government is permitted to commit to by law. To this extent, the national debt ceiling was raised by $800 billion prior to the government's de facto takeover of Fannie Mae and Freddie Mac. The government agencies received in total $116 billion from the US Treasury.

According to his memoir, Henry Paulson learned during the 2008 Olympic Games in Beijing of a scheme in which Russia had urged China to sell together big portions of their holdings in Fannie Mae and Freddie Mac to force the USA to bail out these government agencies.[14] The Chinese declined, though, probably because the Chinese leadership was heedful that a full-blown economic crisis in the USA was not in the interest of the world's most populous nation either. After all, many a manufacturing job in China was solely devoted to stilling the appetite of the American consumer.

The problems for the financial markets did not end with the backstopping of Fannie Mae and Freddie Mac. Little more than a week after Fannie Mae and Freddie Mac were placed in conservatorship, the investment bank Lehman Brothers collapsed overnight. The official reading is that Lehman Brothers was insolvent because of its risky investments in real estate and

---

[14] On the Brink: Inside the Race to Stop the Collapse of the Global Financial System (2010),

the Federal Reserve, therefore, did not have the legal authority to rescue it. However, according to *The New York Times*, Treasury Secretary Paulson, who had endured a lot of criticism for the government bailout of Bear Stearns and the financial support for Fannie Mae and Freddie Mac, had declared beforehand that he would not use public money to rescue Lehman, saying he did not want to be known as "Mr. Bailout."[15]

The question whether or not to bailout Lehman Brothers turned on the valuation of its illiquid assets, a portfolio primarily consisting of real estate. According to estimates of officials of the New York Federal Reserve Bank, Lehman Brothers was narrowly solvent. But other Wall Street banks that were involved in negotiations over a rescue plan for Lehman Brothers were skeptical, arguing that there was a hole in the investment bank's balance sheet. If the latter were true, section 13-3 of the Federal Reserve Act would prohibit that the Federal Reserve lend money to Lehman Brothers. As the British bank Barclays pulled out of the negotiations, Lehman Brothers' fate was sealed. In the end, the political will to save the investment bank was lacking. On September 15, 2008, it filed for Chapter 11 bankruptcy protection in what would become one of the messiest bankruptcies of our time.

In a dramatic turnabout, the federal government bailed out insurance behemoth AIG a day after that in order to prevent a full domino effect. AIG had sold credit default swaps that provided the buyer with insurance against default on bonds. As it turned out, many of these bonds were mortgage-backed securities that offered up subprime mortgages and Alt-A mortgages as collateral. As the housing market soured, the risks of AIG's counterparties materialized all at the same time, rendering the insurance giant unable to make good on the contracts it had sold. The level of the credit risk it had insured through the issuance of credit default swaps was well beyond its means.

This time around, the US government did extract a price from AIG that it did not extract from other businesses that it bailed out. The $85 billion rescue loan to AIG came with a 12 percent interest rate (LIBOR plus 8.5 percent) and gave the USA an 80 percent stake in AIG until the loan was paid off. The chief executive of AIG was told to go. In return, all the creditors of AIG were made whole in the bailout and the contracts with AIG's counterparties, mostly big international banks including

---

[15] "Revisiting the Lehman Brothers Bailout That Never Was," *The New York Times*, September 17, 2014.

Goldman Sachs where Paulson had been chief executive before becoming Treasury Secretary, were honored in full by the US government.

On September 22, a week after the demise of Lehman Brothers, Wall Street behemoths Morgan Stanley and Goldman Sachs gave up their treasured status as investment banks to become traditional deposit-taking banks, allowing them access to the Federal Reserve's discount window. The step by the last investment banks standing marked a dramatic change in the make-up of Wall Street. Two days later, Warren Buffet announced that he had invested $5 billion in Goldman Sachs.

In the weeks after the disorderly default of Lehman Brothers and the subsequent government bailout of AIG, the TED-spread spiked, surpassing 450 basis points in October. It was a clear indication of the extreme amount of distress in credit markets. The prospect that Lehman Brothers' mortgage securities were about to be liquidated sparked a selloff in mortgage-backed securities. Unsure about the value of the collateral that was offered, banks on either side of the Atlantic just would no longer lend each other money. The music had stopped.

THE BIG WALL STREET BAILOUT

As stock markets tanked (the Dow Jones dropped more than 500 points on the day that Lehman Brothers filed for bankruptcy) and images of foreclosed properties and displaced homeowners flooded the television screens, US Congress consented to the Troubled Asset Relief Program that authorized expenditures in the order of $700 billion for the purchase of assets and equity from financial institutions to strengthen the financial sector. President Bush signed the bill into law on October 3, 2008. Under the Troubled Asset Relief Program, the US Treasury could purchase or guarantee up to $700 billion of troubled assets, that is, residential or commercial mortgages and any securities, obligations, or other instruments that are based on or related to such mortgages. By buying up these assets, the federal government wanted to improve the liquidity of these assets, stabilize their prices, and ultimately increase their value so that the financial institutions would be able to stabilize their balance sheets and avoid further losses.

However, within days of the bill's passage, the Federal Reserve and the Treasury unilaterally decided to abandon the plan to purchase troubled assets in favor of direct injections of billions in cash into companies like Goldman and Citigroup. What had been sold to US Congress as a bailout of both banks as well as homeowners became a bank-only operation instead. Not that all Wall Street banks were equally eager to accept the money that was offered to them. The banks feared both the signaling effect of doing so and the strings that came attached to the money. So Treasury Secretary Paulson had to "yank" the Wall Street executives into the Treasury building in Washington D.C. on the Sunday afternoon of November 12, 2008. There, he force-fed them the government funding: Citibank $25 billion, JP Morgan Chase $25 billion, Bank of America $20 billion, Wells Fargo $20 billion, Goldman Sachs $10 billion, and Morgan Stanley $10 billion.[16]

Banks that had received money under the Troubled Asset Relief Program faced restrictions on the bonuses they could give to senior executives, the golden parachute payments, and excessive or luxury spending. At least, rules to that extent were hastily implemented when it became apparent that the bonus bonanza for Wall Street executives continued in spite of the financial crisis, and taxpayers' money was at risk of being spent on the redecoration of Wall Street's executive chambers. Wall Street executives so much loathed this government interference that special rules had to be drawn up to prevent the banks from returning the Troubled Asset Relief Program funds early.[17]

US Congress originally had authorized expenditures of $700 billion. The Dodd–Frank Act, which brought significant changes to financial regulation in the USA in the wake of the financial crisis, reduced that amount to $475 billion. In addition to the big Wall Street banks, the automotive industry received support under the Troubled Asset Relief Program. Of the $75 billion pled for homeowner assistance, less than $15 billion was actually spent. According to the US Treasury, when it closed the program at the end of 2014, it had netted a small profit, returning $441.7 billion on the $426.4 billion invested.

Because of the small profit, the Troubled Asset Relief Program is often deemed a success. But that successful outcome is, to a large degree, an optical illusion. Aware of the fact that the American public was highly critical of the large-scale bailouts of Wall Street banks at the expense of

---

[16] Later that month, Citigroup needed a full-fledged bailout in an asset-relief package worth $306 billion and a further $20 billion recapitalization on top of the earlier $25 billion with the US government ultimately ending up with a 40 percent stake in the Wall Street bank.

[17] "Treasury Issues TARP Repayment Rules," *Business Insider*, May 8, 2009.

Main Street, the Federal Reserve devised more cunning ways to prop up the capital of America's largest banks, thus enabling them to pay the Troubled Asset Relief Program funds back in full. In late November 2008, the Federal Reserve announced that it would buy $600 billion of agency mortgage-backed securities.

In September 2012, the Federal Reserve announced a new and open-ended $40 billion per month bond purchasing program targeted at agency mortgage-backed securities. By the time both bond purchasing programs had been terminated, the Federal Reserve had amassed more than $1.7 trillion in agency mortgage-backed securities, almost a quarter of the total market.[18] By buying up such a large share of agency mortgage-backed securities with newly minted dollars, the Federal Reserve contributed to the balance sheets of banks that still had agency mortgage-backed securities, either by ridding them of these illiquid assets or driving up the price of these assets.

In addition to that, the largest Wall Street banks profited from the Federal Reserve's largesse in the form of emergency loans, which they got at near zero rates.[19] The banks subsequently used the money they borrowed to buy Treasuries or other government-backed debt, earning substantial risk-free profits in a taxpayer-financed arbitrage. In all, the Federal Reserve extended more than $3 trillion of emergency loans to financial institutions, with the latter only having to offer up scantily graded assets as collateral.

The World Beyond America

The financial crisis that originated in the USA reverberated throughout the world. The shock waves were foremost felt in Europe, where commercial banks had *en masse* invested in US mortgage-backed securities. In their relentless search for yield, the European banks had opted for the more risky assets, that is, bundles of commercially securitized Alt-A and subprime mortgages. Although it would take almost another two years before the euro area would find itself in a full-blown crisis, many of the thinly capitalized European banks were hit by the 2007–2008 credit crunch.

---

[18] "Measuring Agency MBS Market Liquidity with Transaction Data," Federal Reserve, 2014.
[19] "Bank Borrowing from the Federal Reserve and Purchases of Securities," Congressional Research Service, 2011.

By the end of September, the insurance giant Fortis was partly nationalized to ensure its survival. It was seen as too big a European bank to be allowed to go under. Authorities in the Netherlands, Belgium, and Luxembourg agreed to pour in €11.2 billion. In Iceland, the government was forced to take control of Glitnir, one of the nation's biggest banks. Dexia was the next European bank that needed a bailout as the deepening credit crisis continued to shake the banking sector. The Irish government took the unprecedented step of guaranteeing all retail deposits. On September 30, stock markets around the world collapsed due to the failure to get a majority of US Congress behind the bailout bill.

The turmoil continued in October. Germany announced a rescue plan Hypo Bank. The Icelandic Internet bank Icesave blocked savers from withdrawing money. By mid-October, the British government announced it would pump £37 billion of emergency recapitalization into the Royal Bank of Scotland, HBOS, and Lloyds TSB while Dutch savings and insurance conglomerate ING got a €10 billion capital injection from the Dutch authorities. The Dutch government obtained full control of all Fortis operations in the Netherlands, i.e., the parts of ABN-AMRO then belonging to Fortis for €16.8 billion. According to the International Monetary Fund, more European banks could fail as private funding had become "virtually unavailable" and banks had to rely on government interventions, asset sales, and consolidation.

In the second week of November, China announced a two-year ¥4 trillion ($586 billion) stimulus package to help boost the economy by investing in infrastructure and social projects and by cutting corporate taxes. The money would be spent on upgrading infrastructure, particularly roads, railways, airports and the power grids throughout the country and raise rural incomes via land reform. The Chinese government also reserved money for social welfare projects such as affordable housing and environmental protection. While the fall in global economic activity due to the financial crisis affected China's economy directly, China did not suffer significant losses on its considerable holdings of US securities as commercial banks in Europe did as it had eschewed the more risky assets.

In December 2008, Iceland's Landsbanki entered bankruptcy. The Irish government provided a fund of €10 billion to recapitalize all its listed banks. A month later, in January 2009, the Anglo Irish Bank was nationalized in a dramatic move by the Irish government. The UK launched a second bank rescue plan as Royal Bank of Scotland recorded the biggest loss in UK corporate history. At the end of January, the German government approved a €50 billion stimulus package. In February 2009, US Congress followed suit, approving a $787 billion economic stimulus package that President Obama would sign into law a week later.

In March 2009, financial authorities closed down the last major Icelandic bank that was still standing after the country's financial collapse. Spain's government had to rescue a regional savings bank. By October 2009, the US Federal Deposit Insurance Company (FDIC) had shut down more than hundred smaller regional banks since the start of the financial crisis. By the end of 2009, the Dubai government said that it would not guarantee the debt of Dubai World, a 100 percent Dubai state-owned holding company that had invested mainly in the glittery real estate, tourism, and shipping, causing a global panic. It was the first harbinger of the sovereign defaults that were about to threaten the world economy.

The Crisis in the Euro Area

In October 2009, a year after the collapse of investment bank Lehman Brothers that brought the financial system near the abyss, the Greek government announced that the country's public finances were in much more dire circumstances than previously disclosed. The Greek deficit over 2009 was estimated to reach 12.7 percent of GDP, more than three times what was permitted under the convergence criteria. Government debt was reported to be at more than 110 percent of GDP, that is, almost double than what was allowed under the convergence criteria. With financial markets already jittery because of the financial problems of Dubai World, they grew instantly concerned about Greece's ability to pay off its debt.

By then, the rating agencies, which had been discredited because of their awarding of triple-A ratings to low-grade mortgage-backed securities, made a comeback with a vengeance. In October, Fitch downgraded Greece from A to A–. In December 2009, Fitch cut Greece further to BBB+. A week later, Standard and Poor's, another of the big three credit rating agencies, cut Greece's rating from A– to BBB+ and left the new rating on credit watch negative. By the end of the month Moody's, the third of the big credit rating agencies, closed the ranks and downgraded Greece from A1 to A2.

That same month, Standard & Poor's cut Spain's credit outlook from stable to negative. To be fair, Standard & Poor's was the first of the three big credit rating agencies to downgrade Spain back in January 2009, cutting its treasured AAA rating by one notch to AA+. With the benefit of hindsight, the move came awfully late, but in real time, it was quite expedient. In April 2010, financial market's attention turned to Spain as it worried over Spain's massive government deficit of more than 11.2 percent of GDP in 2009.

By that time, the Greek parliament had already passed two austerity packages and was in talks with the European Union, the European Central Bank, and the International Monetary Fund—which would later become known as "the troika"—about a possible bailout. On April 23, 2010, the Greek government formally requested an international bailout for Greece. Within ten days, the International Monetary Fund, the EU, and the European Central Bank agreed to what would become the first bailout package for Greece, breaking the "no bailout" clause as laid down in Article 103 of the European treaty.[20] The first bailout for Greece amounted to €110 billion over three years.

Standard & Poor's was also the first of the three big credit rating agencies to strip Ireland of its AAA rating in March 2009, reducing it to AA+ while saying it may be cut further. By August 2010, Ireland's rating was cut to AA–, three notches under AAA. On November 21, 2010, the Irish government petitions with the EU, the European Central Bank, and the International Monetary Fund for a bailout. A week later, as negotiations about deficit reduction and debt restructuring were successfully concluded, Europe sealed the Irish bailout package of €85 billion.

Snowball Effect

By January 2010, the interest rate on Greek 10-year government bonds was already 3 percent higher than the yield on German government bonds of the same maturity, that is, the Greek/German spread was more than 300 basis points. The comparison between the yield on 10-year German government bonds, which are considered very low-risk, and 10-year Greek government bonds is a gauge of the perceived risk that the Greek government will default on its loans. After Greece had formally applied for a bailout on April 23 and Standard & Poor's downgraded Greece's rating on April 27, 2010, below investment grade to junk bond status, the Greek/German spread surpassed 1000 basis points. The higher the interest rate

---

[20] Article 103 of the EU Treaty holds that the Union shall not be liable for or assume the commitments of central governments.

on Greek government debt, and the more precarious Greece's public debt situation, the higher the interest rate on its debt.

The three big rating agencies had been behind the curve for years in the Greek crisis. The first downgrade of Greece sovereign debt happened in October 2009, that is, two days after the Greek government had disclosed that its financial situation was rather bleak. From that moment on, however, the rating agencies also became drivers of events. Every time one of the rating agencies cut Greece's sovereign debt rating by a notch, financial markets would respond by increasing the Greek/German spread, which in turn, would render Greece's sovereign debt increasingly unsustainable.

In a first sign of the contagion effects as a result of the Greek debt crisis, the yields on other peripheral countries' government debt started to rise as well in the first months of 2010. The yield increase was most notable for Irish and Portuguese government bonds whose credit ratings had been cut. Since many investors sought refuge in safe assets, especially German government bonds, the yield on German bonds dropped precipitously, adding to the spread between peripheral government bonds and German government bonds as well.

The downgrades by the credit rating agencies forced the European Central Bank to engage in qualitative easing, meaning that it would accept lower grade collateral (below the standard A–), to avoid a situation where the rating agencies effectively decide whether a euro area country's government bonds can be used as collateral. As Greek was downgraded below investment grade, the European Central Bank in May 2010 was forced to announce that it would accept any Greek government bonds as collateral, regardless of what the rating was.

In the spring of 2010, the European Central Bank engaged in its first round of quantitative easing, buying up around €75 billion of peripheral bonds in the first week of May. As it turned out, the European Central Bank's first brush with quantitative easing only made a small dent in the yield on peripheral government bonds.

Rescue

After the first Greek bailout, the countries of the European Union, in May 2010, created a fund, the so-called *European Financial Stability Facility*, to provide financial assistance to euro countries that found themselves in economic difficulty. The members of the euro area financed the special purpose vehicle that was authorized to borrow up to €440 billion.

Together with funds from the International Monetary Fund and another special purpose vehicle (EMS), the war chest provided by the European Union and the International Monetary Fund to tackle the sovereign debt crisis amounted to €860 billion.

Upon its creation, it was already argued that the European rescue fund fell far short of what was needed. Willem Buiter called in June 2010 for a European rescue fund that would amount to at least €2 trillion as there was a material risk that the sovereign debt crisis would trigger another round of banking crises in the euro area.[21] The banks in the single currency area had a high exposure to government bonds, which once were deemed safe. With the sovereign debt crisis mounting, the government bonds from the euro area's periphery had lost substantial market value in the secondary market. As many of these weakened banks would be unable to attract additional capital from the markets, they would need capital injections from either their governments or other sources.

The creation of the European rescue fund and the bailout packages for Greece and Ireland did little to stem the crisis. In May 2011, the European Union, European Central Bank, and the International Monetary Fund approved a €78 billion bailout for Portugal. After the Irish and Portuguese bailout, the rescue fund had already burned through almost half of it resources. Meanwhile, the yields on not only Greek, Irish, and Portuguese government bonds but also on Spanish and Italian government bonds were on the rise, breaching 6 percent. In August 2012, the European Central Bank resumed buying up government debt, increasing its holdings from more than €50 billion to over €200 billion.

With sovereign defaults of both Spain and Italy in play, two countries that are not only too large to fail but too large to rescue as well, international alarm over the crisis in the euro area grows. With yields well above 6 percent, the government debt of both Spain and Italy would become unsustainable very rapidly. There were increasingly loud calls for the European Union, the European Central Bank, and the International Monetary Fund to give up its policy of forcing austerity upon the periphery, restructure the debt of the periphery, or increase the size of the rescue

---

[21] "Sovereign liquidity facility: Transfer Europe or bank recapitalization fund? What is the EFSF meant to be?," Citi Economics, Global Economics View, June 2010.

fund. These calls did not only come from the most prominent economists in the field but the US government as well.[22]

The crisis in the euro area was at the root of significant political upheaval. In November 2011, the Greek prime minister was pressured to withdraw his promise to hold a referendum on the latest debt deal. That same month, the Italian Prime Minister Silvio Berlusconi was forced to resign as Italy's cost of borrowing hit record levels on bond markets. With Berlusconi out, the European Central Bank started in December 2011 the biggest infusion of credit into the European banking system in the euro's history, lending €489 billion to 523 banks for three years at a rate of one per cent.

By January 2012, the rating agencies started to aim their arrows at France and Austria as well, taking their AAA ratings away. In February, the European Union adopted a second bailout package with the private holders of Greek governmental bonds accepting a haircut of more than 50 percent. The package should enable Greece to bring its debt down to 120 percent of GDP by 2020. That same month, the European Central Bank provided banks in the euro area with further €530 billion in low-interest loans. Net new borrowing under the February auction was around €313 billion.

While the record lending by the European Central Bank offered a short reprieve, by March 2012, the yields on Spanish and Italian government bonds had resumed their relentless climb. Financial markets were clearly betting on an imminent break-up of the euro area. Only when President Draghi told a London audience in the summer of 2012 that the European Central Bank was ready to do "whatever it takes" to preserve the euro while famously adding "believe me, it will be enough," the government bond spreads finally receded.[23]

The yield on peripheral government bonds dropped so quickly, with even the yield on Greek 10-year government bonds dipping below 6 percent for a little while, that one could be forgiven to think that the sovereign debt crisis was something of the past even though economic growth in the euro area remained pretty bleak. Ireland successfully returned in

---

[22] "Exclusive: Geithner to float idea of leveraging euro rescue," *Reuters*, September 15, 2011.

[23] Speech by Mario Draghi, President of the European Central Bank at the Global Investment Conference in London, July 26, 2012.

2012 to the financial markets with a five-year bond auction, which was much sooner than expected, and Spanish yields all but touched 1 percent.

Then a snap election was called in Greece in January 2015, with the radical left-wing party Syriza winning almost an outright majority. It was the pinnacle of the rise of the left-wing populist movement in Southern Europe. With tensions rising between the newly elected, fiercely anti-austerity, Greek government, on the one hand, and the European Union, and the European Central Bank on the other over a new bailout package, the possibility of a break-up of the euro area became once again all too real in the summer of 2015.

CHAPTER 6

The Economic Fallout

WALL STREET

As the global financial crisis unfolded, global stock markets crashed. In September 2008, on the day that Lehman Brothers filed for bankruptcy, the Dow Jones Industrial Average plunged 504 points to close at 10,917.51. The next day, Asian markets follow suit with Japan's Nikkei 225 index closing down 570 points at 11,609. Russia suspended stock market trading for two days as the panic escalated. That week, stock markets around the world shed 5 percent for another day. By the end of that week, as the first contours of a bailout plan began to surface, stock markets recovered somewhat, but not for long. Wall Street continued its rout in the last week of September, as America's biggest savings-and-loan company, Washington Mutual, was seized by the Federal Deposit Insurance Corporation and sold to J.P. Morgan. On September 29, as US Congress failed to pass the $700 billion bailout plan, the Dow Jones plummeted 777 points. Bank shares fell sharply as the credit crunch threatened banks across Europe.

The second week of October, a global stock market rout started in Asia, with Japan's Nikkei index falling almost 10 percent, its biggest drop in 20 years. The Shanghai Composite Index was relatively unperturbed, as the stock market crash in China had already started in October 2007, for mostly domestic reasons unrelated to the financial crisis. The FTSE 100, on the other hand, plunged more than 10 percent, falling under the 4000 mark for the first time in five years. The Dow Jones Industrial Average fell almost 700 points to 7882. While stock markets recovered somewhat the next week as central banks in a coordinated action injected liquidity into the markets, they gave up most of those gains within that same week.

The last week of October, global stock markets resumed their rout. Overnight, the Japanese Nikkei index dropped 9.6 percent. In Hong Kong, stocks fell 8.3 percent. Other Asian stock markets also plunged. In Moscow, the MICEX index slumped 14 percent before the exchange said it was suspending trading till the next week. Germany's DAX index plunged as much as 10.8 percent, France's CAC 40 fell 10 percent, and Britain's FTSE 100 lost 8.7 percent. Although stock markets recovered in early November amid central banks cutting interest rates on both sides of the Atlantic, by mid-November, they were falling again, with shares of Citigroup, once America's largest bank, losing almost 50 percent of their value in the days before the bank being bailed out.

As the year drew to a close, stock markets around the world were down 30 percent or more compared to the beginning of 2008. The FTSE 100 in London wiped out 31 percent, the Dow Jones erased 33 percent, the S&P 500 dropped 37 percent, the DAX index in Frankfurt and the Nikkei index in Tokyo both lost 40 percent, the CAC 40 in Paris fell almost 45 percent, and the Shanghai Composite shed no less than 65 percent in 2008. It would take a few more months for the Dow Jones, the FTSE, and the Nikkei index to bottom out, but by March 2009, most stock markets turned around and found their way up, boosted by what would be the first installment of trillions of dollars in quantitative easing administered by the Federal Reserve. It would, nonetheless, take another four years for the Dow Jones to return to its previous record of 14,093 points.

In the euro area, some stock markets would take much more time to bottom out, depending on the state of the sovereign's finances, and some of them, most notably the stock markets in Athens and Madrid, have yet to return to their pre-financial crisis record. The Shanghai Composite never really recovered from its 2007/2008 crash, that is, not until November 2014, when the Chinese government announced that it would allow foreign investors to trade on stock exchanges on China's mainland.

The global financial crisis did not only rattle stock markets but other financial markets as well. As stress started to build up in credit markets and interbank lending rates rose, there was an enormous flight to safety, that is, US Treasuries. The yield on three-months Treasury bills fell from more than 5 percent in February 2007 to 0.03 percent in December 2008. The yield on 10-year Treasuries dropped as well from 4 percent in August 2008 to slightly over 2 percent in December 2008.

With the flight into US Treasuries came a considerable appreciation of the US dollar as well. The real effective exchange rate of the US dollar rose between March 2008 and March 2009 by 15 percent on a trade-weighted basis. While the 10-year Treasury yield seemed to recover over the course of 2010 and 2011, it came crashing down again in August 2011 as the standoff in US Congress over the debt ceiling brought the world's largest economy on the verge of default. Amid the sovereign debt crisis in the euro area, the 10-year Treasury yield sank even deeper, tipping below 1.50 percent in July 2012 as investors once again sought refuge in US Treasuries.

Main Street

While the financial crisis initially foremost shook Wall Street, soon it began to alter the makeup of Main Street—in the most literal meaning of the word—as well. Foreclosure activity jumped 81 percent in 2008, with one in every 54 households in the USA getting, at least, one notice that the bank was about to initiate the sale of the property. Over 1 million people lost their homes in 2008 alone. Nevada had the highest rate of foreclosure, with more than 7 percent of Nevada housing units, or one in every 14, receiving at least one foreclosure notice in 2008. California had the highest number of foreclosure filings, at 523,624 properties.

Among the 100 largest metropolitan areas, Stockton, California, had the highest rate of foreclosure. Las Vegas was close behind in second place. As home foreclosures are notoriously contagious, especially among strategic defaulters, one home foreclosure could quickly infect an entire neighborhood. As a consequence, the incidence of foreclosures was unevenly spread throughout the USA. Nevertheless, the financial crisis affected the lives of many Main Street people.

Instead of adding between 100,000 and 150,000 new jobs a month, which often is considered the number of jobs needed to keep up with the growth of the working-age population, the US economy shed, month after month, hundreds of thousands of jobs. While the job losses had already mounted before the demise of Lehman Brothers, the pace of job losses accelerated dramatically after that. From September 2008 to September 2009, almost 7 million jobs evaporated.[1] In total, roughly 8.7 million jobs were shed. Expressed as a percentage of the number of jobs at peak employment in January 2008, job losses amounted to 6.3 percent, by far worse than during any post-war recession.

Not only the extent of the job losses stood out, but the slow recovery of the job market was remarkable as well. It would take more than six years, that is, until March 2014, for the US job market to just recoup the jobs that had been lost since the previous peak in January 2008. Still, a significant number of the jobs that had been recovered were only on a part-time basis, leaving many an employee underemployed, albeit not unemployed. With the notable exception of the economic recession of 2001, post-war economic recoveries had been V-shaped, meaning that the job market would bounce back very rapidly, generally within two years.[2]

The official unemployment rate hit 10 percent in October 2009. Other employment statistics painted an even more worrisome picture. The U-6, for example, which is the underemployment rate and includes both part-time workers who want a full-time job as well as those not in the labor force who would take a job if one were available, reached 17.2 percent in April 2010. That same month, the share of the long-term unemployed, that is, those who have been out of work for 27 weeks or longer, reached 45.3 percent. Most worrisome, perhaps, is that the labor force participation rate, that is, the labor force as a percentage of the working-age population has fallen off a cliff since the beginning of the financial crisis, dropping from 66.1 percent in September 2008 to 62.4 percent in September 2015.

In Europe, the housing bubbles started to deflate as well in the wake of the credit crunch. With the exception of Ireland, the housing markets peaked later and the downturn was more protracted compared to the USA. The same applies to the unemployment rate in the euro area and the European Union, which peaked not once but twice, first as a result of the 2008 financial crisis, and subsequently, at the occasion of the sovereign debt crisis. The euro area unemployment rate initially rose from

---

[1] Bureau of Labor Statistics.
[2] "Percent Job Losses: Great Recession and Great Depression," *Calculated Risk*, February 12, 2012.

7.3 percent in 2008 to 10.3 percent in 2010. Although the unemployment rate declined for a short while, it climbed to reach just over 12 percent amid the sovereign debt crisis.[3]

Underneath the average unemployment rate, however, was a bunch of disparate statistics as well as statistical methods, with registered unemployment rates as high as 25 percent in Spain and Greece and as low as 5 percent in Germany. In part, the differences between the USA and Europe in the aftermath of the financial crisis can be attributed to cultural and structural differences, most notably the fact that European countries have more generous welfare states, stricter labor market protection laws, more stringent bankruptcy laws, and lower labor mobility compared to the USA.

A more important distinction between the USA and Europe is that, during the boom years, labor costs in the peripheral countries increased much faster than in the rest of the euro area. When the boom went bust, the countries in the periphery, most notably Greece, Spain, Ireland, and Portugal, were settled with an uncompetitive tradable sector. Because external devaluation through currency depreciation was no longer on the table, the peripheral countries had to regain competitiveness through internal devaluation, that is, renegotiating individual wage contracts.

As the euro area was still very much an unfinished project, there was no meaningful fiscal integration, that is, a supranational or federal component to spending at the national level. So the sovereign, instead of Brussels, had to cover the unemployment benefits and other social expenditures whereas in the USA Washington D.C. would pick up the bill. There was no harmonization of social policies either, which eroded the popular basis for fiscal transfers to the periphery at the expense of the core countries; nor was there a banking union. So, when banks in the periphery found themselves on the verge of bankruptcy, it was once again up to the sovereign to recapitalize the faltering banks, while the recapitalization as such brought the sovereign once again closer to default. Only President Draghi's assurance in July 2012 that the European Central Bank would, in fact, act as lender of last resort could stop the peripheral countries from spiraling downward.

---

[3] The unemployment figures for the European Union as a whole follow the same trajectory, albeit a half to a full percentage point below the unemployment rate in the euro area.

Government

After the bailout of the big Wall Street banks, US public finances were in dire straits. The budget deficit that had meandered around 3 or 4 percent of GDP in the years before the global financial crisis, exploded in the years after the big meltdown of Wall Street, topping 13 percent of GDP in 2009. The government money spent on bank bailouts, outlays for unemployment benefits, food stamps and other social programs together with the $898 billion stimulus plan and the plunging tax revenues resulted in a tripling of the deficit. In the euro area, the overall budget deficit reached 6.2 percent of the euro area's GDP.[4] It then receded rather quickly, reaching 2.9 percent of GDP in 2013. In terms of government debt as a share of GDP, the euro area and the USA did not outrun each other by much, with gross government debt reaching more than 90 of GDP in 2012 in the euro area and more than 100 percent of GDP in the USA in 2012. Not only did the euro area start out with a somewhat higher debt-to-GDP level compared to the USA, economic growth in the years after the financial crisis in the euro area was also lower, affecting the debt to GDP ratio through the denominator effect.[5]

But again, underneath the euro area's pavement, things were considerably worse than on the surface. In 2007, none of the euro area countries was running a deficit in excess of 3 percent, again with the exception of Greece that had a deficit of 6.5 percent of GDP and Portugal that had a tiny transgression with a deficit of 3.1 percent.[6] By 2009, virtually all countries had a deficit in excess of 3 percent, with Greece reporting a deficit of 15.8 percent, closely followed by Ireland with 14.2 percent and Spain with 11.2 percent. In 2007, many euro area countries had government debt that exceeded the norm of 60 percent of GDP as laid down in the Stability and Growth Pact. Nonetheless, Greece and Italy stood out, with government debt ratios of more than 100 percent of GDP even before the financial crisis.

The countries with the largest increases in debt to GDP ratio from 2007 to 2010 were Ireland, Portugal, and Greece. It was the main reason that these three countries needed bailouts. While Greece was quite

---

[4] International Monetary Fund, WEO Database, October 2015.

[5] The government debt to GDP ratio for the European Union as a whole follows the same trajectory, albeit about 5 percentage points below the debt to GDP ratio in the euro area.

[6] Eurostat.

successful in reducing the budget deficit, it was much less so when it came down to reducing the government debt to GDP ratio, which reached 175 percent by 2013. It is what Barry Eichengreen, early on in the crisis, predicted would happen—namely, that without debt-restructuring, the drive for austerity would be self-defeating as it would shrink a country's GDP and thus increase the debt to GDP ratio.[7] Ireland, on the other hand, was able to grow its economy in the face of austerity in spite of net emigration since 2009 and thus bring down government debt as a share of GDP.[8]

China and Beyond

Although China's stock market in 2007/2008 crashed mostly for domestic reasons that had little to do with the global financial crisis, the impact of the financial crisis on global trade was such that China's leadership did not want to take any chances. In October 2008, the People's Bank of China began to ease monetary policy to stimulate the economy. The next month, the government announced a ¥4 trillion ($586 billion) stimulus program, increasing public expenditures on infrastructure (highways, railways, and airports), affordable housing, public health and education, the environment, and technological innovation. Lower reserve ratios for the banks, interest rate cuts, and the lowering of mortgage down-payment requirements led to substantial increases in household borrowing.

Even though China's GDP growth dropped from 14.2 percent in 2007 to 9.2 percent in 2009, the reported unemployment rate rose during that same period from 4 to 4.3 percent.[9] China's government debt remained around 20 percent of GDP as the stimulus was financed primarily by bank credit, rather than deficit spending. Private debt, however, defined as household debt plus debt of non-financial companies, increased between 2009 and 2010 from 120 percent to 150 percent of GDP.[10] While China's economy did not return to consecutive years of double-digit growth after

---

[7] Barry Eichengreen, "Going Beyond Austerity Measures," *The New York Times*, May 24, 2011.

[8] Central Statistics Office of Ireland.

[9] Ministry of Human Resources and Social Security of the People's Republic of China.

[10] "Is China Leading the World into Recession?," Citi Research, Global Economics View, September 2015.

the financial crisis, it was a beacon of prosperity in the aftermath of the global financial crisis.

Japan was still licking its wounds from the bursting of the asset price bubble in 1993 when the global financial crisis struck. Although Japan's banking sector emerged relatively unscathed, the Japanese economy nonetheless contracted sharply due to a steep fall in external demand. When the economy bounced back, it resumed its path of lackluster growth of the previous decade. Only this time around, the Japanese economy found itself in the good company of most other advanced economies that, in turn, feared a Japanese decade.

In the years after the financial crisis, emerging and developing economies grew three to four times as fast as advanced economies.[11] The economic growth in emerging economies was aided in part by China's economic stimulus package and in part by commodity prices that, after an initial drop-off, quickly bounced back. While in 2000, advanced economies accounted for almost 60 percent of global GDP and emerging and developing economies slightly over 40 percent, by 2020, the latter are forecasted to account for 60 percent of GDP and advanced economies for what is left.[12]

Great Recession

As financial markets unraveled, pundits and economists alike were quick to point out the parallels between the Great Depression of the 1930s and the economic recession in the wake of the global financial crisis. But a comparison of the fall in global industrial production from its peak in mid-1929 to the fall in global production from its peak in late-2007, a year after the collapse of Lehman Brothers, showed that this time around, the situation was only half as bad as it was during the Great Depression.[13] Hence, this economic crisis was quickly dubbed the Great Recession.

---

[11] On a formal exchange rate basis, International Monetary Fund, WEO Database, October 2015.

[12] On a purchasing power parity basis, International Monetary Fund, WEO Database, October 2015.

[13] Paul Krugman, "The story so far, in one picture," *The New York Times* blog, November 3, 2009.

As there is no commonly accepted definition of a recession, not at the global level nor at the level of individual nations, there is no agreement on the extent and the timing of the Great Recession. If the strict definition of a recession as a growth contraction is used, then, according to the International Monetary Fund, the Great Recession spanned the calendar year 2009.[14] In case the more common definition of a global recession is used, that is, global growth at lower than 2 percent, then the Great Recession spanned two calendar years.

The National Bureau of Economic Research determined that the beginning of the recession in the USA was in December 2007. The bottom was reached in June 2009, which was the final month of the recession. The euro area went through a double-dip recession, with the first recession lasting 15 months, starting in the second quarter of 2008 and ending in the second quarter of 2009, and the second recession lasting 18 months, beginning in the fourth quarter of 2011 and ending in the first quarter of 2013.[15] The UK also went through a double-dip recession, with the first recession lasting 18 months and the second recession lasting nine months.[16] GDP levels in the advanced economies declined permanently since 2008 by as much as 10 percent below their respective long-run trends.

Under the strict definition of a recession as a growth contraction, China's economy did not go into a recession. Under the prevailing definition of a recession in China, which is a growth rate of less than 4 percent, there was no recession either. Although GDP growth in China initially fell off sharply in 2008, it quickly rebounded to its double-digit pre-crisis rate in late 2009 at 11.4 percent per year, less than a year after unveiling its ¥4 trillion stimulus package. Despite weak international demand and a 45 percent drop in exports, total industrial production in China nearly doubled between 2007 and 2013. During the crisis years, China's economic growth contributed 50 percent to the growth of global GDP even though its income accounted for less than 10 percent of global GDP.[17]

---

[14] Others have argued that the global economic contraction started in the third quarter of 2008 and lasted three quarters, that is, until the first quarter of 2009.
[15] The European Union experienced a triple-dip recession, Eurostat.
[16] Office for National Statistics in the United Kingdom.
[17] On a formal exchange rate basis, International Monetary Fund, WEO Database, October 2015.

Secular Stagnation

In spite of the fiscal stimulus programs implemented in many advanced economies that were worth up to 5 percent of GDP and massive monetary stimulus by way of quantitative easing, five years after the demise of Lehman Brothers GDP growth in advanced economies remained sluggish at best and stagnant in most cases. It was then that economists, most notably Larry Summers, raised the specter of secular stagnation.[18]

Alvin Hansen coined in 1938, that is, the latter stages of the Great Depression, the term "secular stagnation."[19] Hansen argued that, because of the apparent slowdowns in population growth and the pace of technological advance, firms were unlikely to see much reason to invest in new capital goods. He concluded that tepid investment spending, together with subdued consumption by households, would likely prevent the attainment of full employment for many years.

Secular stagnation occurs if there is a persistent shortfall of demand, which cannot be overcome with near-zero interest rates. As such, it needs to be distinguished from the argument that the growth of economic potential is slowing. Secular stagnation is a demand-side, not a supply-side concept, although the persistent lack of demand can eventually contribute to the lack of potential supply. This is, for example, the case if the long-term unemployed lose their skills or give up looking for work, a phenomenon known as hysteresis. There is no guarantee that market economies when plunged into a downturn, will revert to the growth rate that was considered normal before.

The episodes over the past decades that exhibited satisfactory economic growth proved financially utterly unsustainable. In the years before the global financial crisis, economic growth was to a large extent driven by the housing bubble, which was associated with an ultimately unsustainable increase in the share of residential investment in GDP (from just under 4 percent of GDP in 2000 to 6.5 percent of GDP in 2005). The rising house prices in the USA were associated as well with an equally unsustainable increase in the debt-to-income ratio for households (from 95 percent of GDP in 2000 to more than 130 percent of GDP in 2007). Viewed

---

[18] Lawrence Summers, "U.S. Economic Prospects: Secular Stagnation, Hysteresis, and the Zero Lower Bound," *Business Economics*, Vol. 49, No. 2, 2014.

[19] Alvin Hansen, "Economic Progress and Declining Population Growth," American Economic Association presidential address, 1938.

through the prism of the housing bubble, the real growth rate of the US economy before the global financial crisis was mediocre at best.

Europe's economic performance after the introduction of the euro in 1999 was surprisingly strong. For a while, it seemed that all doomsayers about the single currency had been mistaken. Compared to the USA, the euro area appeared almost entirely balanced. But as the financial sector on both sides of the Atlantic crumbled, it became apparent that house prices in Europe had lost touch with reality just as much as house prices in the USA. The stellar economic performance of the euro area, especially the periphery, in the years leading up to the global financial crisis thus proved to be at least as unsustainable as the economic growth in the USA before the crisis. Since then, the countries in the euro area have done considerably worse than the already sluggish US economy amid worries over the sovereign debt crisis.

The "new economy" of the late 1990s, which was characterized by high growth, low inflation, and high employment, turned out to be largely unsustainable as well because it was the dot-com bubble rather than fundamentals that propelled economic growth and labor demand. It was the first time in decades that wages and salaries as a share of GDP made considerable inroads at the expense of corporate profits, increasing from 44 percent of GDP in 1994 to almost 47 percent of GDP in 2000. As the stock market bubble was less leveraged than the housing bubble, the fallout from the stock market crash was less severe compared to the housing bubble.

Of course, the housing bubble in the new millennium cushioned the effect of the 2000 stock market crash. Some commentators have even suggested that that was the entire purpose of the Federal Reserve's loose monetary policy in the early 2000s. As Paul McCulley in July 2001 mused: "There is room for the Fed to create a bubble in housing prices, if necessary, to sustain American hedonism. And I think the Fed has the will to do so, even though political correctness would demand that Mr. Greenspan denies any such thing."[20] When the housing bubble ultimately popped, the American satirical newspaper *The Onion* in July 2008 ran an article with the eerily deft headline: "Recession-Plagued Nation Demands New Bubble To Invest In." That was still years before the debate about secular stagnation began.

---

[20] Paul Krugman, "Running Out of Bubbles," *The New York Times*, May 27, 2005.

Summers suggests that a decline in the real interest rate is at the root of the increasing financial instability which encourages risk-seeking by investors. The decline in real interest rates, in turn, may be traced back to three developments, according to Summers. First, it may be a reflection of the changing character of economic activity, that is, the rise of technological behemoths like Apple and Google who are swimming in cash. An Internet company like Instagram has a market value comparable to that of Sony, with just a fraction of the capital investment required to achieve it, or workers for that matter. The reduced demand for investment, in turn, affects the levels of interest rates.

Second, a declining rate of population growth induces a decline in the natural rate of interest as it lowers investment demand. Just like it has already happened in Japan, over the next two decades, the population in Europe and the USA will grow at a substantially lower rate than in the previous two decades, and hence, depress investment demand. Third, Summers points to the changes in the distribution of income, both between labor income and capital income and between those with more wealth and those with less. These changes have raised the propensity to save, and so have the rising earnings that corporations retain. The increase in inequality and the capital income share of GDP result in an increase in the level of savings. The reduced investment demand and the increased propensity to save both operate in the direction of a lower equilibrium real interest rate.

Other economists have offered up alternative explanations for the economic stagnation that has affected virtually all advanced economies in the aftermath of the global financial crisis. Some have argued that advanced economies are stuck in a "safety trap." To make banks more robust, regulators raised the capital requirements for large banks that could be too big to fail, thus forcing institutional investors to invest in triple-A assets. At the same time, the supply of these assets has gone down by half due to the financial crisis as many assets lost their triple-A status, pushing the real interest rate down.[21] Richard Koo has argued that secular stagnation is nothing else than a balance sheet recession, which is an economic recession that occurs when high levels of private sector debt in the wake of an asset price bubble cause individuals

---

[21] Ricardo Caballero and Emmanuel Farhi, "On the role of safe asset shortages in secular stagnation," in *Secular Stagnation: Facts, Causes, and Cures*, VOXEU eBook, p. 111, 2014.

or companies to collectively focus on saving rather than spending or investing to shore up their balance sheets.[22]

Robert Gordon, on the other hand, has argued that the US economy may have stumbled upon a problem even bigger than secular stagnation—namely, stagnant or slow-growing potential output. In his view, the US economy is already operating close to potential output. According to Gordon, economic growth in the USA will continue to be sluggish for the next 25–40 years—not because of a slowdown in technological growth, but rather because of four "headwinds": demographics, education, inequality, and government debt.[23]

The evolution of inequality at the bottom takes the form of endless downward pressure on wages, with two-tier wage systems and workers forced into part-time work when they want full-time work. The channels to lower labor productivity are, for example, part-time workers who lose skills and the opportunities for promotion, or college students from low-income families who have to work while going to school, and drop out of both, thus losing the chance to gain human capital and future productivity.

---

[22] Richard Koo, "Balance sheet recession is the reason for secular stagnation," in *Secular Stagnation: Facts, Causes, and Cures*, VOXEU eBook, p. 131, 2014.

[23] Robert Gordon, "The turtle's progress: Secular stagnation meets the headwinds," in *Secular Stagnation: Facts, Causes, and Cures*, VOXEU eBook, p. 47, 2014.

CHAPTER 7

Unlimited Supplies of Labor

Arthur Lewis' Essay

The integration of China and India in the global market added more than 2.3 billion consumers and producers to the global economy. They entered as suppliers of core goods and services and as demanders of non-core commodities. Even today, more than a decade after China's accession to the World Trade Organization, more than a third of Chinese still work in the primary sector, which besides farming also includes forestry, logging, and fishing. In India, the primary sector provides employment to 60 percent of the country's total population.

As Arthur Lewis pointed out, the neoclassical framework is not suitable to analyze the growth dynamics of such economies. In his 1954 essay "Economic Development with Unlimited Supplies of Labor," Arthur Lewis proposed a framework for the economic development of an emerging economy that had abundant supplies of labor. In 1979, Lewis won the Nobel Prize in Economics for his contributions to the field of economic development.

Lewis' theory of economic development with unlimited supplies of labor is a classical model. In case labor is in unlimited supply, the neoclassical model, which assumes that labor is in short supply, is useless, according to Lewis. The same goes for Keynesianism, which addresses a shortfall in aggregate demand in the short run. Once the remedies that Keynes proposed have successfully been applied to the ailing economy, the neoclassical framework becomes germane again. While Lewis' essay addresses the economic development of developing and emerging economies, and closed economies for that matter, his work is also useful to analyze the contemporary global economy with a secular underemployment of labor.

An unlimited supply of labor exists in countries where the population is large relative to capital and natural resources so that there are large sectors of the economy where the marginal productivity of labor is negligible, zero, or even negative. In developing and emerging economies, such "disguised" unemployment can often be found in the agricultural sector because the piece of land that a family has to tend to is so small that if some members of the family find other employment, the remaining members could cultivate the holding just as well, although they might have to work harder.

This phenomenon played a significant role in the development of China during the great transformation. Prior to the opening up and reform under Deng Xiaoping, China suffered from chronic shortages of food supply. During the first half of the 1970s, the number of households that failed to meet the required grain production quota increased. This resulted in smaller grain stocks and cross-provincial shipments, which raised the fears of "repeating the error of 1959," a clear reference to the Great Leap Forward famine that suggests that China was on the verge of another food crisis.[1]

Before the policy of reform and opening up in 1978, China's economy operated well below its potential, partly because its labor force, perceiving that their effort hardly affected their incomes, withheld a substantial fraction of its available energy, which in turn, was reduced by chronic under-nutrition. Once the link between effort and reward was restored, work effort multiplied and food production expanded. Labor productivity increased so rapidly that soon, millions of Chinese started looking for employment beyond the countryside, resulting eventually in the migration of hundreds of millions of Chinese.

The phenomenon of disguised unemployment is by no means confined to the countryside. As Lewis already pointed out in 1954, there are the wives and daughters of the household too. Most advanced economies

---

[1] Loren Brandt and Thomas G. Rawski, "China's Great Transformation," in Brandt, Loren; Rawski, G. Thomas, *China's Great Transformation*, Cambridge University Press, 2008.

have experienced a considerable rise in female labor force participation over the past few decades. However, the differences in levels of female labor force participation across countries are still considerable, especially if the number of hours worked is taken in account as well, and well below the level of male labor participation, suggesting that female labor is still underutilized in many countries.

Disguised unemployment is found elsewhere too, such as in the domestic sector. In developing and emerging economies, the line between employees and dependents is thin. It is considered a moral duty to keep as many servants on the payroll as possible. In China, middle-class families usually employ one or more "*ayi*" (maid). The subsistence sector is evident in public spaces too. In China's big cities numerous, albeit less and less, people are employed to sweep public squares and tend to public restrooms. These are the so-called *urban underemployed*.

Another source of labor supply is the increase in the population resulting from the excess of births over deaths or net immigration. As prosperity is an important method of birth control, most advanced economies are facing an aging population and an either stagnant or shrinking working-age population, resulting in an increase in the dependency ratio. Emerging economies experience a shift in the population's age structure during which the share of the working-age population (15–64) is larger than the non-working-age share of the population (14 and younger, and 65 and older).

This transition is known as the demographic dividend. Due to China's one-child policy, which was implemented between 1978 and 1980 and was formally being phased out in 2015, the demographic shift in China occurred relatively and quickly, with birth rates falling from, on average, six births per woman in 1965 to 1.5 births per woman in 2000. As a result, China enjoyed a relatively large albeit short-lived demographic dividend that by now has almost run its course.[2]

THE MODEL

According to Lewis, in an over-populated economy, that is, an economy with a large population relative to the stock of capital, there can be an

---

[2] According to the United Nations, the demographic dividend accounted for 15 per cent of China's economic growth between 1982 and 2000.

enormous expansion of new industries or new employment opportunities without any shortage of unskilled labor becoming apparent in the labor market. From the point of view of the effect of economic development on wages, the supply of labor is practically unlimited. This applies only to unskilled labor. There may at any time be a shortage of skilled workers, from electricians to engineers, biologists, doctors or lawyers. However, a shortage of skilled labor is only a "quasi-bottleneck" in the sense that it is temporary. If the capital is available for development, then the capitalists or the government will soon provide the facilities to train more skilled people. In an open economy, one can also attract skilled workers from abroad.

The real bottlenecks to expansion are therefore capital and natural resources, and so long as these are available, the necessary skills will be provided as well, though perhaps with some time lag. If unlimited labor is available while capital is scarce, the law of diminishing returns dictates that only so much labor will be used with capital until the marginal productivity of labor is zero. In practice, however, labor is not available at a zero wage. The price of labor, in economies with unlimited supplies of labor, is a wage at the subsistence level. Workers in the capitalist sector earn a wage that is somewhat higher than the subsistence level, or the so-called *capitalist wage* . Capital will, therefore, be applied up to the point where the marginal productivity of labor equals the subsistence wage. Labor supply at the capitalist wage is also perfectly elastic, meaning that extra demand for labor will not lead to higher wages because workers can be drawn from the subsistence sector as long as labor is in unlimited supply.

Lewis uses a simple two-sector model to analyze the economic development with unlimited supplies of labor—namely, the capitalist sector and the subsistence sector. The capitalist sector is that part of the economy— either private or public—that uses reproducible capital and pays capitalists for the use thereof. The subsistence sector is that part of the economy that is not using reproducible capital, generally the agricultural sector. The implication of unlimited supplies of labor is that the capitalist sector can hire even more workers without the need to raise real wages. All that the capitalist sector has to pay is the capitalist wage. Under these conditions, any gains in labor productivity do not translate into higher wages, as mainstream economic theory has it, but in higher profits instead, which Lewis calls the "capitalist surplus." The capitalist surplus is the difference between the marginal productivity of labor and the capitalist wage, symbolized by WNP in Fig. 7.1. In economies with unlimited supplies of labor, capital formation, and technical progress do not result in rising wages but in a rising share of profits in the national income instead (Fig. 7.1).

The key to Lewis' model of expansion is the use of the capitalist surplus. In so far as the capitalist surplus is reinvested in creating new capital, the marginal productivity of labor increases at every level. Therefore, the curve representing the marginal productivity of labor shifts outwards as the capitalist sector expands, taking even more people into capitalist employment out of the subsistence sector. The surplus becomes even bigger, the capital formation even greater, and the process will continue until the labor surplus has disappeared. As the supply of labor is perfectly elastic in a situation of unlimited supplies of labor, workers continue to be available at the capitalist wage rate.

In the beginning, the national income of the developing or emerging economy consists almost entirely of subsistence income. This subsistence wage remains constant in real terms throughout the expansion since labor can, by definition, be ceded to the expanding capitalist sector without reducing subsistence output. The process, therefore, increases the capitalist surplus as a share of the national income. The model says, in effect, that if unlimited supplies of labor are available at a constant real wage,

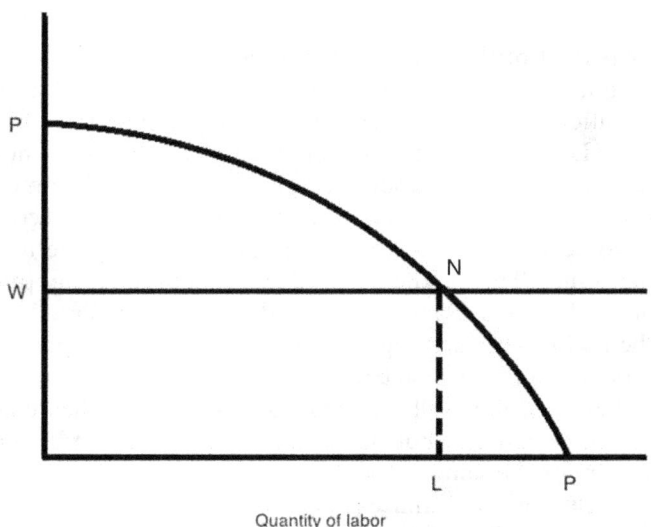

Fig. 7.1 Capitalist surplus with unlimited labor supplies (*Source*: Arthur Lewis)

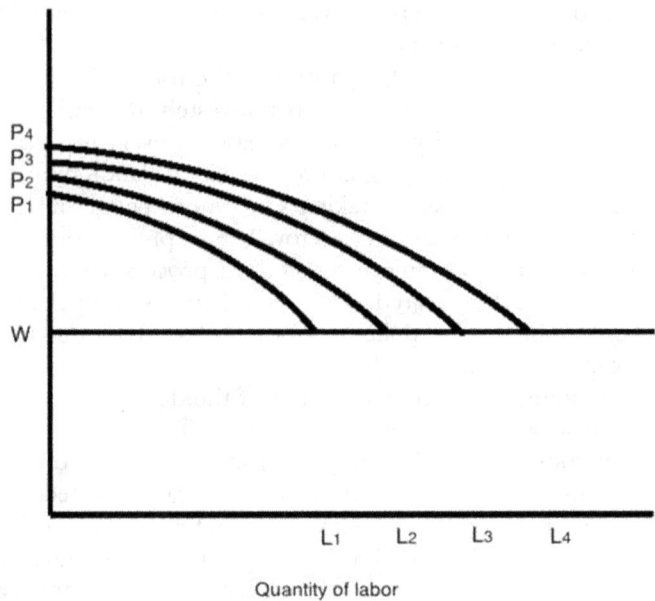

Fig. 7.2 Capitalist surplus with unlimited labor supplies (*Source*: Arthur Lewis)

and if any part of profits is reinvested in productive capacity, profits will grow continuously as a share of national income, and capital formation as a share of national income will also increase (Fig. 7.2).

In Arthur Lewis' model, the primary source of national savings is profits. In case savings are increasing as a share of national income, it often happens because profits as a share of national income are increasing. In his view, workers' savings are very small as they earn (little more than) subsistence wages. The middle classes do save, but the savings out of their salaries are of little consequence for productive investment. Most members of the middle class are engaged in the perpetual struggle to keep up with the Joneses; if they manage to save enough to buy the house in which they live, they are doing well. They may save to educate their children, or to subsist in their old age, but this saving is virtually offset by the savings being used up for the same purposes.

Only the elite save a significant portion of their income. In countries with unlimited supplies of labor, the top 10 percent with the highest incomes, that is, the upper-income decile, receive up to 40 percent of national income. People in the top decile do not get all of a sudden thriftier or consume less. The most plausible explanation is that people save more because they have more to save. Saving increases relatively to the national income because the incomes of the savers increase relatively to the national income. The important fact of economic development with unlimited supplies of labor is that the distribution of incomes is altered in favor of the saving class.

The Use of the Capitalist Surplus

In Arthur Lewis's model for economic development with unlimited supplies of labor, the capitalist surplus is the *sine qua non* for economic development. According to Lewis, rapid capital accumulation is the prerequisite for economic development so a country could not go through the industrial revolution until savings increased relatively to national income. The model effectively predicts that as long as unlimited supplies of labor are available at a constant real wage and if any part of profits is reinvested in productive capacity, profits will grow continuously relatively to the national income, and capital formation will also grow relatively to the national income.

While the rising share of profits in national income at the expense of labor's share is instrumental to economic development according to Lewis, it is also where his model is most vulnerable. As Lewis himself clearly realized, there is no guarantee that the capitalists will use the capitalist surplus for capital formation. Malthus, the eternal pessimist, imagined that the capitalist surplus would lead to a commodities glut, that is, a widespread excess of supply over demand. Ricardo, more optimistically, rebutted that there would be no such glut as what the capitalists did not consume themselves they would use (to pay the wages of workers) to create more fixed capital.

Marx agreed with Ricardo, as he believed that capitalists have a passion for accumulating capital. The new fixed capital would then, in the next stage, make possible the employment of more people in the capitalist sector. Ricardo added that if capitalists did not want to accumulate, they would consume instead of saving. Employment in the next stage would not be as big as it would have been if they had created more fixed capital and so brought more workers into the capitalist sector, but so long as there is no hoarding, it makes no difference to the current level of employment, whether capitalists decide to consume or to save.

Part of the capitalist surplus is consumed. As for the part which is consumed, Arthur Lewis realized that some of it is a genuine payment for service rendered for managerial or entrepreneurial services, as well as for the services of public administrators, whether these are paid salaries out of taxes, or whether they live off their rents. However, Arthur Lewis also acknowledged that these managerial and entrepreneurial services, as well as the public services, might well be overpaid. The solution to such overpayment was in Lewis's eyes progressive taxation. He saw the overpayments of managers and administrators also as an argument for nationalization, albeit a dubious one.

When an economy eventually runs out of its unlimited supplies of labor, it reaches the Lewis Turning Point, named after Arthur Lewis. Beyond the Lewis Turning Point, additional demand for labor will raise the equilibrium wage rate, and the economy will conform to the neoclassical model.

Open Economy

Lewis wrote his model for a closed and emerging economy. However, in a globalized world the effects of unlimited supplies of labor spill over to advanced economies as well. Lewis envisaged this possibility also and suggested what capitalists in an emerging economy could do once capital accumulation would catch up with the labor supply, wages would begin to rise substantially above the subsistence level, and the capitalist surplus would negatively be affected. According to Lewis, as long as there is still surplus labor in other countries, the capitalists can avoid the capital surplus being adversely affected either by encouraging immigration or by exporting their capital to countries where there is still abundant labor at a subsistence wage.

In the case of relatively small immigrations, the effect on wages is negligible and immigrants will enjoy the higher wages in the host country. Mass migration, however, may pull the wage level in the host country down. In a competitive model and absent labor protection laws, the wage level, for example, in the USA could exceed the wage level in India and China only by an amount covering migration costs. All the benefits of decreasing wages and, increasing returns on capital go into the capitalist surplus. For this reason, labor unions in countries where the wage level is relatively high are bitterly hostile to immigration. Without immigration, real wages are higher than they otherwise would be while profits, the capital surplus, and total output are smaller than they otherwise would be.

As Arthur Lewis already noted in his landmark essay and recent history underscores, exporting capital from a country with a labor shortage to a country with a labor surplus is less controversial and, therefore, easier to organize for the capitalists. Labor unions are quick to restrict inflows of immigrants but much slower in bringing the export of capital under control even though the export of capital reduces the build-up of fixed capital at home, and thus reduces the demand for labor. However, if the capital abroad is used in ways that raise the standard of living of the capital-exporting country, this effect may be offset wholly or partially.

Capital export may benefit workers on balance if it is used for increasing the supply of things they import or raising wage costs in the capital-importing country. The reduction in wages in capital-exporting countries, however, is aggravated if the capital is invested in ways that increase the productivity of competing exports. Capital-importing countries with surplus labor do not gain an increase in real wages from having foreign capital invested in them unless this capital results in increased productivity in the commodities they produce for their own consumption.

CHAPTER 8

China's Economic Development

INTERNATIONAL COMPARISON

From 1980 to 2015, the growth rate of the Chinese economy averaged 9.7 percent per year. By 2015, China's GDP in real terms was 28 times as large as it had been in 1980.[1] By comparison, the US economy grew over that same period on average 2.6 percent per year, and US real GDP in 2015 was only 2.5 times as large as it had been in 1980. Maddison and Wu have argued that China initially underestimated the size of its economy because the initial data ignored large swaths of output, particularly in the service sector. When this previously unrecorded output was included in the official data, the past GDP data were not revised upward. As a consequence, the official growth rate suggests more economic growth than has taken place. According to Maddison and Wu, the actual growth rate in China was on average almost 2 percent points lower than the official growth rate as published by the International Monetary Fund.[2]

The discussion of growth rates is not only relevant for the international comparisons of emerging economies over the past 35 years. It has implications for the projections that are based on past official growth rates as well. If these past growth rates have been overstated, forecasts that are based on previous official growth rates bring into question the value of

---

[1] Formal exchange rate basis, International Monetary Fund, WEO Database, October 2015.
[2] Angus Maddison and Harry Wu, "China's Economic Performance: How Fast has GDP Grown? How Big is it Compared with the USA?," 2006.

projections such as in what year China's economy is set to overtake the US economy on a formal exchange rate basis. China skeptics are eager to cite Vice Premier Li Keqiang, who in 2007 famously proclaimed China's GDP figures to be "man-made" and "for reference only." China at the time was experiencing its fifth year of double-digit economic growth, reaching over 14 percent that same year. Therefore, Vice Premier Li's remarks may just as well have been intended to quell Western fears over China's robust rise.[3]

A comprehensive comparison of economies by the International Comparison Program, which made use of estimates of the real cost of living, concluded in 2014 that China's economy had in fact grown faster than previously projected, overtaking the US economy in 2014 instead of 2019.[4] Extensive research on the prices of goods and services showed that money goes further in poorer countries than previously thought, prompting an increase in the relative size of emerging market economies. The study was carried out under the auspices of the World Bank, and its results are used by, among others, the International Monetary Fund.

The growth in output flows from an increase in the numbers of workers/hours worked or an increase in the output per worker (labor productivity). Labor productivity, in turn, flows from an increase in the contribution of capital (capital deepening), an increase in the contribution of human capital, or greater efficiency (total factor productivity). Comparing the economic development in China, India, Mexico, and Brazil from 1980 to 2004, it is noticeable that during that period, output per worker in China tripled and that the high pace of productivity growth continued after that.[5] The growth in output in India, Brazil, Mexico, and the rest of the world was modest at best by comparison. India is the only country that comes somewhat close to China as output per worker in India almost doubled during that same period. Research by the Conference Board puts labor productivity growth in China from 1995 to 2006 at 110 percent, in

---

[3] The 10th and 11th Five-Year Plan called for average annual GDP growth of 7 and 7.5 percent for the period from 2001 to 2005 and 2006 to 2010, respectively. It seems, therefore, that China's explosive economic growth may also have taken its leaders by surprise.

[4] According to a report in *The Financial Times* of May 1, 2014, China fought for a year to undermine the International Comparison Program's report showing it was poised to usurp the USA as the world's biggest economy in 2014, based on purchasing power.

[5] Alan Heston and Terry Sicular, "China and Development Economics," in Brandt, Loren; Rawski, G. Thomas, *China's Great Transformation*, Cambridge University Press, 2008.

India at 60 percent and in the USA and the European Union-15 at 22 and 15 percent, respectively.[6]

Since 2007, productivity growth has been declining worldwide, including in China.[7] In the USA, labor productivity growth slowed to 1 percent between 2007 and 2014 compared to 2 percent between 1999 and 2006. In the euro area, labor productivity growth slowed to 0.2 percent from an already meager 1 percent. In China, productivity growth slowed from 9.9 percent between 1999 and 2006 to 8.9 percent between 2007 and 2014. India saw labor productivity growth doubling from 3.2 to 6.4 percent per year while in Brazil, labor productivity increased from 0.3 to 1.5 percent, and in Mexico, labor productivity growth declined from 1.3 to 2 percent. Even though the labor productivity growth in China slowed somewhat in the aftermath of the financial crisis, compared with other emerging economies like India, Mexico, and Brazil, China still stands out.

Sources of Productivity Growth

Since 1978, the beginning of the reform and opening up of China, its economy has gone through different stages, each contributing in its way to labor productivity growth. In the first half of the 1980s, amid the introduction of the household responsibility system where rural land was divided into private plots, agriculture was the main source of economic growth in China. As the link between effort and reward was effectively restored, grain output rapidly multiplied. Substantial increases in official output prices, especially for grain, added to the reward. During that period, income distribution changed in favor of rural areas.

Under Mao, China had been stripped from any and all private enterprises, even street vendors. As Orville Schell (1984) recounts, the streets looked as if a neutron-bomb-like had been detonated, destroying small business while leaving everything else intact. Any groceries had to be bought from dreary state-owned companies. By 1983, the streets of Beijing had visibly changed even though urban development and manufacturing would only take over as the main engines of growth from the

---

[6] Pieter Bottelier and Gail Fosler, "Can China's Growth Trajectory be Sustained?," The Conference Board, 2007.

[7] Bart van Ark et al., "Prioritizing Productivity to Drive Growth, Competitiveness, and Profitability," The Conference Board, June 2015.

mid-eighties. Street-side merchants were selling food and apparel while pedicabs, private barbers and shoemakers were offering their services.

The rising productivity in agriculture resulted in a shift in employment from farming toward industry, just as Arthur Lewis had envisaged. It was the beginning of an exodus from the countryside. Because of the success of the partial reform of the rural economy, officials pressed ahead with urban reform efforts focused on improving the performance of the state-owned industry. Instead of eliminating the planned economy, China created a dual price system that split transactions for most commodities into a plan component and a market component. Once producers had satisfied the plan quota, they could sell the remaining output at increasingly flexible prices.

The dual price system familiarized Chinese households and businesses with a market economy while avoiding the economic and political pitfalls associated with privatization (which threatens people's livelihood) or full liberalization of prices (which eliminates long-standing subsidies and undercuts the authority of plan agencies).[8] With the dual price system, China overcame the supply and demand problems associated with rigid prices and created incentives for innovation. Income distribution changed in favor of urban areas and growth was higher in coastal provinces where the experiments with the Special Economic Zones had started in the 1980s and most foreign direct investment and international trade was concentrated.

In the early 1990s, foreign investment became a major factor in China. Between 1990 and 1997, inwards net foreign direct investment rose from a meager $3.5 billion per year to $44 billion per year.[9] By welcoming foreign investment, China added power to the economic transformation as foreign money was used to build factories, create jobs, link China to international markets, and the transfer of technology. Strong export growth, in turn, appears to have fueled productivity growth in domestic industries. The economic liberalization boosted export growth, which, in turn, fuelled productivity growth in domestic industries. While foreign direct investment abated in the second half of the 1990s amid the 1997 financial crisis in Asia, in the early 2000s, it accelerated again in the new century.

According to the International Monetary Fund, a sustained increase in worker efficiency, or total factor productivity, was the driving force behind

[8] Brandt and Rawski 2007.
[9] OECD.

the productivity boom between 1979 and 1994.[10] Although capital accumulation and the number of Chinese workers both played their role, the efficiency gains accounted for more than 42 percent of China's growth. As such, it was a more important source of growth than capital deepening or the number of workers added. Although new machinery, better technology, and more investment in infrastructure have helped to raise output, the capital-output ratio has hardly budged. This pronounced lack of capital deepening suggests a constrained role for capital. While capital formation alone accounted for over 65 percent of the economic growth before 1978, with labor adding another 17 percent, together they accounted for only 58 percent of the post-1978 boom, a slide of almost 25 percentage points. Productivity increases made up the rest.

The restructuring of the industrial sector took off in the mid-1990s with large-scale layoffs for redundant workers and privatization of state-owned enterprises. As a result of the restructuring, total recorded employment in manufacturing, including both state as well as non-state enterprises, fell by an estimated 18 million jobs between 1995 and 2003 even though output continued to grow.[11] The number of job losses in manufacturing was, at least, five times higher than in the USA during the same period. In spite of the job losses in the manufacturing sector, total employment in China did not fall by much during the period of industrial restructuring because other sectors, in particular, construction and the service sectors, took in many of those who had been laid off in manufacturing.

Foremost in private Chinese firms and foreign invested enterprises, manufacturing employment started growing again from 2004 on, albeit very slowly. By 2005, the manufacturing sector in China employed approximately 100 million workers compared to 14 million in the USA.[12] China's industrial restructuring (involving management changes, layoffs, plant closures, plant resizing, mergers, the privatization of numerous state-owned enterprises, and pervasive technological upgrading) led to sharply improved productivity from around the mid-nineties, both in state and in non-state enterprises. When the restructuring of state-owned enterprises got under way in the mid-1990s, initial productivity gains were mainly

---

[10] Zuliu Hu and Mohsin S. Khan, "Why Is China Growing So Fast?," International Monetary Fund, 1997.

[11] China Statistical Yearbook, 2006.

[12] Judith Bannister and George Cook, "China's employment and compensation costs in manufacturing through 2008," *Monthly Labor Review*, 2011.

due to the shedding of redundant labor, but in later years, technological, managerial, and labor improvements combined with falling logistics costs became more important factors.

Since non-state enterprises are on average more efficient than state-owned enterprises, the rapidly growing share of private enterprise in total industrial output accelerated average productivity growth. For workers, the new jobs were in growing competitive firms, many of which could provide rising real wages and some benefits. The restructuring process had an enormous impact on the state-owned sector, substantially reducing the number of loss-making firms. In both state as well as non-state enterprises, technological upgrading, made easier by relatively inexpensive capital, was seen as the only way to stay in business. Domestic competition became even more intense as a result of China's accession to the World Trade Organization in December 2001 and contributed to falling prices, which was reflected in a decrease in the real exchange rate for the renminbi.

According to research by The Conference Board, during the period from 1995 to 2003 labor productivity in large- and medium-sized industrial enterprises increased on average 20.4 percent per year. The number is consistent with the findings of other empirical studies undertaken by Chinese researchers at Peking University. Although high labor productivity growth is not necessarily matched by a corresponding improvement in overall production efficiency, in China, there are nonetheless strong indications of sharply improved competitiveness in numerous Chinese industries since the mid-nineties. Labor productivity growth in the manufacturing sector was reinforced by reforms in China's financial sector that led to a more efficient allocation of resources. Another important factor contributing to labor productivity growth was the large increase in government spending on infrastructure as part of a fiscal stimulus program aimed at avoiding a steep domestic recession following the Asian financial crisis in 1997/98, which lowered the cost of logistics for enterprises.

The actual sources of labor productivity growth in China from the mid-1990s on are hard to measure because the rapid increase in labor productivity was associated with capital deepening and a sharp relative decline in the share of state enterprises in total output. Scholars disagree on the precise numbers and even the trend. Some have suggested that total factor productivity growth, or workers' efficiency, accelerated in China's industrial sector since the mid-1990s. Others have suggested that the trend has been mostly flat or even declining.

The global slowdown in productivity in the aftermath of the global financial crisis seems to be the result of weak aggregate demand and the fact that there is less room for productivity growth in emerging markets. In the case of China, factors contributing to the declining productivity growth include a high base effect, demographics, the shift from manufacturing to services, the declining returns on capital investment, and diminishing efficiency gains. The Conference Board expects productivity growth in China to slow down further in the coming years to an average of 5.5 percent per year in the period from 2015 to 2019 and to an average of 4 percent per year in the period from 2020 to 2024.

China's Savings Rate

Savings as a share of the economy in China have traditionally been higher than in other emerging economies. The savings rate is much higher compared to advanced economies as well. In 1980, China's national savings rate already stood at 33 percent of GDP, compared to 27 percent in Mexico, 23 percent in Brazil and 18 percent in India.[13] The savings rate in most advanced economies in 1980 was between 20 and 25 percent. In 2008, China's savings rate reached 52 percent of GDP, compared to a savings rate of 32 percent in India, and respectively, 22 and 20 percent of GDP in Brazil and Mexico. At the time, the average national savings rate was 15 percent in the USA, 23 percent in the euro area, and 26 percent of GDP in Japan.

Initially, government savings was the primary driver of the national savings rate in China, making up two-thirds of the national savings rate in 1980.[14] After the introduction of the household responsibility system in the early 1980s, household savings rose from 10 percent of GDP in 1980 to over 15 percent of GDP in 1985. During that period, corporate savings stood at only 2 percent of GDP. By 1995, the overall savings rate had increased to 41 percent of GDP. By then, household savings and corporate savings were the main drivers. The savings rate may have been somewhat overstated because of the significant contribution of inventory accumulation to the national savings rate, reflecting the accumulation of unsellable output produced by state-owned enterprises. After China's entry into the World Trade Organization, the national savings rate accelerated rapidly,

---

[13] International Monetary Fund, WEO Database, October 2015.
[14] Aart Kraay, "Household Saving in China," *World Bank Economic Review*, 1990.

leaping from just below 38 percent in 2000 to 53 percent in 2007, with household and corporate savings amounting to, respectively, 23 and 25 percent of GDP, and government savings contributing around 5 percent of GDP.

Gross investments as a share of GDP in China is also high compared to other emerging economies and advanced economies, although the gross investment rate did not keep up with the savings rate. By the early 2000s, China began to run substantial current account surpluses, reaching 10 percent of GDP in 2007. In the aftermath of the global financial crisis, the current account surplus quickly receded, reflecting both a somewhat lower national savings rate as well as a significant pick up in gross investments as a share of the economy.

Government Savings

Since the start of the economic reforms in 1978, aggregate savings in China have remained at a high level of above 33 percent of GDP for the entire period, although the weight of the different components of the high savings rate varied. The surge in the national savings rate by almost 17 percent since was entirely driven by an upsurge in savings by corporations and high-income households, just as Arthur Lewis' model predicts. Between 1999 and 2008, the share of corporate savings rose from 15 to 25 percent of GDP, household savings increased from 17 to 23 percent, and government savings ticked up from 3 to 5 percent of GDP.[15] The share of government saving in GDP fluctuated at a level below 4.4 percent in the period of 1992–1999, reaching the lowest point at 2.6 percent in 1999. However, the figure had climbed since then, reaching 5.2 percent in 2007.

Rising revenues from the tax on production were the largest contributor to the growth in government income between 1999 and 2007, accounting for two-thirds of the increase in the disposable income of government.[16] The second largest contributing factor to government disposable income was net current transfers. In 2007, the government collected twice as much income taxes and social insurance fees than it spent on social wel-

---

[15] Sectoral savings rates are based on the Flow of Funds Accounts in the China Statistical Yearbook. There may be a slight discrepancy with the national savings rate as reported in the International Monetary Fund, WEO Database.

[16] Dennis Tao Yang, Junsen Zhang, and Shaojie Zhou, "Why Are Saving Rates so High in China?," NBER Working Paper No. 16771, 2011.

fare payments, social insurance provisions, and other transfers. Overall, the combined increases in taxes on production and transfers added to about 90 percent of the growth in government revenues from 1999 to 2007.

Compared with the increase in government income, the total growth in public spending was modest between 1999 and 2007.

In 2008 and later years, the government savings rate remained around 5 percent of GDP in spite of the ¥4 trillion ($586 billion) two-year stimulus package that was announced in the aftermath of the financial crisis. The stimulus package was financed primarily by way of state-owned banks' credit, spurring private debt, rather than through public deficit spending. Even though tax revenues increased considerably in the new millennium, tax revenues as a share of GDP in China are still well below tax revenues as a share of GDP in major developed economies, such as Japan, Germany, and the USA.

Household Savings

China's household savings rate has risen substantially since 1978 amid the economic reforms and fast income growth. Household savings only accounted for 6 percent of GDP in the late 1970s but grew to about 23 percent of GDP in 2007. Chinese households save on average 30 percent of disposable income while US households save around 6 percent of disposable income. There has been a myriad of research into the household savings rate, linking it to the breaking of the iron rice bowl, China's one-child-policy, and to economic growth in general, to rising household incomes and the increasing income inequality in China.

Before 1978, the government assigned most jobs in China. The government paid the workers subsistence wages and guaranteed lifetime employment along with near-free housing, education, health care, and pension. This is what generally is called the "iron rice bowl." Before the large-scale reform of state-owned enterprises in the late 1990s, workers in state-owned enterprises enjoyed similar job security as government employees. Since the reform, over 35 million workers in state-owned enterprises have been laid off. The rise in unemployment risk and income insecurity for workers in state-owned enterprises is associated with an increase in precautionary savings.[17]

---

[17] Hui et al., "Breaking the "Iron Rice Bowl" and Precautionary Savings: Evidence from Chinese State-Owned Enterprises Reform," 2014.

The economic transitions in China not only involved the reform of state-owned enterprises, but also signaled the end of fully government-supplied education, healthcare, and housing. The uncertainty associated with the costs of education, healthcare, retirement, and housing may have induced precautionary savings. Although the Chinese government in recent years has spent billions of dollars on better health care, expanding a pension program, building schools, and hiring teachers in rural China, the household savings rate kept rising.

Demographic changes induced by China's one-child-policy could affect household saving through two transmission mechanisms. First, as the non-working-age population consumes but does not earn an income, a fall in their share in the population tends to increase the household savings rate. Second, in an emerging economy without a mature social security system, children often provide old-age security to their parents. Children thus act as an effective substitute for life-cycle saving. As the one-child-policy reduces the number of children, it may increase the household savings rate as well.

Economic growth and rising household incomes are associated with higher household savings rate. This is not easily reconcilable with classical models of saving, such as Modigliani-Brumberg's life-cycle theory, and Friedman's permanent-income hypothesis. These classical models of household saving predict that—faced with higher future earnings—households will consume more and save less in order to smooth lifetime consumption. Chinese households, on the contrary, continued to save more in spite of the anticipation of higher future incomes.

The growing income inequality in China during the economic transition contributed to the rise in household savings. The savings rate of the highest income group is much greater compared to the savings rate of the lowest income group. Between 1988 and 2007, the savings rate of the lowest quartile (0–25 percent) fluctuated between 5 and 10 percent of disposable income in most years, ending at 7 percent in 2007. In contrast, the savings rate of the highest income quartile (75–100 percent) began at only 10 percent in 1988 and increased rapidly to more than 34 percent of disposable income in 2007. That is almost fivefold the savings rate of the lowest income group in that year. The savings rate of the highest income decile (90–100) in 2007 was 38 percent of disposable income, and the savings rate of the highest income quintile (95–100) was 43 percent of disposable income.[18]

---

[18] Heleen Mees and Raman Ahmed, "Why Do Chinese Households Save So Much?," 2012.

Based on a representative Chinese household survey carried out in 2010 and 2011, Gan Li finds much higher savings rates for the high income groups than the National Bureau of Statistics of China. According to Gan Li, the highest income decile (90–100) had an average savings rate of 66.5 percent, representing 74.9 percent of total household savings while the highest income quintile households (95–100) had an average savings rate of 69.0 percent representing 61.6 percent of total household saving.[19] Most of these high income households belong to the capitalist class and not to the class of wage earners. In the aftermath of the global financial crisis, the savings of households continued to rise, reaching more than 25 percent of GDP in 2012, in spite of the Chinese government's increased spending on healthcare and education, and the government's entreaties to Chinese families to save less and consume more.[20]

Corporate Savings

Corporate savings were at 2 percent of GDP only a small component of national savings before the economic reforms in 1978. Amid the restructuring of the state-owned enterprises, corporate savings rose rapidly. By the end of the 1990s, corporate savings stood at 13 percent of GDP. Between 1999 and 2007, corporate savings increased to 25 percent of GDP. The corporate savings are a direct reflection of the increased profitability of enterprises. Corporate profits rose more than 15-fold from 1992 to 2007 in nominal terms while the ratio of profits to industrial value added rose from about 21 percent in the late 1990s to close to 30 percent in 2007. Just as Arthur Lewis predicted, the share of enterprise income in GDP rose during that period from 13 percent to above 18 percent while the share of household income declined from about 70 percent of GDP in 1992 to 58 percent of GDP in 2007.

The rise in corporate profitability is primarily the result of the unlimited supplies of labor that allowed businesses to expand without having to pay higher wages. In particular, labor costs were kept low, thanks to the immigrant workers who had abandoned the countryside for the cities. The flow of immigrants, which was estimated at around 135 million in 2007, ensured relatively low labor costs for businesses in China, a major factor behind China's emergence as the workshop of the world.

The economic reforms played an important role as well. The dual price system, the flow of foreign direct investment, the privatization of state-owned enterprises, and the growth of private enterprises all increased

---

[19] China Household Finance Survey, 2010–2011.
[20] China Statistical Yearbook, 2014.

competition among businesses in China, inducing innovative efforts and raising the efficiency of the corporate sector. The breaking of the iron rice bowl and the implementation of labor market incentives suppressed labor costs, and hence, contributed to corporate profitability.

China's remarkable growth in exports, which allowed enterprises in China to sell their products at First-World prices while paying Third-World wages, was an important factor as well. As China removed barriers for foreign direct investment in the late nineties to gain access to the World Trade Organization, export growth accelerated. The momentum for exports continued after China's accession to the World Trade Organization in 2001. Between 1999 and 2007, the export increased on average more than 25 percent per year, allowing China to make full use of its comparative advantage.[21] In spite of the global financial crisis, China's export of goods and services as a share of all exports rose from 3 percent in 2000 to 7 percent in 2008 and continued to grow to reach 10 percent of the world's exports in 2014.[22]

Cost benefits enjoyed foremost by state-owned enterprises contributed to rising profitability. State-owned enterprises were able to take out loans at interest rates much lower than the prevailing market rates. If state-owned enterprises had paid market interest rates, their profits would have been significantly reduced.[23] The Chinese government also subsidized the energy sector, leading to much lower energy costs, not only for state-owned enterprises but for private and foreign-invested enterprises as well.

Weak corporate governance structures and underdeveloped financial markets are often cited as reasons that in China few dividends get distributed.[24] Although some stockholders earn dividends, total dividend payments accounted for only a small proportion of the enterprise value added. Moreover, state-owned enterprises did not have to pay dividends at all to the Chinese government before 2008 in spite of the fact that their profitability had increased since the reforms of the state sector in the mid-1990s. Lower dividends translate to more retained corporate earnings, that is, higher corporate savings.

---

[21] Dennis Tao Yang, Junsen Zhang, and Shaojie Zhou, "Why Are Saving Rates so High in China?," NBER Working Paper No. 16771, 2011.

[22] World Bank, World Development Indicators.

[23] Guonan Ma and Yi Wang, "China's High Saving Rate: Myth and Reality," *BIS Working Papers No. 312*, 2010.

[24] Louis Kuijs, "Investment and Saving in China," World Bank, 2006.

Enterprises in China, in particular small and medium-size enterprises, rely on their own savings to finance most of the investments in fixed assets because of weaknesses in China's financial markets. Contrary to the conventional wisdom that bank credits are the main source of financing in China, the share of domestic loans remained below 21 percent of total investments in the period from 1995 to 2008 while self-raised funds, which also includes funds raised through the issuance of equity, accounted for the largest share of investment. The share of self-raised funds in total investment increased over time, rising from just below 50 percent in the mid-1990s to almost 65 percent in 2008. During that period, the share of domestic loans was declining. This indicates a lower degree of bank financing to enterprises and associated financial sector exposure than is usually thought. Between 2008 and 2013, the weight of domestic loans in the funds for fixed investment has decreased to 12 percent while the weight of self-raised funds increased to 68 percent. These self-raised funds also include trust funds, corporate bonds, and equity financing.

Absorption Constraints

The explanations offered in the economic literature for China's high savings rate so far are rather fragmented. The most robust outcome is that China's savings rate correlates positively with economic growth, profitability, and household income. While China's national savings rate is indeed remarkably high, China's experience is not entirely unique. China's trajectory over the past 30 years is actually quite similar to the experiences of—for example—Singapore, Japan, and Malaysia, which also had average national savings rates of about 45 percent of GDP during their era of high growth. It suggests that China's savings rate is merely a reflection of its sizeable capitalist surplus. China is only different because its economy is vastly larger, and has gotten much more scrutiny because of its role in the years leading up to the global financial crisis and ensuing economic recession.[25]

China's savings rate also does not stand out compared to the savings rates of resource-rich countries. During natural resource booms, the national savings rates in Norway, Saudi Arabia, and the United Arab Emirates are comparable to China's savings rate. Just like China, these resource-rich countries enjoy large capitalist surpluses. Resource-rich

---

[25] Mees, Heleen, "Why Do Chinese Households Save So Much?," 2012.

countries tend to run large current account surpluses too just as China did in the years leading up to the global financial crisis. The International Monetary Fund invariably advises resource-rich countries to use the windfall of foreign exchange to build up a sovereign wealth fund large enough so that the revenues of the fund raise a country's income in perpetuity, just as the permanent income hypothesis dictates.[26]

In the case of China, supply constraints and bottlenecks in the domestic economy may help explain both the high savings rate as well as the current account surplus. A country's ability to absorb additional consumption and investment is limited because it has a shortage of skilled workers, physical capital, and infrastructure.[27] Arthur Lewis already acknowledged that a shortage of skilled labor might prove the bottleneck in an expansion. According to Lewis, it's a "quasi-bottleneck" for it is only a temporary bottleneck, in the sense that if the capital is available for development, the capitalists or their government will soon provide the facilities for training more skilled people.

How quickly an economy can overcome quasi-bottlenecks depends on whether the various sorts of capital—skills, capital equipment, and infrastructure—can freely be moved around the globe or bought and sold in the world markets. In reality, physical capital is embedded so it cannot move free of cost around the globe, and some sorts of capital are not for sale, and therefore, cannot be acquired in the world markets.

By all means, China has done quite a job of making capital tradable. Entire factories have been transported to China, like the ThyssenKrupp steel factory in Dortmund, Germany. As James Kynge describes in *China Shakes The World* (2006), in 2004 about a thousand Chinese workers came to the little city of Hörde and worked twelve hours a day, seven days a week, six weeks in a row, to ready the factory for transportation. Something similar happened to Chinese investments in Africa. China shuttles workers and equipment to Africa to construct infrastructure as payment for securing sufficient natural resources for its 1.3 billion population.

Often the problem is that creating new capital requires non-traded capital. A shortage of this so-called *homegrown capital* is believed to be the quintessential determinant of absorptive capacity. Even if an economy

---

[26] Jeffrey Davis et al., "Stabilization and Savings Funds for Non-Renewable Resources: Experience and Fiscal Policy Implications," International Monetary Fund, 2002.

[27] Rick van der Ploeg and Anthony Venables, "Absorbing a windfall of foreign exchange: Dutch disease dynamics," 2010.

has perfect access to international capital markets, the requirement that it accumulates capital goods with a domestic component means that it cannot jump instantaneously to a new steady state. This homegrown capital can be physical capital, but it may also be human capital. After all, it takes teachers to produce teachers.

China has been very creative with regard to raising home-grown capital as well. Since the start of the economic reform program under Deng Xiaoping, more than 3 million Chinese have gone overseas to study. More than a quarter of Chinese students went to the USA. At the same time, Chinese universities try to lure academic talent back to China by offering one-off bonuses, promotion, competitive salaries and free housing under the so-called *Thousand Talents Program*. The policies start to bear fruit. China's share in the world's total academic submissions has increased from 6.1 percent to 11.3 percent between 2005 and 2010; the number of patents granted went up eightfold.[28]

Over the past decades, China has been building thousands of museums, even to such an extent that people speak of the "museumification" of China.[29] In 1949, when the Communist Party took control, China had just 25 museums. During the Cultural Revolution of 1966–1976, many of them were demolished. But the rapid growth and urbanization that accompanied Deng Xiaoping's reform policies after 1978 also launched a museum-building boom. By 2012, China had more than 3500 museums. But building up and displaying art collections, planning exhibitions, training curators, conservators and other museum staff take more time. Because of a shortage of this type of homegrown capital, many a museum in China ends up empty.

The ability to increase consumption and investment may also be curbed because of institutional constraints, including the way a country manages its budget, accounting, and procurement processes, and the way it manages its capital account. In the case of China, households and businesses do not have perfect access to international capital markets as extensive capital controls are in place, limiting households and corporations' ability to borrow and invest abroad. These restrictions include outright restrictions, ownership limits, and administrative approval requirements. In a

---

[28] "Global Publishing: Changes in submission trends and the impact on scholarly publishers, Thomson Reuters, 2012.
[29] "Mad about museums," *The Economist*, 2013.

2005 list of countries by capital controls drawn up by the International Monetary Fund, China ranked 57 out of 61.[30]

If households and enterprises cannot spend their income in its entirety because of absorption constraints, any windfall will translate into higher levels of household savings and corporate savings. These are so-called *forced savings*; consumers and enterprises do not spend all of their disposable income or retained profits, not because they want to save but because the (capital) goods and services they seek are not available. The fact that the savings rate of the highest income groups is very high (69 percent according to the Gan Li household survey) while the savings rate of the lowest income groups is very low (below 5 percent), suggests that the forced savings hypothesis is indeed an important explanation in China. It explains why China's housing market and stock markets are prone to speculative bubbles. It also suggests that a redistribution of income in favor of the lowest income groups would aid consumption and significantly reduce the overall savings rate.

The mechanism of absorption constraints is most apparent in small, oil-rich countries such as the United Arab Emirates, Kuwait, and Qatar. In Dubai, an ATM dispenses gold bars and in Abu Dhabi, a $11 million Christmas tree was unveiled. While the Gulf States have made essentially all capital tradable, they are often unable to spend it all. In as far as national savings cannot be absorbed nationwide these countries run large current account surpluses just like China did in the years leading up the financial crisis.

---

[30] The question is whether it would have made a large difference in terms of the national savings rate, given the extent to which foreign investors tried to circumvent the capital controls and pour money into the country, resulting in billions of dollars of hot money flows making their way into China.

CHAPTER 9

Corporate Cash Piles and Falling Interest Rates

Ballooning Current Accounts

In the years leading up to the global financial crisis, the USA was borrowing heavily on international capital markets, with the US current account deficit reaching almost 6 percent of GDP in 2006. The US current account deficit was mirrored in China's and oil exporting countries' current account surpluses. As Ben Bernanke pointed out in his 2005 Sandridge Lecture, it would have been more natural for the world's largest economy to be a net lender. According to Bernanke, the deterioration in the US current account had little to do with domestic economic policies or other economic developments within the USA itself.

Instead, a combination of diverse forces created a significant increase in the global supply of savings that could help explain both the increase in the US current account deficit and the relatively low level of long-term real interest rates in the world. Not the fact that the US national savings rate had declined from 18 to less than 14 percent of GDP was to blame, but the fact that emerging and developing economies had moved from a collective deficit of 1.5 percent of GDP to a net collective surplus of 4 percent of GDP.[1]

In the view of Bernanke, one factor contributing to the high level of global savings was the aging of the baby boom generation in some

---
[1] Emerging and developing markets' collective GDP in 2004 was about three-fourths of US GDP.

large industrial economies, notably Germany. A more important explanation, however, was the reversal in the flows of credit to developing and emerging-market economies, a shift that transformed those economies from net borrowers on international capital markets to large net lenders. Bernanke ascribed the change in the current account positions of developing and emerging countries to the series of financial crises those countries had experienced in the 1990s.

In the mid-1990s, most emerging economies were net importers of capital just as economic theory would predict. In 1996, emerging Asia and Latin America borrowed about $80 billion net on world capital markets. Loss of lender confidence in combination with short-term debt that was denominated in foreign currencies resulted in painful financial crises. The countries that were hardest hit included Mexico in 1994, Indonesia, Malaysia, Korea, and Thailand in 1997–1998, Russia in 1998, Brazil in 1999, and Argentina in 2002. These crises had the shared characteristics of rapid capital outflows, currency depreciation, tumbling domestic asset prices, weakened banking systems, and economic recession.

In response to these crises, some emerging economies in Asia, such as South Korea and Thailand, began to pay down foreign debt and build up large quantities of foreign exchange reserves. These are assets held by a central bank or other monetary authority, usually in various reserve currencies, most importantly the US dollar, and to a lesser extent, the euro, the pound sterling, and the Japanese yen. To amass official foreign reserves, a country generally has to run large current account surpluses. While China escaped the worst effects of the Asian financial crisis, it nonetheless started to build up reserves as well. This "war chest" of foreign reserves was initially seen as a buffer against potential capital outflows. However, by 2006, the foreign reserves of China, South Korea, Malaysia, and India were double of what was deemed the adequate level of foreign reserves while Russia's foreign reserves were even four times the adequate level.[2]

The growth of foreign exchange reserves since 1995 accelerated most notably in emerging economies. Between 1995 and 2006, international reserves more than tripled, with China leading the pack. In the oil-exporting countries of the Middle East, the accumulation of international reserves has been quite modest compared to that of most non-

---

[2] Onno Wijnholds and Lars Søndergaard (2007), "Reserve Accumulation – Objective or By-Product?," European Central Bank Occasional Paper Series No. 73, 2007.

industrialized countries. There are two main reasons for this. First, these oil exporters have channeled a substantial share of their foreign exchange revenue into sovereign wealth funds. The assets of these funds lack the character of international reserves because they are less liquid because the money is, for example, invested in shares instead of US Treasuries. Second, oil-exporting countries in the Middle East often place their assets in offshore financial centers and are for that reason not counted as belonging to the central. This leads to an underestimation of their reserve holdings.

Exchange Rate Regimes

Bernanke and many others have suggested that the reason for the build-up of foreign reserves was that countries like China were pursuing policies aimed at achieving export-led growth by means of an undervalued exchange rate. Countries typically pursue export-led growth if domestic demand is insufficient to use all domestic resources in full. During the Asian financial crisis of 1997–1998, several countries were forced to adopt a floating exchange regime. However, they often chose to manage their float quite actively through interventions in the foreign exchange market. By either pegging their currencies to the US dollar or conducting a heavily managed float, these countries contributed to substantial reserve accumulation and global imbalances in external current accounts, according to Bernanke.

In 1995, China effectively fixed the exchange rate at 8.3 renminbi to the US dollar. As China was not severely affected by the Asian financial crisis, it continued to peg the renminbi to the dollar. For that reason, many accused China of currency manipulation. However, in real terms, the renminbi weakened vis-à-vis the US dollar between 2002 and 2005, casting doubts on the assertion that the renminbi was substantially undervalued during those years. When China gradually started to introduce some flexibility in its exchange rate regime in the summer of 2005, the renminbi rose by 18.6 percent in real effective trade-weighted terms between June 2005 and August 2008.

In spite of the appreciation of the renminbi, China continued to make very substantial additions to its reserves, leading many commentators to insist that the renminbi was still undervalued. The views about the extent of the undervaluation of the renminbi varied widely, ranging between 5 and 40 percent. Some economists argued that the fact that the current account surplus kept rising in spite of the appreciation of the renminbi—from almost 6 percent of GDP in 2005 to more than 10 percent of GDP in 2007—showed that the undervaluation of the renminbi was not the core of the problem.

Several economists have cautioned that the matter of the undervaluation or overvaluation of a currency should be treated gingerly. It is not easy to establish what the equilibrium real exchange rate of a currency is as any estimate is highly sensitive to small changes in model specifications, explanatory variable definitions, and time periods used in the estimation.[3] Others have argued that the renminbi may appear undervalued on the basis of relative prices but in the context of large stocks of nonperforming loans, the reverse may be true.[4] Still others have argued that, while every fixed or managed nominal exchange rate by definition is manipulated, a country the size of China cannot influence its effective real exchange rate in a lasting manner by managing/manipulating its effective nominal exchange rate, let alone some bilateral nominal exchange rate.[5]

In 2015, the International Monetary Fund declared that the Chinese renminbi was no longer undervalued even though the US government continued to insist that the renminbi was significantly undervalued.[6] By then, the renminbi had gained 25 percent against the US dollar since it was allowed to adjust upward within a narrow band a decade before while the real broad effective exchange rate of renminbi had gained over 50 percent compared to June 2005. Since July 2015, China has let the renminbi drop, in what appears to be an attempt to set the broad-based exchange rate closer to the rate that reflects China's fundamentals.

Natural Resources and Current Account Surpluses

In his 2005 Sandridge Lecture, Bernanke also pointed to the sharp rise in oil prices as a factor that contributed to the swing toward current account surpluses among the non-industrialized nations. At $60 a barrel, oil was still well below the peak price of $140 a barrel that it reached in July 2008.

---

[3] Steven Dunaway, Lamin Leigh, and Xiangming Li, "How Robust are Estimates of Equilibrium Real Exchange Rates: The Case of China," International Monetary Fund, 2006.
[4] Yin-Wong Cheung, Menzie Chinn and Eiji Fujii, "Why the Renminbi Might be Overvalued (But Probably Isn't), 2005.
[5] Willem Buiter, "When all else fails, blame China," *The Financial Times* blog, 2009.
[6] International Monetary Fund, Press Release No. 15/237, 2015.

The current account surpluses of oil exporters, notably in the Middle East but also in countries such as Russia, Nigeria, and Venezuela, rose as oil revenues surged. Current account surpluses in the double digits, even up to 42 percent, were the rule rather than the exception.

However, nobody would argue that oil-exporting countries, for which oil is the main export product, could reach a balanced current account simply by floating their currencies. After all, the price of oil is being determined on world markets and set in US dollars. An increase in the exchange rate of the Russian ruble would not affect the oil price in US dollars, and thus it would not alter the demand for Russian oil and the volume of Russian oil exports. An appreciation of the ruble would have increased the demand for imports, but the effect would likely not be large enough to make a dent in the double-digit current account surpluses that Russia was running for most of the past decade.

A similar mechanism seems to have been at play in China as well. After all, China's exports mainly consist of manufactured products for which the most important input is labor. Since China in the early 2000s still had unlimited supplies of labor, meaning that it could add as many workers as it needed without paying much more than the subsistence wage. The subsistence wage is not defined in monetary terms but rather in terms of a basket of food and energy. The prices of food and energy are, just like the price of oil, set in the global marketplace. An appreciation of the renminbi would therefore not alter the subsistence wages in real terms, leaving the competitiveness of China's manufacturing sector and its current account surplus largely unchanged.[7]

The same reasoning does not apply to most of the other, smaller, Asian economies that have pegged their currencies to the US dollar or maintained a heavily managed float. Both Malaysia as well as Thailand had an income per capita measured on a purchasing power parity basis in the early 2000s that was a multiple of income per capita in China, suggesting that workers in Malaysia and Thailand were paid more than the subsistence level. The same is, of course, even more true for Hong Kong and South Korea, where income per capita based on purchasing power parity in the early 2000s was almost tenfold the income per capita in China. Although GDP per capita in China has risen considerably since the early 2000s, there is still a pool of unutilized and underutilized labor for which subsistence wages or slightly above subsistence wages may apply.

---

[7] Downward wage rigidity could in principle explain an increase in real wages amid a renminbi appreciation, and hence, a deterioration of China's competitiveness.

Feedback Loops

The People's Bank of China has by far the largest holding of foreign exchange reserves, at $3 trillion per January 2016 while the Bank of Japan is a distant second with $1.2 trillion. The other central banks have around $500 billion or less in foreign exchange reserves. Central banks still hold part of the foreign exchange reserves in gold although the role of gold in the international monetary system has substantially declined over time. The rest is predominantly held in other liquid assets. Per 2006, about 65 percent of foreign exchange reserves were held in US dollar-denominated assets, mostly US Treasuries but also US agency debt (such as the debt issued by government-sponsored enterprises Fannie Mae and Freddie Mac). About 25 percent of foreign exchange reserves were held in euro-denominated assets, predominantly the bonds issued by the governments of the euro area, while about 5 percent was held in Japanese yen-denominated assets and another 4 percent in UK pound-denominated assets.

According to Bernanke, the reasons why the global savings glut was felt disproportionately in the USA were the depth and sophistication of US financial markets (which, among other things, allowed households easy access to housing wealth) as well as the special international status of the US dollar. Because the dollar is the leading international reserve currency and because some emerging-market countries use the dollar as a reference point when managing the values of their own currencies, the saving flowing out of emerging and developing economies was directed relatively more into dollar-denominated assets, such as US Treasuries securities. The effects of the savings outflow may thus have fallen disproportionately on US interest rates.

Bernanke also suggested that the US dollar was stronger than it would have been if it had not been the leading international reserve currency. However, the US dollar lost 35 percent of its value between February 2002 and June 2008, based on the broad trade-weighted exchange rate. Initially, the US dollar dropped amid the Federal Reserve cutting the fed funds rate from 6.5 percent in late 2000 to 1 percent in June 2003. But in spite of the Federal Reserve raising the fed funds rate again from 1 percent in July 2004 to 5.25 percent in June 2006, the US dollar continued to fall. There seems to have been three feedback loops at play.

First, the low fed funds rate between June 2003 and July 2004 resulted in a home refinancing boom with two-thirds of the mortgages that were originated during that period being used for refinancing.[8] Spending out of

---

[8] Heleen Mees, "U.S. Monetary Policy and the Housing Bubble," 2012.

home equity rose from around 1 percent of GDP in the 1990s to almost 5 percent of GDP by 2005. Two-thirds of the cash out of home equity was used for personal consumption, home improvements, and credit card debt. US spending on products imported from China fuelled the capitalist surplus in China, which was reflected in rising corporate profitability and household incomes of the Chinese elite. The increased demand for products made in China also fuelled the profitability of Western companies that benefitted from low labor costs in China, thus adding to the corporate savings glut in the advanced world. The extra savings by China and Western companies were, in turn, predominantly invested in government debt, thus contributing to the low interest rate environment.

Second, the low interest rate environment put downward pressure on the US dollar and—as the Chinese currency was pegged to the US dollar—on the renminbi as well. The lower exchange rate of the renminbi vis-à-vis most currencies fuelled demand for China-made products in much of the rest of the world, giving rise to a larger capitalist surplus in and beyond China, adding to corporate savings and the foreign exchange reserves held by the People's Bank of China.

Third, as China started to make a significant impact on the global demand for oil in the early 2000s, oil prices began to rise. The rising oil prices prompted increases in the trade deficits of oil-importing countries and the accumulation of foreign exchange reserves in oil-exporting countries. The latter were predominantly invested in US Treasuries, contributing again to the low interest rate environment and low US dollar alike. The lower US dollar, in turn, put upward pressure on the dollar-denominated oil prices, adding to the US current account deficit and the accumulation of foreign exchange reserves in oil-exporting countries.

Causality

In his Sandridge Lecture and in his speech at the Annual Meeting of the American Economic Association in January 2010, Ben Bernanke suggested that the foreign capital inflows triggered the housing boom. However, research by François Geerolf and Thomas Grjebine shows that causality runs from rising house prices to the deterioration of the current account, not the other way around.[9] A positive shock to house prices does cause a

---

[9] François Geerolf and Thomas Grjebine, "House Prices Drive Current Accounts: Evidence from Property Tax Variations," 2013.

deficit in the current account in the next period while capital inflows do not cause increases in house prices. Across time and countries, there is a very large and significant impact of house prices on current accounts but not the other way. The mechanism is simple. If housing prices rise, consumers will spend more money because of the wealth effect. That means that imports increase while exports decrease as the trading sector becomes less competitive.

The USA did not experience a housing bubble because of capital inflows from China and other emerging markets. Instead, the sustained increase in house prices, which already started in 1998, triggered the capital inflows. The deterioration of the US current account was less than a simulation based on the change in national house prices would suggest.[10] It is also not the case, as many economists have alleged, that the massive capital inflows from the core countries in the euro area triggered the housing bubbles in Ireland and Spain.[11] In Ireland, house prices saw their biggest increase in the 1990s, that is, before the introduction of the euro. In Spain, the deterioration of the current account lagged the rise in house prices.

The argument has, therefore, to be phrased more carefully. It can still be argued that the housing booms that affected virtually all countries in the Western hemisphere would not have happened had it not been for China joining the World Trade Organization. Without China's accession to the World Trade Organization, there would not have been a corporate savings glut that created a low interest rate environment in the first place. Moreover, US monetary policy in the early 2000s would have been more effective in stimulating domestic demand and bringing about full employment had it not been for China's accession to the World Trade Organization. Core inflation would also have been higher.

In that scenario, the Federal Reserve would have raised interest rates sooner, which would have cooled the housing market, curbed household debt, and restrained financial institutions' reach for yield. Other central banks would no doubt have followed the Federal Reserve's lead and raised rates sooner as well. Instead, US demand fueled the manufacturing sector and economic growth in China, adding to the capitalist surplus, which in turn drove up the Chinese savings rate. Absent China, the USA would have had to pay higher interest rates on foreign capital inflows, which would have affected the interest rate on home mortgages as well.

---

[10] Geerolf and Grjebine, 2013.
[11] Paul Krugman, "Deflation As Betrayal," *The New York Times* blog, January 10, 2015.

In a similar vein, without the single European currency, the central banks of Ireland and Spain would have raised interest rates sooner as inflation was too high for comfort. Ireland and Spain would also either have faced higher interest rates on foreign capital inflows or have incurred exchange rate risk on foreign loans, which probably would have cooled the housing markets. Causality notwithstanding, housing markets would not have gone out of control the way they did without China's accession to the World Trade Organization and absent the introduction of the euro.

An important aspect that tends to be overlooked in the economic literature, and which is intimately related to the issue of causality, is that housing bubbles are, to a large extent, domestically financed. That is why countries with structural current account surpluses also experienced housing bubbles. Take for example the Netherlands, where the female labor participation rate was very low until the end of the 1980s. By the mid-1990s, due to a change in the so-called *social pact* between trade unions and employers' organizations, Dutch women entered the labor market in droves (albeit on a part-time basis).

The female labor supply resulted in lower wage costs and higher profitability of Dutch companies, improving the competitiveness of the traded sector and generating extra economic growth. The rising corporate profitability was not accompanied by an equivalent rise in corporate investment. Instead, the corporate savings glut in the Netherlands lowered the yield on Dutch government bonds and home mortgage loans. This process was reinforced because of the dwindling budget deficit that curbed the supply of Dutch government bonds. Between 1990 and 2000, house prices in the Netherlands more than doubled with most of the increase happening in the latter half of the nineties.

The same seems to have occurred in Ireland and Spain as the governments in the 1990s brought down the budget deficit in a push to meet the convergence criteria for joining the euro. Ireland and Spain started to run budget surpluses in 1996 and 2004 respectively. Government debt as a share of GDP ratio dwindled as a result. It is easy to see that Spanish and Irish investors who normally bought government bonds switched to either bank debt or mortgage-backed securities when the supply of government bonds dried up. Vice versa, countries that were much less fiscally sound, like Greece, Italy, and Portugal, did not experience housing bubbles to a similar extent during the pre-crisis years.

Falling Interest Rates

While interest rates had been declining steadily since the early 1980s, the 10-year US Treasury dropped from more than 15 percent in the early 1980s to under 5 percent in the early 2000s, it was not until 2004 that the then Federal Reserve Chairman Alan Greenspan argued that something was amiss. According to Greenspan, the failure in 2004 and 2005 of the 400 basis point increase in the fed funds rate to carry the yield on the 10-year Treasury note along with it (as it historically almost invariably did) dramatically changed the long-held view that US long-term interest rates were significantly influenced, if not largely determined, by monetary policy. The failure to lift the 10-year Treasury yield posed a problem, as the Federal Open Market Committee desperately needed higher interest rates to cool the housing market.

The correlation coefficient in the USA between the fed funds rate and the 30-year mortgage rate from 1963 to 2002 had been a tight 0.83. In the early 2000s, however, the 30-year mortgage rate clearly delinked from the fed funds rate with the correlation between the funds rate and the 30-year mortgage rate falling to an insignificant 0.17 during the years 2002–2005. The correlation between the fed funds rate and the 10-year Treasury yield was 0.87 from 1982 to 2001 and fell to an insignificant 0.24 during the years 2002–2005. From 2002 to 2008, the correlation was, at 0.51, still much smaller than during the period dubbed the Great Moderation.

Not only in the USA but also in the UK, long-term and short-term interest rates decoupled. The correlation between the Bank Rate (the monetary policy rate of the Bank of England) and the yield on 10-year Gilts was 0.79 from 1982 to 2001 and 0.30 from 2002 to 2008. In Germany, the correlation between the discount rate and the yield on 10-year Bonds was 0.61 from 1982 to 2001. Both the reunification of East and West Germany in 1990 and the introduction of the single currency impacted the term structure during this period. From 2002 to 2008, the correlation between the European Central Bank's monetary policy rate (the so-called *Main Refinancing Minimum Bid Rate*) and the yield on 10-year Bonds was 0.40.

Research by the Federal Reserve Bank of New York shows that the term premium, that is the amount by which the yield-to-maturity of a long-term bond exceeds that of a short-term bond, on 10-year Treasuries dropped 2 percentage points during the 2004–2005 monetary tightening cycle, compared to a drop of only 0.5 percentage points during the 1994 and 1999 monetary tightening cycles.[12] The term premium rose modestly in the first six months of the 1994 and 1999 tightening cycles before declining by approximately 0.5 percentage points in the following six months. This contrasts with the 2004 tightening cycle, dubbed "the conundrum period," when the term premium dropped steadily in the face of rising short-term interest rates.

Taken over a 24-month period, the term premium dropped almost 3 percentage points between July 2003 and July 2005 compared to a 1.5 percentage point drop from 1993 to 1995 and a 0.5 percentage point increase in the term premium from 1998 to 2000. This result suggests that the 10-year Treasury yield was between 1.5 and 3.5 percentage points lower during the conundrum years than what was to be expected on the basis of the two previous rounds of monetary policy tightening. The finding is comparable to the outcome of a simple regression where the projected 10-year Treasury is a function of the fed funds rate and a constant.[13]

Emerging Economies' Savings

In his Sandridge Lecture, Bernanke faulted the reversal in the flows of credit between advanced economies and developing and emerging economies for the interest conundrum. In doing so, Bernanke blamed emerging economies for the Federal Reserve's inability to cool the US housing market and the ensuing global financial crisis. In particular, Bernanke blamed China and other Asian emerging market economies and oil producers like Saudi Arabia for the low global interest rates. Bernanke's remarks set off tons of research into foreign capital flows although researchers quickly started to focus on the effectiveness of quantitative easing as large-scale official purchases of US Treasuries and US agency debt no longer were seen as the culprit but as the solution to the financial crisis.

According to early research dating back to 2004, foreign capital flows had only a small or no impact on US long-term rates.[14] This research formed the basis for Greenspan's remark that the foreign buying of US bonds probably depressed US long-term rates by "less than 50 basis points."[15] However, it made use of a partial measure of foreign flows from

[12] Tobias Adrian, Richard Crump, and Emanuel Moench, "Do Treasury Term Premia Rise around Monetary Tightenings?," Liberty Street Economics blog, 2013.
[13] Mees, 2012.
[14] Bernard Sack, "Regression Evidence on the Effects of Foreign Official Purchases of U.S. Treasury Securities," Federal Reserve Board, 2004.
[15] Response to Senator Shelby, Senate Banking Committee hearing, July 25, 2005.

the Federal Reserve Bank New York, which did not include financial flows that are channeled through financial centers or sovereign wealth funds. The same is true for research in 2006 that concluded that foreign official purchases of US Treasuries appeared to have played little or no role.[16]

Later research, using an estimate of total foreign capital flows, concluded that foreign purchases of US government bonds had an economically large and statistically significant impact on long-term interest rates in the new millennium.[17] By one estimate, the 10-year Treasury yield in 2004 and 2005 was 0.8 percentage points lower than it would have been in the absence of foreign inflows into US government bonds. This outcome still only explains half of the (lower range) drop in the term premium that the Federal Reserve Bank of New York found in the 2004–2005 monetary tightening cycle. Foreign purchases of US government bonds have an impact of similar magnitude on other interest rates such as corporate bond yields and 30-year mortgage rates.

Other research shows that both the purchases of US government debt by the Federal Reserve as well as the purchases by foreign central banks significantly affected the level and the dynamics of US real interest rates. In particular, by 2008, foreign purchases of US Treasuries are estimated to have had cumulatively reduced long-term real yields by around 80 basis points. The subsequent impact of total purchases, that is, including the Federal Reserve's asset purchase, in 2008–2012 has been even larger: the quantitative easing depressed the real 10-year Treasury yields by around 140 basis points.[18] Of course, the research showing that foreign purchases of US government bonds that had an economically large and statistically significant impact on long-term interest rates must be treated with caution. After all, causality runs from rising house prices to a deterioration of the current account balance, and hence, foreign purchases of government debt, not the other way around, according to research by Geerolf and Grjebine (2011).

Some have objected that the global savings rate—that is world savings as a fraction of world GDP—was actually low in the 2002–2004 period and that the increase in global savings largely played out after

---

[16] Glenn Rudebusch, Eric T. Swanson and Tao Wu, "The Bond Yield Conundrum from a Macro-Finance Perspective," Monetary an Economic Studies, pp. 83–129, 2006.

[17] Francis Warnock and Veronica Warnock, "International capital flows and U.S. interest rates," *Journal of International Money and Finance*, Vol. 28, 903–919, 2009.

[18] Iryna Kaminska and Gabriele Zinna, "Official Demand for U.S. Debt: Implications for U.S. real interest rates," International Monetary Fund, 2014.

2004. However, they overlook the changing composition of world savings. In 2000, advanced economies accounted for 78 percent of global savings. By 2008, the share of emerging economies in global savings had doubled to 44 percent while advanced economies accounted for a mere 56 percent of global savings.[19] Emerging economies' savings have been heavily skewed toward fixed-income assets, either because emerging economies' investors are genuinely more risk averse, and/or because they are institutionally constrained to invest in equity capital. Institutional constraints include emerging economies' underdeveloped capital markets and the reluctance of most Western countries to allow emerging economies' sovereign wealth funds to invest in equity capital of Western companies.

Total debt securities outstanding started rising at a higher rate from 2002 onward even though the global savings rate was relatively low at the time. China's current account surpluses were used almost wholly to acquire assets in the USA; more than 80 percent of which consisted of very safe US Treasuries and US agencies debt. The other emerging economies used their current account surpluses to purchase roughly equal amounts of safe US assets and European bank deposits. The 2000s saw a sharp increase in the global return on physical capital and a rise in the yield on quoted equity as a result of emerging economies' portfolio preferences.[20]

Europe as such did not run a current account surplus and thus was not a net exporter of savings to the rest of the world. But Europe leveraged up its international balance sheet significantly, issuing, among other instruments, considerable sovereign debt and bank debt, and using the proceeds to buy substantial amounts of triple-A rated US mortgage-backed securities. The strong preference of the emerging economies for US Treasuries and US agency debt pushed Europeans and US investors, who were in a desperate search for yield, into the toxic US debt securities. The amount outstanding of triple-rated mortgage-backed securities rose to $1.7 trillion from 2003 to 2007, of which US residents took $1.1 trillion and Europeans $0.4 trillion.[21]

---

[19] Mees, 2012.
[20] Kevin Daly and Ben Broadbent, "The Savings Glut, the Return on Capital and the Rise in Risk Aversion," Goldman Sachs Global Economics Paper No: 185, 2009.
[21] Ben Bernanke et al., "International Capital Flows and the Returns to Safe Assets in the United States, 2003-2007," Federal Reserve, 2011.

Corporate Savings

By focusing solely on foreign central banks' purchases of US Treasuries, Bernanke overlooked a more important player in the market for government debt. As a JP Morgan research note in June 2005 already noted, the real driver of the savings glut was the corporate sector in advanced economies.[22] Between 2000 and 2004, the increase in G-6 corporate savings was five times greater than the increased savings by emerging economies. During those years, corporate profits around the globe surged while capital spending remained relatively weak. As a result, companies in aggregate became net savers on a huge scale and as such important players in the government debt market. The corporate sector in advanced economies turned from being big borrowers to being net savers as their profits exceed their capital spending.

As corporate savings make up a large part of emerging economies' savings as well, the global savings glut is not so much a *geographical* phenomenon but a *sectoral* phenomenon instead. The total increase in net savings by non-financial corporates in advanced economies between 2001 and 2005 was more than $1 trillion, that is, 3 percent of annual global GDP and five times the increase in net savings by emerging economies over that same period. Just like China does with its foreign exchange reserves, corporations invest their stockpiles of cash predominantly in riskless assets such as US Treasury bills.

Ultimo 2007, China's $1.5 trillion of foreign exchange reserves compared to $1.7 trillion of corporate cash reserves hoarded by US companies (both financial and non-financial) alone.[23] The corporate cash hoarding was not limited to the USA. By 2007, non-financial companies in Europe, the Middle East, and Africa had amassed approximately $0.9 trillion in cash reserves. The savings behavior of companies in the advanced world was remarkably similar despite the fact that the economies experienced wildly diverging growth rates.

Instead of investing to boost future output and incomes, firms across the globe were running large financial surpluses, using their spare money to repay debts, buy back shares or build up cash. A more natural thing would be for companies to be net borrowers and for households as a group to be net savers, providing firms with the capital to invest. The global financial crisis did not change that. By 2014, publicly listed non-financial companies

---

[22] "Corporate savings are driving the global savings glut," JP Morgan, June 24, 2005.
[23] Heleen Mees, "Interest rates should take blame for recession," *The Financial Times*' Economist Forum, 2013.

in Europe, the Middle East, and Africa had amassed almost $1.3 trillion in cash reserves, a 50 percent increase compared to 2007, and just shy of the $1.5 trillion in corporate cash piles held by US non-financial companies.

The pile of unspent corporate cash that has been built up since the turn of the century is in the hands of an increasingly smaller number of companies. About a third of the world's biggest non-financial companies are sitting on most of the $2.8 trillion gross cash pile.[24] With $1.5 trillion, non-financial US companies account for 45 percent of the corporate cash reserves. Next in line are Japanese companies that account for 14 percent of the cash reserves globally, followed by companies based in France, Germany, and the UK. Much of this cash is held in secure but low-yielding US Treasury securities, earning these companies a steady stream of interest payments. It is estimated that Apple, Microsoft, Google, and Cisco alone have around $163 billion invested in US Treasuries and US agency debt.

Other than in the case of foreign purchases, there are no official records of companies' purchases of US Treasuries or government agency debt. Therefore, there are no estimates of the impact that these corporate purchases of government debt have on real interest rates. Given the size of the corporate cash piles in advanced economies, it is safe to assume that the impact of the corporate savings on interest rates in the years leading up to the global financial crisis was at least as large as the foreign purchases of US Treasuries or US agency debt. That would put the combined effect of foreign central banks purchases and corporate purchases of government debt in 2005 at least at 1.6 percent, which is similar to the lower range of the drop in the term premium that the Federal Reserve Bank of New York found.[25]

Natural Rate of Interest

In a study for the Bank of England, Rachel and Smith put the decline in global real interest rates in a long-term perspective.[26] Since the 1980s, the long-term risk-free real interest rate has dropped by around 450 basis points in both emerging and developed economies. Although there are

---

[24] "The cash paradox: How record cash reserves are influencing corporate behavior," Deloitte, 2014.

[25] The corporate savings glut is a good example of how the availability of data shapes the policy debate. Had more data been available, corporate savings would undoubtedly have shared the blame for the global financial crisis.

[26] Lukasz Rachel and Thomas Smith, "Secular drivers of the global real interest rate," Bank of England, 2015.

differences across countries, the global pattern is basically the same wherefore Rachel and Smith conclude that global factors are at work. Changes in the rate of growth can't explain the fall in interest rates because global growth was fairly steady in the pre-crisis decades. Rachel and Smith attribute two-thirds of the 450 basis points fall in real rates since the 1980s to shifts in preferences for saving and investment.

In an expansive but somewhat fragmented analysis, they attribute the increase in desired global savings to demographic forces, higher inequality and to a lesser extent to the glut of precautionary saving by emerging economies. Meanwhile, the desired levels of investment have fallen as a result of the falling relative price of capital, lower public investment, and due to an increase in the spread between risk-free and actual interest rates. As these forces are likely to persist or build even further, Rachel and Smith expect that the global natural rate of interest may remain low and perhaps settle at or slightly below 1 percent in the medium-to-long run.

Tobias Nangle and Charles Goodheart tie the decline in interest rates to the erosion of workers' bargaining power.[27, 28] The Nangle-Goodheart hypothesis is that a combination of the demographic dividend, that is the rising proportion of the population being of working age, and globalization resulted in a global glut of labor. Faced with an oversupply of workers, the relative price of labor fell, pushing down the labor share of national income in the advanced economies and depressing wage growth. The availability of cheap labor reduced the need for labor-saving, productivity-enhancing capital investment in advanced economies. According to Goodheart and Nangle, the lower demand for capital and less inflationary pressure from wages reduced real interest rates. However, as demographics have turned, they expect that the trends of low wages, falling real rates and rising inequality should, therefore, turn too.

Two caveats should be raised with regard to the Nangle-Goodheart hypothesis. First, the proportion of working-age population is not decisive. Without the economic transformation of China, which also included the introduction of the one-child policy between 1978 and 1980, the proportion of the working-age population would undoubtedly have been higher than it actually is. The effect on workers' bargaining power in

---

[27] Toby Nangle, "Labor power sets the neutral real rate," VoxEU, May 9, 2015.
[28] Charles Goodhart, Pratyancha Pardeshi, and Manoj Pradhan, "Workers vs pensioners: the battle of our time," *Prospect Magazine*, December 2015.

advanced economies would nonetheless have been negligible. The proportion of the working-age population is not the key, but the proportion of the working-age population that can be drawn into the capitalist sector. Globally, there still is a huge pool of un- or underutilized labor, even though demographics have turned. Moreover, if the future sees a rise of the robots, labor's share of GDP will continue to decline.

Second, as gross investments as a share of GDP are at their long-term average of 13 percent of GDP, it is not so much the declining demand for capital goods that caused interest rates to fall. Rather, it was wage growth trailing labor productivity growth that led to the rise in corporate profits. As there was no countervailing rise in corporate investment, the excess profits resulted in a global corporate savings glut that in turn contributed to the falling interest rates.

CHAPTER 10

The Shortfall in Demand

LABOR SHARES FALLING EVERYWHERE

Not only China but industrialized economies also experienced a substantial rise in the capitalist surplus. The capitalist surplus does not only translate in rising corporate profits but rising incomes for the global elite, or the top 1 percent, as well. Although the trend has been apparent since the beginning of the 1980s, it has become much more pronounced since the turn of the century. In a globalized world, the effects of unlimited supplies of labor spill over to advanced economies. Western companies moved production facilities and offices to China, India, and Eastern Europe, and the so-called *offshoring* or *outsourced* work to companies in those countries. The International Monetary Fund reckoned that, by 2005, almost a billion people in the world's labor force were engaged in export-oriented, and therefore, competitive markets, an almost threefold increase since the fall of the Berlin Wall.[1]

Between 1980 and 2013, wages and salaries as a share of GDP dropped 9 percentage points in the USA while over the same period, profits after tax as a share of GDP increased by roughly the same amount. Corporate profits after tax as a share of national income more than doubled since the eighties. This phenomenon is by no means confined to the USA. It is apparent in virtually every other industrialized nation as well. In Japan, labor's share in GDP fell from 80 percent of GDP in 1978 to 65 percent of GDP in 2010.

---

[1] International Monetary Fund, *World Economic Outlook*, April 2007, Chap. 5, p. 162.

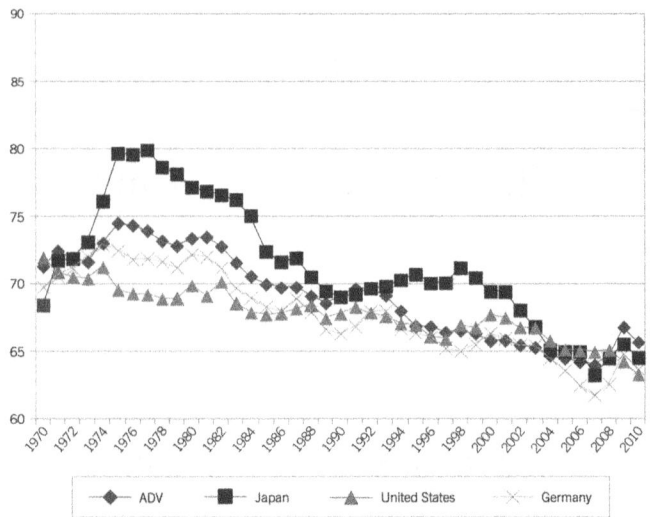

Fig. 10.1 Adjusted labor income shares in developed economies, Germany, the USA and Japan, 1970–2010. The adjusted labor income share makes an adjustment for the self-employed. Note: ADV = unweighted average of 16 high-income OECD countries (Australia, Austria, Belgium, Canada, Denmark, Finland, France, Germany, Ireland, Italy, Japan, the Netherlands, Spain, Sweden, the United Kingdom, and the United States. The Republic of Korea is excluded) (*Source*: ILO, Stockhammer, AMECO)

In Germany, labor's share in GDP dropped from 73 percent in the early 1970s to 63 percent in 2007. In other high-income countries, labor's share in GDP declined on average almost 10 percentage points since the mid-1970s.[2] Over the period from 1990 to 2009, the share of labor compensation in national income declined in 26 out of 30 developed economies with a corresponding rise in corporate profits as a share in national income.

As wages and salaries also include the salaries of the so-called *super-managers*, the actual position of wage earners has deteriorated more than can be deduced from the decline in wages and salaries as a share of GDP. If the labor compensation of the top 1 percent of income earners is excluded, the drop in the labor share is even greater. This reflects the

---

[2] International Labor Organization, "Wages and equitable growth," *Global Wage Report 2012/13*, 2013.

sharp increase, especially in English-speaking countries, of the wage and salaries (including bonuses and exercised stock options) of top executives, who now cohabit with capital owners at the top of the income hierarchy.[3] In 2015 alone, the chief executive of JP Morgan Chase, Jamie Dimon, and the chief executive of Goldman Sachs, Lloyd Blankfein, both made it to the billionaires list. Top executives like them can no longer be considered wage earners; they firmly belong to the class of capitalists.

Studies that look at labor compensation by categories of workers invariably find that the falling wage shares of low- and medium-skilled workers are the primary drivers of the decline in labor's share in GDP. In the ten developed economies for which data are available, the wage share for low-skilled workers fell by 12 percentage points between the early 1980s and 2005 while it increased by 7 percentage points for highly skilled workers. Between 1980 and 2005, the wage share for unskilled workers in the USA, Japan, and Europe fell by 15 percent, 15 percent, and 10 percent, respectively, but it increased for skilled workers with higher education by 7 percent, 2 percent, and 8 percent, respectively.

The fact that labor as a share of GDP is falling does not necessarily mean that real wages are falling, although that has certainly been the case for groups of low- and unskilled workers. It means that wages do not keep up with productivity growth, adding to profit growth instead. Between 1999 and 2011, average labor productivity in developed economies rose more than twice as much as average wages. In the USA, real hourly labor productivity in the non-farm business sector increased by about 85 per cent since 1980, while real hourly compensation increased by only around 35 percent. In Germany, labor productivity surged by almost a quarter over the past two decades while real monthly wages remained flat.[4]

Arthur Lewis imagined that mass labor migration from India and China, with workers moving to high-wage countries, might bring down the wage level in a country like the USA. The reverse happened, with producers moving production facilities or outsourcing work to China and India. It brought the wage costs in advanced economies down all the same. Although nominal wages as such are downward rigid, groups of unionized workers got fired en masse and replaced by temporary workers with no benefits. The Mott's applesauce factory in Rochester, New York tried in 2010 to cut its union workers wage in half, and when they balked, the factory replaced them with substitute workers.

[3] *Id.*
[4] *Id.*

Before the mid-1980s, a 1 percent change in the output gap would generate roughly a response of 0.45 percent in the similarly defined gap of the employment-population ratio.[5] The rest of the 1 percent shortfall of real GDP would show up in declining productivity and in hours per employee. The observed ratios are roughly consistent with the predictions made by Arthur Okun in what is known as "Okun's Law." After the mid-1980s, however, the response ratio jumped from 0.45 percent during the 1954–1986 to 0.78 percent during 1986–2011. These days, employment drops much more during economic recessions than it would have done previously.

The decline in labor's share in GDP is not confined to industrialized countries. On the contrary, it is even more pronounced in many emerging and developing economies, with considerable declines in Asia and North Africa and more stable but still declining wage shares in Latin America. The average labor shares in a group of 16 developing and emerging economies declined from around 62 percent of GDP in the early nineties to 58 percent just before the crisis.[6] Even in China, a country where wages of paid employees roughly tripled over the last decade, the total economy increased at a faster rate than the total wage bill. Hence, labor's share of national income went down.[7]

TECHNOLOGY VERSUS GLOBALIZATION

The two most important explanations for the fall of labor's share of rich countries' income are the rise of robots, which made it cheap to replace humans with automation and the rise of China and India, which resulted in a labor glut that put downward pressure on wages in industrialized countries. A third explanation is the decline of organized labor, which was most acute in the 1980s during the reign of Thatcher and Reagan although the de-unionization has continued since then.

Karabarbounis and Neiman put the global decline in labor's share of income since the early 1980s at roughly five percentage points, to just

---

[5] Robert J. Gordon, "The case of the US jobless recovery: Assertive management meets the double hangover," VoxEU, 2011.
[6] International Labor Organization (2013).
[7] Wage growth is only measured in so-called "urban units," which in practice cover mostly state-owned enterprises, collective-owned units and other type of companies linked to the state.

over 50 percent of GDP.⁸ They argue that neither international trade nor offshoring or outsourcing is primarily responsible for the labor share declines in rich countries such as the USA, because labor-abundant countries such as China, India, and Mexico also experienced significant declines in their labor shares. Instead, they conclude that at least half of the global decline in the share of labor is due to the plummeting cost of capital goods, particularly those associated with computing and information technology.

Elsby, Hobijn, and Şahin, in a study of the US labor market, highlight the offshoring and outsourcing of the labor-intensive component of the US supply chain as the most important explanation for the decline in the US labor share over the past 25 years.⁹ They find little support for explanations based on the substitution of capital for (unskilled) labor to exploit technical change embodied in new capital goods. The acceleration of the decline in the labor share in the 2000s in the USA was not accompanied by an increase in the rate of capital deepening. Moreover, growth in real wages and labor productivity, in fact, slowed during that period rather than accelerated. Elsby, Hobijn, and Şahin also find little evidence for institutional explanations based on the decline in unionization (Fig. 10.2).

Autor, Dorn, and Hanson, in a paper that juxtaposes the effects of trade and technology on the US labor market between 1990 and 2007, find similar results as by Elsby, Hobijn, and Şahin.¹⁰ Labor markets that are exposed to rising Chinese import competition experienced significant falls in employment, particularly in manufacturing and among non-college workers. Labor markets that are susceptible to computerization due to specialization in routine task-intensive activities did not experience a net employment decline. Autor, Dorn, and Hansen conclude that the impact of trade increases in the 2000s as imports accelerate.

The reasoning by Karabarbounis and Neiman— that because labor's share declined in labor-abundant economies like China, India, and Mexico, offshoring and outsourcing cannot be the culprit—shows a limited under-

---

⁸ Loukas Karabarbounis and Brent Neiman, "The Global Decline of the Labor Share," NBER Working Paper No.19136, 2013.

⁹ Michael Elsby, Bart Hobijn and Aysegül Sahin, "The Decline of the U.S. Labor Share," Brookings Papers on Economic Activity, 2013.

¹⁰ David Autor, David Dorn, and Gordon Hanson, "Untangling Trade and Technology: Evidence from Local Labor Markets," NBER Working Paper No. 18938, 2013.

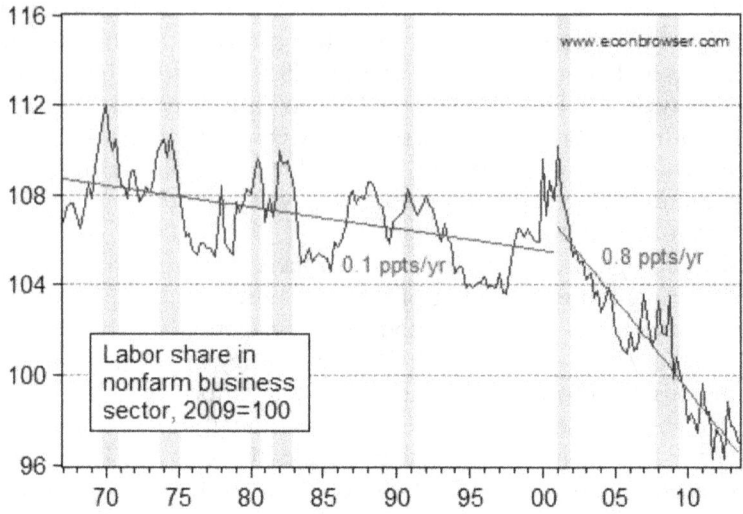

Fig. 10.2 Labor share of non-farm business in the USA (*Source:* EconBrowser)

standing of the economic development of emerging economies. As Arthur Lewis noted in his landmark essay, the capitalist surplus in emerging and developing economies will rise when more workers are taken out of the informal sector and added to the official workforce.

As long as labor is in unlimited supply, the more workers are added to the capitalist sector, the higher the share of profits. If the capitalist surplus is also used for capital deepening, labor productivity will grow, adding to profits once again. The workers in China, India, or Mexico who abandon the informal sector to work in manufacturing or a back office are better off as they see their incomes rise from the subsistence wage to the higher capitalist wage. In Fig. 4.3, this is represented by the real income growth, up to 80 percent, in emerging economies. However, while the workers advance, the capitalists who employ them advance even more. They are dubbed the booming global elite.

In rich countries, workers have gone from a situation where labor was in short supply and wages in keeping with labor productivity, to a situation where wages lag behind labor productivity growth because there is a worldwide labor glut, at least of the low-skilled variety. When jobs in the traded sector in rich countries vanish, it naturally puts downward pressure on the wages in the non-traded sector, which may help explain why Karabarbounis and Neiman saw labor's share decline across industries. In emerging economies, both the laborers as well as the capitalists advance in spite of the declining share of labor in GDP. In advanced economies, however, the capitalists advance while the laborers lose out. The decline of labor's share in advanced economies' GDP and emerging economies' GDP are two sides of the same offshoring/outsourcing coin.

This is not to say that the rise of Internet companies did not change the rules of the game. The world has moved toward a winner-takes-it-all economy because technology has increased the size of the market that can be served by a single person or firm. It is for that reason that Internet companies like Facebook and Instagram, to name a few, have a multibillion dollar market valuation. It does not arise from capital deepening but rather from the winner-takes-it-all effect through which small differences in skills (or simply luck) can mean enormous differences in returns. Internet technology that reduced transaction costs has enabled the sharing economy, making the sharing of assets cheaper and easier than ever—and, therefore, possible on a much larger scale. Airbnb and Uber are multibillion dollar network companies, with a market value that exceeds the market value of their respective old-economy pendant the Hyatt Hotels Corporation and the Ford Motor Company plus General Motors combined. However, the sharing economy has little to do with capital deepening—rather the opposite.

It is also not to say that the rise of the robots does not pose a threat to jobs. However, this may be more of a concern for the future than the past. After all, the observed pattern in the 2000s with high labor productivity growth in China, and to a somewhat lesser extent, in other emerging economies and slowing productivity growth in advanced economies clearly favors the narrative of globalization over robotization.[11]

---

[11] Andrew McAfee and Erik Brynjolfsson argue that the measurement of GDP is fundamentally flawed because it does not include the fact that information is now free due to the growth in Internet sources, which is somewhat of a red herring as GDP has always been understated as it missed the value of new inventions like electric lights, the subway, and the automobile.

Challenging Economic Orthodoxy

Economic orthodoxy has it that while some jobs may be lost in the short run due to international trade, gross domestic product of each country that engages in trade will increase in the long run because of the economic laws of comparative advantage. The gains of the winners from free trade, properly measured, will exceed the losses of the losers as a result of the trade-induced rise in total global vectors of the goods and services that people in a democracy want. While some groups may be hurt by dynamic free trade, the gains of the winners are big enough to more than compensate the losers. Therefore, in the long run, everybody will gain from international trade.

In 2004, Paul Samuelson sounded the alarm, arguing that mainstream economics is "dead wrong" about the necessary surplus of winnings over losings in each country that engages in trade when it comes to free trade.[12] Using a classic Ricardo-Mill two-country (USA, China), two-good model, Samuelson demonstrates that a low-wage nation that is rapidly improving its technology, like China, has the potential to change the terms of trade with the USA in ways that reduce per capita income in the USA. This version of dynamic fair free trade lowers the new labor-market-clearing real wage. To bring about that result, China's technology would need to improve in the industries that the USA exports. Such improvement would deteriorate US terms of trade, and as such, it would help labor and hurt capital in the USA, relative to the situation before the improvement in China's technology.

That is not what happened. In fact, technology in China improved mostly in sectors that the USA imports, such as manufacturing, not in sectors that the USA exports.[13] As a result, the US terms of trade, excluding oil, improved significantly in the early 2000s amid China's accession to the World Trade Organization. Between 2000 and 2008, the US Bureau of Labor Statistics index of import prices (excluding oil) rose by 10.3 percent while export prices increased by 21.7 percent. This result is not sensitive for what period is chosen. Therefore, US terms of trade vis-à-vis

---

[12] Paul A. Samuelson, "Where Ricardo and Mill Rebut and Confirm Arguments of Mainstream Economists Supporting Globalization," *Journal of Economic Perspectives*, Volume. 18, Number. 3, pp. 135–146, 2004.

[13] Avinash Dixit and Gene Grossman, "The Limits of Free Trade," *Journal of Economic Perspectives*, Volume 19, Number 3, pp. 241–245, 2005.

China improved, meaning that the price of goods that the USA imports from China fell.

In a two-factor model, the Stolper-Samuelson theorem predicts that trade with China benefits US capital and hurts US labor with the gains to capital exceeding the harm to labor.[14] Low-skilled workers in the US manufacturing sector are worse off as a result of trade with a low-wage country like China because factor prices will tend to even out across countries in sectors that do not differ in technology.[15] As the US capitalists' gains exceed the losses to US labor, the capitalists can, in theory, compensate the low-skilled workers.[16] Hence, trade between the USA and China conforms to economic orthodoxy.

If we look at the US terms of trade including oil, however, the picture is quite different. Between 2000 and 2008, the US Bureau of Labor Statistics index of import prices including oil increased by 32.1 percent while export prices increased by 21.7 percent, indicating that the overall US terms of trade deteriorated because of the rising oil price. Although the result is sensitive to what period is chosen, it is valid for most intervals between 2000 and 2014. American workers at the lower end of the skills spectrum experienced a double whammy: first they were hit by trade with China, and then by an oil shock that was, by all means, related to the rise of China.

Lower Tax Rates

In practice, workers in advanced economies were not compensated for the losses they suffered due to international trade.[17] Rather, the opposite happened. The capitalist surplus increased not only because of lower wage costs but also due to profound changes in taxation. In the mid-1980s, a trend toward a reduction in corporate income tax rates started with tax reforms in the UK and the USA. The reforms were aimed at broadening the tax base by reducing depreciation allowances and lowering the

---

[14] The theorem states that, under certain conditions, a rise in the relative price of a good will lead to a rise in the return to that factor which is used most intensively in the production of the good, and conversely, to a fall in the return to the other factor.

[15] This is the so-called *factor price equalization theorem*, also by Samuelson.

[16] In practice, workers at the lower end of the skills spectrum were not compensated for their loss but rather the opposite.

[17] The bailouts of banks during the global financial crisis exacerbated the shift from labor to capital.

statutory tax rates. The changes fitted neatly in the at the time developing Washington consensus, which argued for less distortionary taxation. Other industrialized countries followed suit with the most pronounced reductions of corporate tax rates occurring in Europe. The statutory corporate income tax rates in member countries of the Organization for Economic Cooperation and Development dropped on average 7.2 percentage points between 2000 and 2011, from 32.6 percent to 25.4 percent.[18]

According to the Organization for Economic Cooperation and Development, the corporate tax burden, measured as corporate income tax revenues as a share of GDP, did not fall. The un-weighted average of revenues deriving from taxes on corporate income as a share of GDP increased from 2.2 percent in 1965 to 3.8 percent in 2007. In light of the dramatic rise in corporate profits as a share of GDP, the corporate tax burden expressed as a share of corporate profits has fallen. In the USA, for example, profits before tax as a share of GDP rose from 6 percent at the end of 2001 to 13.7 percent of GDP in the third quarter of 2006 while the revenues from corporate income tax during that period only rose from 2.2 percent of GDP to 2.7 percent of GDP. The effective corporate tax rate in the USA dropped from 31.7 percent of corporate income under President Reagan to 20.5 percent of corporate income under President Obama while after-tax profits almost doubled.[19]

In Europe, in a competitive race to the bottom among European Union member countries, the effective average corporate income tax rate dropped from 28 percent in 1996 to 18 percent in 2007. The Netherlands, a country notorious for its tax planning opportunities, saw profits of non-financial corporations increase from 20 percent of GDP in 1990 to over 25 percent of national income in 2012.[20] Including financial corporations, profits rose from 26 percent of national income in 1990 to a whopping 41 percent of national income in 2012. The increase in profits is, however, not reflected in the tax revenues of the Dutch Treasury. Between 1990 and 2012, corporate income tax revenues dropped from 3.1 percent to 1.8 percent of GDP.

The Organization for Economic Cooperation and Development estimates that the effective tax rates paid by large multinational enterprises are

---

[18] OECD, *Addressing Base Erosion and Profit Shifting*, 2013.
[19] "Corporate Profits Grow and Wages Slide," *The New York Times*, April 4, 2014.
[20] OECD, Revenue Statistics.

4 to 8½ percentage points lower than the effective tax rates paid by similar enterprises with only domestic operations.[21] The companies that most likely are able to benefit from the cheap labor in emerging economies and reap the capitalist surplus are also most capable of reducing the burden of corporate income taxes by using tax havens and international tax treaties. The worldwide loss in corporate income tax revenue due to tax base erosion is estimated to be in the range of 4 to 10 percent of global corporate income tax revenues, that is, a loss in revenues of $100 billion to $240 billion annually.

An even more dramatic decrease in tax rates, which also springs from the Washington consensus, is apparent in the personal income tax. Compared to the late seventies, top tax rates on upper-income earners have declined significantly in many rich countries, from around 70 percent to around 50 percent.[22] Although the lower top tax rates were, in part, offset by measures that broadened the income tax base, they were also paid for by shifting the relative tax burden to lower income groups. The English-speaking countries, in particular, cut top income tax rates aggressively.[23] For example, the US top marginal federal individual tax rate was 91 percent in the 1950s and 1960s but is only 39.6 percent in 2015. In the UK, the top tax rate dropped from more than 90 percent in the late 1970s to 40 percent in the 2000s while income over £150,000 is taxed at 45 percent in 2015.

The reductions in top tax rates came with a concentration of income among the top 1 percent. For example, the USA experienced a 35 percentage point reduction in its top income tax rate and a very large ten percentage point increase in its top 1 percent pre-tax income share. By contrast, France or Germany saw little change in both the top tax rates and as well as the top 1 percent income shares during the same period. Countries that made large cuts in top tax rates such as the UK or the USA have not grown significantly faster than countries that did not cut top tax rates to that extent. This suggests that the concentration of income among the top 1 percent is not so much due to extra effort by the top 1 percent earners but mostly due to rent-seeking.[24]

---

[21] OECD, *Measuring and Monitoring BEPS, Action 11 – 2015 Final Report*, OECD/G20 Base Erosion and Profit Shifting Project, 2015.

[22] Tax Policy Center, Historical Top Marginal Personal Income Tax Rate in OECD Countries, 2014.

[23] Thomas Piketty and Emmanuel Saez, "Optimal Labor Income Taxation," NBER Working Paper No. 18521, 2012.

[24] Thomas Piketty, Emmanuel Saez and Stefanie Stantcheva, "Optimal Taxation of Top Labor Incomes: A Tale of Three Elasticities," CEPR Discussion Paper No. 8675, 2011.

The Use of the Capitalist Surplus – China

In the case of China, the majority of the capitalist surplus is indeed used to create more capital. Even in China's boom years, at least 80 percent of China's national savings were reinvested domestically, and since the percentage has been 90 percent or even more. Notable are the major infrastructure investments like airports, harbors, railways, and highways, the new urban residential housing, and (renewable) energy. Gross capital formation rose from 36 percent of GDP in 2001 to 48 percent of GDP in 2011, more than double the rate in advanced economies and well above the peaks of roughly 40 percent of GDP hit by South Korea and Taiwan when they went through a period of rapid industrialization. In spite of rapid growth, China's capital-to-output ratio is within the range of other emerging markets, suggesting that it had very little capital to start with.

It is not easy to overstate the role of the Chinese government, both at the central as well as the local level, in the investment drive. In the strict sense, government accounts for less than a quarter of total gross fixed investment, that is, investments that are formally part of the central, provincial, and village government budgets, and are financed either by taxation or public borrowing. The lion share of investment, however, is carried out by state-owned enterprises and quasi-private enterprises, which can borrow money on more favorable terms than private companies. It has been dubbed capitalism with Chinese characteristics or Leninist capitalism.

Economists—using a neoclassical approach—have argued that China's fixed investment has been consistently too high: as a share of GDP, it should be closer to 40 percent of GDP instead of 50 percent of GDP.[25] However, the neoclassical approach presumes that labor is in short supply, which is not quite the case in China. China today compares roughly with the USA at the start of the twentieth century and Japan in 1950, with almost 35 percent of the labor force still working in the primary sector.[26] A relaxation of the hukou-standards will draw more workers from the subsistence sector into the capitalist sector. Urbanization has not run its course yet in China. At 56 percent, China's degree of urbanization is

---

[25] Il Houng Lee, Murtaza Syed, and Liu Xueyan, "Is China Over-Investing and Does it Matter?," IMF Working Paper WP/12/277, 2012.

[26] In the USA, only 2 percent of the labor force works in the primary sector nowadays.

well below the 70 percent expected for a country with its income level per person.

In Arthur Lewis' model, as long as labor is in unlimited supplies, there is no over-investment. The capitalists are supposed to use the entire capitalist surplus for the formation of new capital to draw ever more workers out of the subsistence sector into the capitalist sector. Even though China's working-age population has already peaked, the International Monetary Fund estimates that China will only reach the Lewis Turning Point somewhere between 2020 and 2025.[27, 28] Higher labor force participation rates and increased fertility may push the moment China's economy runs out of unlimited supplies of labor to 2030.

Part of the capitalist surplus in China is redistributed from capital to labor through minimum wage hikes. In China, local governments have the task of setting minimum wages as the different regions have very different standards of living. Each province, municipality, or region sets its own minimum wage in accordance with its own local conditions. The monthly minimum wage in 2015 varied from ¥860 in one of the poorest provinces, Anhui, to ¥2200 in Shanghai. Under the Chinese Employment Promotion Plan, minimum wages are supposed to increase in accordance with local living standards and should fall between 40 and 60 percent of the average local wages. Between 2008 and 2012, minimum wages increased by an average 12.6 percent rate per year.[29]

Part of the capitalist surplus in China is used for consumption. This may represent reasonable payment for managerial and entrepreneurial services rendered as well as public services. However, the conspicuous consumption displayed by the super-rich in China suggests that many of these services are significantly overpaid. Especially the brassiness of the *"fu-erdai,"* which is a Chinese term for the second generation of the rich in mainland China, is considered one of the bigger social and moral problems that are associated with modern Chinese society.

---

[27] Mitali Das and Papa N'Diaye, "Chronicle of a Decline Foretold: Has China Reached the Lewis Turning Point?," IMF Working Paper, 2013.

[28] Fang Cai and Meiyan Wang argued in 2010 that labor shortages were emerging, suggesting that the Lewis Turning Point would be reached rather sooner than later (see Fang Cai and Maiyan Wang, "Growth and Structural Changes in Employment in Transitional China.," *Journal of Comparative Economics*, 2010).

[29] "A Complete Guide to 2015 Minimum Wage Levels Across China," China Briefing, May 26, 2015.

Oil-Exporting Countries

In times of oil booms, oil-exporting countries have high savings rates and corresponding current account surpluses, meaning that the capitalist surplus is hardly used for capital formation but for foreign reserve accumulation instead. Part of the capitalist surplus is used for lavish consumption spending as well but, relative to the oil revenues during boom years, consumption is almost negligible. Accumulating foreign exchange reserves is in accordance with the policy recommendations issued by the International Monetary Fund, and it may be an optimal policy path from the standpoint of the resource rich country, but it is hardly so from the standpoint of aggregate global demand. By investing the money in foreign government bonds, resource rich countries contribute to asset bubbles in the rest of the world.

Advanced Economies

In advanced economies, the capitalist surplus is not used for capital formation. While investment as a share of GDP remained relatively stable, as a share of profits, it almost dropped by half. There clearly is a profits and investment disconnect. This experience in advanced economies is at odds with the thinking of the classical economists, whose models were—in fairness—not designed for advanced economies. Malthus' prediction that the capitalist surplus would lead to a commodities glut, that is, a widespread excess of supply over demand, seems more apposite. In the USA alone, non-financial corporations had hoarded $1.6 trillion in cash and cash equivalents at the end of 2011. The cash holdings increased particularly fast between 2002 and 2004, growing at an annual rate of 19 percent (from $822 billion to $1.17 trillion), then plateaued until the end of 2008.[30] At that point, they rose fast again, growing at an annual rate of about 10 percent, reaching $1.7 trillion in 2014. Corporations in Europe, the Middle East, and Africa are hoarding similar amounts of cash, as are corporations in, most notably, China and Japan.

Economists have offered a number of disparate explanations for the corporate cash piles. Some say that the increase in the cash-to-assets ratio of firms is related tightly to precautionary motives and that the recent rise

---

[30] Juan M. Sánchez and Emircan Yurdagul, "Why Are Corporations Holding So Much Cash?," Federal Reserve bank of St. Louis, 2013.

in cash holdings is the result of increased uncertainty in the cash flows of firms. Others tie the corporate cash piles to repatriation taxes. The USA taxes corporations on their worldwide income. However, such taxation only takes place when earnings are repatriated. Therefore, firms may have incentives to keep foreign earnings abroad. As a consequence, in times of limited foreign investment opportunities and high profitability, these funds are likely to be held abroad in the form of cash. Other economists, however, dismiss the claim that differences in the way that countries tax foreign income alter the cash-holding behavior of the firms. They find, instead, that multinational firms with high R&D tend to hold the highest abnormal cash ratio.

Joseph Gruber and Steven Kamin of the Federal Reserve conclude that the corporate savings glut is the result of the sharp decline in corporate investment as a share of profits, so it is more a dearth of investment. In the years leading up to the global financial crisis, corporate investment rates had fallen below levels that would have been predicted by models estimated in earlier years that use economic growth, interest rates, profits, and other relevant determinants.[31] Only in the period from 2005 to 2007, corporate investments picked up so corporate cash holdings in advanced economies plateaued.

Corporate payouts to investors, in the form of dividends and share buy-backs, have generally gone up since the turn of the century and remained strong even after the global financial crisis, which suggests that the weakness in investment spending does not reflect corporate caution in response to either the bursting of the dot-com bubble or the global financial crisis, as some have suggested. The emergence of the corporate savings glut may be more related to a perceived absence of profitable investment opportunities than to a tightening of financial conditions or surge in corporate caution, which is consistent with the secular stagnation hypothesis.

A rise in short-termism, meaning that the focus of companies is on short-term results, has been blamed for the relative drop investment. Companies listed on stock exchanges face more short-term pressure from asset managers and investors, compared to privately-held firms that are held by a smaller group of individuals and for a longer period of time.[32]

---

[31] Joseph Gruber and Steven Kamin, "The Corporate Saving Glut in the Aftermath of the Global Financial Crisis," International Monetary Fund, 2015.

[32] John Asker, Joan Farre-Mensa, and Alexander Ljungqvist, "Corporate Investment and Stock Market Listing: A Puzzle?," *Review of Financial Studies*, 28 – 2, pp. 342–390, 2015.

Some economists argue that short-termism is a direct consequence of shifting incentives for companies' executives. In particular, the rise of the bonus culture and pay incentives at the managerial level may have led to an excessive focus on short-term results, hurting investment and longer-term growth.[33]

While a chronic shortfall in investment is part of the secular stagnation thesis, relative to assets, sales and GDP, American firms' investment has held steady. As *The Economist* points out, while the mix has shifted from plant and machines to things like software and research and development due to the drop in the costs of capital goods, gross private non-residential investment today is almost exactly at its long-run average of 13 percent of GDP.[34] There was a shift in the composition of investment, toward intellectual property. But, relative to GDP, investment as a whole has held steady.

Since investment as a share of national income did not fall, only as a share of rising profits, the excess of corporate savings over investment seems to be the result of the decline in labor's share of GDP and the relative fall in consumer demand associated with that. The temporary surge between 2005 and 2007 in investment, in both residential as well as business investment, may well have been triggered by the rise in debt-fuelled consumer spending, both in Europe and the USA, which in turn, was triggered by falling interest rates and rising housing wealth. Not without a reason, one used to quip at the time that Americans (and Europeans alike) treated their houses as ATMs. When the global financial crisis erupted and the housing markets in the Western hemisphere went in full meltdown mode, households started to pay down debts and companies began to pile up cash again.

The subsequent contraction in private investment during the global financial crisis was primarily a phenomenon of the advanced economies, not of the emerging economies.[35] For the former, private investment has declined by an average of 25 percent since the crisis compared with pre-crisis forecasts. In contrast, private investment in emerging and developing economies has only gradually slowed in recent years. The investment slump in the advanced economies has been broad-based. Though the

---

[33] Roland Bénabou and Jean Tirole, "Bonus Culture: Competitive Pay, Screening, and Multitasking," 2013.

[34] "As a share of GDP, investment is not in decline," *The Economist*, December 4, 2015.

[35] International Monetary Fund, *World Economic Outlook*, April 2015, Chap. 4, p. 111.

contraction has been sharpest in the housing sector, business investment accounts for two-thirds of the investment slump.

The overall weakness in demand since the global financial crisis appears to be the primary reason for businesses not to invest more. This finding is consistent with the findings of Blanchard and Summers, who found that fundamentals rather than the cost of capital drive investment.[36] In surveys, more than 40 percent of businesses in Europe and 10 percent of businesses in the USA in 2014 cited low consumer demand instead of financial constraints as the dominant factor.[37] In 2009, the numbers were 80 and 35 percent respectively. Or, as the chief executive of Unilever, Paul Polman, sighed, the Anglo-Dutch multinational consumer goods company is not investing because consumers are not spending.

The Inverse of Say's Law

In the world of Jean-Baptiste Say, the classical economist, there were no output gaps or unemployment because one could always produce things. In the process of producing them, one would create income and the people who got the income would then spend the income and so there would be no problem, he argued. This is what is now known as Say's law, namely, supply creates its own demand. In the aftermath of the Great Depression, however, John Maynard Keynes showed that in a world where the demand could be for money and for financial assets, there could in the short run be a shortfall in aggregate demand and, hence, unemployment.

Larry Summers argued that what we see in advanced economies is actually the inverse of Say's Law, that is, the lack of demand creates, over time, the lack of potential supply.[38] In 2014, the US economy operated about 10 percent below what the Congressional Budget Office had projected back in 2007 about the US economy's capacity in 2014. Of the 10 percent that the US economy was operating below its previously estimated potential, approximately half was the result of a continuing shortfall relative to the economy's potential while the other half was lost potential. Research into the effectiveness of labor market policies shows that any gains from labor

---

[36] Blanchard, Olivier, Changyong Rhee, and Lawrence Summers, "The Stock Market, Profit, and Investment," *The Quarterly Journal of Economics*, Vol. 108, No. 1, pp. 115–136, 1993.

[37] International Monetary Fund, *World Economic Outlook*, April 2015, Chap. 4, p. 111.

[38] Larry Summers, "Lack of Demand Creates Lack of Supply," Center on Budget and Policy Priorities, 2014.

market policies are only transitory and that those gains come through displacement at the expense of other eligible workers. Overall, labor market policies seem to have very little net benefits in terms of job creation as there is, in fact, job rationing due to a lack of demand.[39]

The crucial question is whether the shortfall in aggregate demand is indeed Keynesian in nature, that is, whether the shortfall in demand is the result of people temporarily hoarding cash. Keynes argued that there was no guarantee that the goods that individuals produced would be met with demand because individuals could decide to hoard cash in times of financial distress. As the economy would be unable to maintain itself at full employment, it was necessary for the government to step in and put underutilized savings to work through government spending. However, as Arthur Lewis pointed out, once the remedies that Keynes proposed had been successfully applied to such a shortfall, the economy should conform to the neoclassical model again with its defining characteristic that labor is in short supply.

On the face of it, the current shortfall in demand is not the result of US households hoarding cash. At 5 percent of disposable income, the household savings rate in the USA is low compared to the earlier decades. Between 1960 and 1980, the US household savings rate was between 10 and 12.5 percent of disposable income. Since 1980, the US household savings rate has dropped precipitously from 10 percent of disposable income to less than 2 percent in July 2005 when the US housing market had peaked. Although the household savings rate rose to 7.5 percent of disposable income in the wake of the global financial crisis as households paid down debt, since the beginning of 2013, the household savings rate is down to 5 percent again, the same level it had at the start of the twenty-first century.[40]

In as far as anemic growth was the result of a balance sheet recession, that no longer appears to be the case. Household debt as a share of disposable income has stabilized at below 110 percent since 2012 compared to 130 percent on the eve of the financial crisis. To make up for the drop in wages and salaries as a share of GDP in terms of effective demand, house-

---

[39] Bruno Crépon, Esther Duflo, Marc Gurgand, Roland Rathelot, and Philippe Zamora, "Do labor market policies have displacement effects? Evidence from a clustered randomized experiment," 2012.

[40] In the European Union, the average household savings rate is just a few percentage points higher compared to the USA.

holds in the USA would have to dis-save up to 5 percent of disposable income annually. Between 2000 and 2007, US household debt as a share of disposable income rose from 95 percent to more than 130 percent. As the global financial crisis has taught, such a path is utterly unsustainable.

In Europe, the total debt of households, non-financial enterprises, and the general government sector as a share of GDP has increased compared to the beginning of the global financial crisis. There has been some shift of debt from the private sector to the public sector but the overall debt burden remains unprecedentedly high for an economy in peacetime. The fact that the euro area remains highly leveraged is probably the main reason why the wealth effect associated with rising asset prices has been muted at best so far.

Keynesian Remedies – Monetary Stimulus

Keynes argued that the solution to the Great Depression was to induce investment through a combination of monetary policy and government spending on infrastructure, or more in general, fiscal policy.

Monetary policy affects the real economy through a number of transmission mechanisms. First, if the interest rate at which businesses and consumers can borrow is lowered, investments that were previously unprofitable may become profitable, increasing investment demand. Second, consumer purchases that are financed through debt become more affordable, increasing consumer demand. Third, lower interest rates typically inflate the prices of long-lived assets like houses and stocks, which in turn, may increase consumer demand through the so-called *wealth effect*. Consumers tend to spend more when prices of those assets are rising because rising asset prices make them feel wealthy. Fourth, lower interest rates may induce capital outflows that may result in a depreciation of the currency, which will, in turn, stimulate a country's export sector and curb imports. Fifth, monetary policy may well shore up the balance sheets of retail banks, which in turn may increase bank lending to both businesses as well as consumers.

In the months following the collapse of Lehman Brothers, central banks around the world started to cut interest rates, with the Federal Reserve leading the pack. By December 2008, the Federal Reserve cut the fed funds rate to virtually 0 percent (officially between 0 and 0.25 percent). The Bank of England cut the official bank rate to 0.5 percent, and the European Central Bank's main policy rate was lowered to 1 percent in the course of 2009. The Bank of Japan and the People's Bank of China also eased monetary policy. With the main policy rate near zero and the US economy still teetering, the Federal Reserve resorted to unconventional monetary policy, buying up US Treasuries and illiquid mortgage-backed securities. The purchases lowered the yield on long-term government bonds and helped to shore up banks' balance sheets. The Bank of England did so too, but the European Central Bank embarked on quantitative easing only much later in the crisis.

The first round of quantitative easing in the USA, also known as QE1, ran from November 2008 until June 2010 was extremely effective in calming financial markets and preventing further panics, by propping up prices of illiquid assets and shoring up banks' balance sheets.[41] By the end of 2010, financial markets in the USA were orderly again and a modest economic recovery was underway. A number of studies have confirmed that beyond calming financial markets, the central banks' asset purchase programs did indeed succeed in driving up the price and lowering the yields of the underlying assets. Although the central banks purchased mostly government bonds and agency debt, the central banks' asset purchases have also led to an increase in the demand for other assets, including corporate bonds and shares, driving up the prices of a wide range of assets, not just government bonds.

According to an analysis by the Bank of England, the bank's asset purchases have pushed up the price of equities by at least as much as they have pushed up the price of government bonds.[42] By pushing up a range of asset prices, asset purchases have boosted the value of households' financial wealth. During the 2010 Jackson Hole conference, Ben Bernanke cited this wealth effect as the most important transmission mechanism of monetary policy.[43]

In practice, the benefits from these wealth effects will accrue to those households holding most financial assets. The distribution of these assets outside pension funds is heavily skewed, with the top 5 percent of households owning 40 percent or more of these assets, exacerbating the income inequality in advanced economies. As the savings rate of the top income

---

[41] Vladimir Klyuev, Phil De Imus, and Krishna Srinivasan, "Unconventional Choices for Unconventional Times: Credit and Quantitative Easing in Advanced Economies," International Monetary Fund, 2009.

[42] Bank of England, "The Distributional Effects of Asset Purchases," 2012.

[43] Ben Bernanke, "The Economic Outlook and Monetary Policy," At the Federal Reserve Bank of Kansas City Economic Symposium in Jackson Hole, Wyoming, August 27, 2010.

households is much higher than the savings rate of low-income households, the response of real economic activity to rising asset prices will be low.

Wealth inequality has risen since the global financial crisis, according to research by the Bank of International Settlements. While low interest rates and rising bond prices have had a negligible impact on wealth inequality, rising equity prices have been a key driver of inequality. To the extent that monetary policy has boosted equity prices, it may have added to inequality.[44] Therefore, the central banks' bond buying programs may have compounded the ailments of advanced economies by raising the returns on assets compared to labor.

The central banks also used communication as a tool to drive down interest rates. Most famous is President Draghi's reassurance in the summer of 2012 that the European Central Bank would do "whatever it takes" to preserve the single currency. Two summers earlier, the Federal Open Market Committee caused great consternation in financial markets by declaring that it expected the fed funds rate to stay near zero percent until mid-2013 (in fact, the fed funds rate stayed near zero until December 2015). Economists like Kenneth Rogoff and Paul Krugman suggested raising the target for the inflation rate, and the Federal Open Market Committee did, suggesting that they would allow inflation to run around 2.5 percent, but to little avail. By then, declining commodity prices relentlessly pulled inflation rates far below the standard Federal Open Market Committee's inflation target of 2 percent headline PCE.

Out of frustration that the zero-lower bound curbed central banks' room for maneuver, some economists have suggested banning cash altogether as a cashless society would enable negative interest rates. But central banks have been testing the zero-lower bound in a world full of cash. In June 2014, the European Central Bank lowered the deposit rate that it pays commercial banks on their reserves, to minus 0.1 percent, meaning that it was in effect charging commercial banks to hold their excess deposits at the central bank. Three months later, the European Central Bank cut the deposit rate again, to minus 0.2 percent, and in December 2015 again, to minus 0.3 percent. The European Central Bank is not the only central bank going below zero with interest rates. Denmark's central bank has held the main policy rate below zero for almost three years to

---

[44] Dietrich Domanski, Michela Scatigna and Anna Zabai, "Wealth inequality and monetary policy," BIS, *Quarterly Review*, March 2016.

safeguard its exchange-rate peg with the euro. The Swiss National Bank uses negative interest rates to deter investors from buying francs and the Swedish Riksbank to stoke inflation.

Commercial banks did not en masse withdraw their reserves from the central banks once the deposit rate dipped into negative territory, as theory has it. The costs associated with holding large swaths of money and settling payments in cash are simply too high. The banks would have to move the cash between themselves each day and the costs of counting, storing, and insurance are prohibitive. Since all banks are awash with cash, they cannot lend it to each other either. In credit markets, the yields on European government bonds from the northern countries have gone negative as well. In November 2015, the Chair of the Federal Reserve Janet Yellen told US Congress that if the US economy soured, negative interest rates would be on the table as well as they could be an incentive for banks to lend.[45]

The Bank for International Settlements has pointed out that if negative policy rates do not feed into lending rates for households and firms, they largely lose their rationale.[46] On the other hand, if negative policy rates are transmitted to lending rates for firms and households, then they will affect the banks' profitability unless negative rates are also imposed on deposits, raising questions as to the stability of the retail deposit base. The Bank for International Settlements also cautioned that it was hard to predict how institutions or individuals would behave if interest rates were to go further into negative territory.

If business investment does not depend on the costs of capital but on effective demand instead, as Olivier Blanchard and Larry Summers concluded in 1994, low interest rates may do little to stimulate corporate investment directly. Blanchard and Summers showed in a 1994 empirical study that fundamentals (i.e., consumer demand) rather than the cost of capital drive corporate investment. In that case, monetary policy's main transmission mechanism is indeed through the prices of assets, such as the stock market and the housing market.

To the extent that monetary policy brings about changes in the exchange rate, historical experience in advanced and emerging economies

---

[45] Hearing Committee on Financial Services of the U.S. House of Representatives, November 4, 2015.

[46] Morten Linnemann Bech and Aytek Malkhozov, "How have central banks implemented negative policy rates?," BIS, *Quarterly Review*, March 2016.

suggests that these movements typically have sizable effects on export and import volumes. A 10 percent real effective depreciation of an economy's currency is associated with a rise in real net exports of, on average, 1.5 percent of GDP, with substantial cross-country variation around this average. Although these effects fully materialize over a number of years, much of the adjustment occurs in the first year.[47] However, the change in exchange rates will only redistribute demand from countries whose currencies are depreciating to those that are appreciating. It is a beggar-thy-neighbor policy. It will do little to nothing to increase aggregate demand at the global level.

Keynesian Remedies – Fiscal Stimulus

When the economy is at the zero lower bound, raising the level of demand at any given level of interest rate is considered the preferable strategy. Expansionary fiscal policy, either by cutting taxes or increasing government spending, raises demand for businesses' products and employment, making up for the shortfall in demand. In general, government spending is preferred to tax cuts because in an economic recession, households and businesses alike may use the tax cuts to pay down debts instead of using the windfall to invest or consume. Keynesians assume that in a depressed economy, government spending raises GDP by more than the government's spending increase. The philosophy behind it is simple. If the government increases spending to carry out major repairs on the Brooklyn Bridge, not only will the construction workers see their income rise, but the companies where the construction workers spend their wages will see income rise as well.

The question is how large the fiscal multiplier is. This measure captures how effectively tax cuts or increases in government spending stimulate output. A multiplier of 1 means that a $1 million increase in government spending will increase a country's GDP by $1 million. Economists are deeply divided about how well, or indeed whether, fiscal stimulus works. According to economists of the Chicago School, the multiplier tends to be negligent, as higher interest rates and taxes associated with government spending crowd out private spending, regardless of the state of the economy. Keynesian economists assume that during a recession, when capital and labor are underutilized and the real rate of interest is below zero, a

---

[47] International Monetary Fund, *World Economic Outlook*, October 2015, Chap. 3, p. 105.

fiscal stimulus will increase overall demand. If the initial stimulus triggers a cascade of expenditure among consumers and businesses, the multiplier may be well above one. As long as the economy is in a liquidity trap with the equilibrium interest rate below zero, government spending will not crowd out private spending.

The fiscal multiplier is likely to vary according to the type of fiscal action as well. Government spending on infrastructure may have a bigger multiplier than a tax cut if consumers save a portion of their tax windfall. A tax cut targeted at lower income households will generally have a bigger impact on spending than a tax cut for high-income households as the former are credit constrained and tend to spend a higher share of their income. Crucially, the overall size of the fiscal multiplier also depends on how people react to higher government borrowing. If consumers expect higher future taxes in order to offset the debt-financed fiscal stimulus, they may choose to spend less today, which would reduce the fiscal multiplier.

Estimating the effects of fiscal policy is hard. The reason is that fiscal actions are often taken in response to other events in the economy. Separating the impact of those other events from the impact of the tax changes or government spending increases is very difficult.[48] One approach is to use microeconomic case studies to examine consumer behavior in response to specific tax rebates and cuts. These studies, largely based on tax changes in America, find that permanent cuts have a bigger impact on consumer spending than temporary ones and that consumers who find it hard to borrow, such as those close to their credit card limit, tend to spend more of their tax windfall. But case studies do not measure the overall impact of tax cuts or spending increases on output.

An alternative approach is to try to determine the statistical impact of changes in government spending or tax cuts on GDP. The difficulty here is to isolate the effects of fiscal stimulus measures from the rises in social security spending and falls in tax revenues that are associated with recessions. This kind of studies also allows for cross-country comparisons. Multipliers are bigger in closed economies compared to open economies because less of the stimulus leaks abroad via imports. It is why it is generally better that the governments of open, smaller economies coordinate fiscal stimulus to ensure a maximum impact.

The International Monetary Fund concluded in 2012 that the multiplier in the aftermath of the global financial crisis was probably larger

---

[48] "Much ado about multipliers," *The Economist*, September 24, 2009.

than previously estimated. Instead of a fiscal multiplier ranging from 0.4 to 1.2, the actual multipliers may be higher, in the range of 0.9 to 1.7 with the lower end of the estimate applying to tax cuts and the higher end to government spending.[49] The fiscal consolidation undertaken by most advanced economies after the global financial crisis posed a much greater drag on the economy than the economic forecasts thus far had taken into account.

Dutch Disease

The push for austerity in the euro area, especially in the countries of the periphery, has been fiercely criticized. With interest rates near zero, it is often argued that governments should instead boost spending to offset the collapse in private spending. That way, the economy would recover by itself and grow sufficiently for government debt levels to become sustainable. In this view, the economic recession in the aftermath of a housing bubble is simply the result of a lack of demand, with no role for the supply-side of the economy.

In reality, the housing bubbles that plagued virtually all countries in the Western hemisphere came with Dutch disease-like symptoms, that is, a deterioration of the traded sector. In 1977, *The Economist* coined the term Dutch disease to describe the woes of the Dutch economy. A large gas field had been discovered in 1959. Dutch exports soared. However, there was a contrast between the external health of the economy and the internal ailments. After the first oil crisis in 1974, the Dutch economy entered a stage of stagflation with simultaneously high inflation and high unemployment. The average growth rate of the economy declined from 5 percent to 2 percent per year and the unemployment rate jumped from 1.1 percent to 5.1 percent. The small government budget surplus turned into a deficit of 3 percent in 1975.

According to the British magazine, the high value of the guilder, the Dutch currency at the time, was the primary cause of the problems. Gas exports had led to an influx of foreign currency, which increased demand for the Dutch currency and thus made it stronger. That made other parts of the economy less competitive in international markets. The problems for the Dutch economy did not stop there. The new investments designed for gas extraction generated few jobs and the Dutch central bank kept

---

[49] International Monetary Fund, *World Economic Outlook*, October 2012, Chap. 1, p. 41.

interest rates low in an attempt to stop the guilder from appreciating too fast. That prompted investment to rush out of the country, shrinking future economic potential. Moreover, the natural gas resources were spent to finance government transfers, including a large disability insurance scheme that drew away almost a million workers from labor supply.

Since the initial article in *The Economist*, economists have built models and done empirical research to analyze the effects of a resources boom. The economic analysis of a natural resources boom was subsequently extended to foreign aid as the country that receives foreign aid also experiences an influx of foreign exchange that may trigger effects similar to a natural resources boom. But the analysis can be extended to housing bubbles too. The mechanism is as follows. First, research shows that a housing bubble often coincides with a construction boom, increasing wages in the construction sector and drawing skilled labor into the non-traded sector, increasing overall wages. Given that the international price of traded goods is fixed, the higher wage in terms of traded goods will reduce the traded sector's profitability and competitiveness, and result in a decline in exports. This is the resource movement effect.

Second, higher wages will increase spending and raise the price of non-traded goods relative to traded goods, which is an increase in the real effective exchange rate. The higher real effective exchange rate hurts the competitiveness of the traded sector once again because of the so-called *spending effect*. Third, higher house prices in and of themselves will induce higher spending because of the wealth effect, raising the real exchange rate once more and further deteriorating the tradable sector. Rising house prices are thus associated with rising employment in the construction sector, declining employment in the manufacturing sector, declining exports, rising unit labor costs and rising real effective exchange rates. This is exactly what happened in the 2000s. Figs. 10.3, 10.4, 10.5, and 10.6 show, respectively, the change in construction employment, manufacturing employment, exports, and unit labor costs versus the change in house prices between 2000 and 2007.

Because technological progress is higher in the traded sector compared to the non-traded sector, a decline in the traded sector will affect a country's learning-by-doing induced technological progress and therefore structurally hurt a country's long-term productivity growth. [50] This means that it is only natural for a country to find itself on a lower growth path after the bursting of a housing bubble, as Summers pointed out has happened to the USA. To paraphrase a remark Paul Krugman made in the context of

---

[50] Sweder van Wijnbergen, "The 'Dutch Disease': A Disease After All?," *The Economic Journal*, Vol. 94, No. 373, pp. 41–55, 1984.

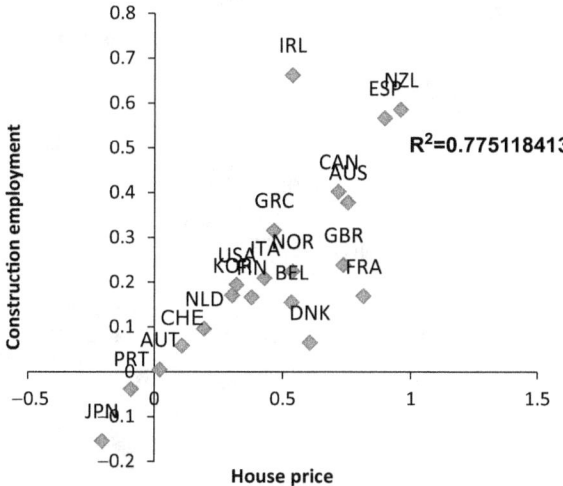

Fig. 10.3 Construction employment versus house price 2000–2007 (*Source*: OECD)

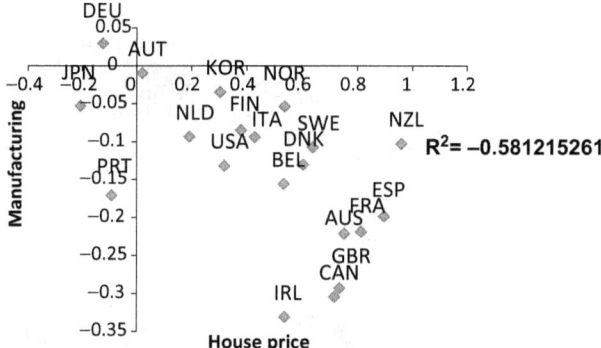

Fig. 10.4 Manufacturing employment versus house price 2000–2007 (*Source*: OECD)

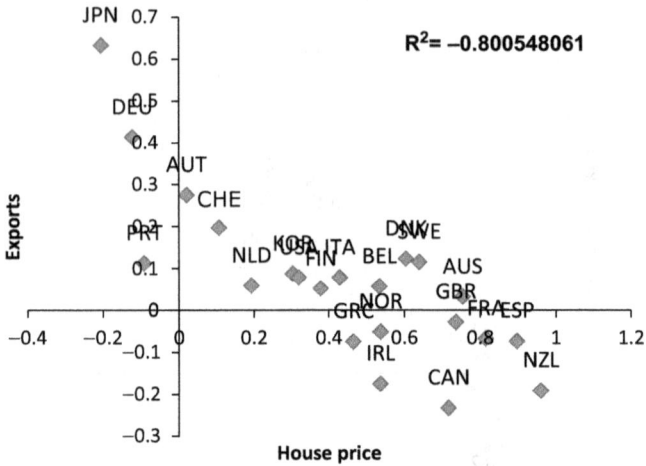

Fig. 10.5 Exports versus house price 2000–2007 (*Source*: OECD)

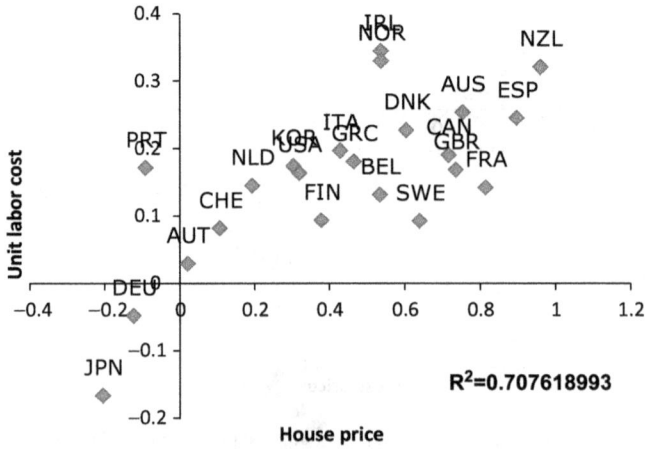

Fig. 10.6 Unit labor costs versus house price 2000–2007 (*Source*: OECD)

Japan's industrial policies in the 1970s and 1980s, if the housing bubble lasts long enough, some or all of the industries that move abroad in the short run will remain abroad even after the housing bubble has burst.[51]

Not only did the rise of China contribute to the housing bubbles that affected virtually all countries in the Western hemisphere, it also eroded the competitiveness of advanced economies. In light of the damage already done to the traded sector, it is doubtful that debt-financed government spending to offset the collapse in private spending is the right answer to an economic depression that flows from the bursting of a housing bubble. After the bursting of a housing bubble, an economy not only faces demand-side problems but supply-side problems as well. Since government spending will mainly benefit the non-traded sector, driving up wages or, at least, preventing wages to decline to the equilibrium wage, it will prolong the problems in the traded sector, especially so if the option of currency depreciation is not on the table.

Much of the imbalances within the euro area involved trade with non-euro countries. Germany saw a sharp increase in the exports to Asia and Eastern Europe because of strong demand for German durable manufactures. Southern Europe, on the other hand, experienced a sharp increase in imports from low-wage countries. For southern Europe to regain its competitiveness, internal devaluation was as necessary as it was painful. Debt-fuelled public spending would only delay the much-needed adjustment, posing a drag on the economic recovery. This argument is reinforced by the fact that the housing booms in Ireland and Spain were associated with high levels of construction and infrastructure spending. If anything, Ireland and Spain have more airports and high-speed railroads than the size of their respective economies warrants.

By the same token, it is not clear either that it would contribute to the strength of the euro area's economy if Germany were to prize itself out of the market to meet the euro area's periphery halfway, as many economists have suggested. A better course of action for the euro area is to focus on debt restructuring and reinforcement of the tradable sector in the periphery. Internal devaluation generally leads to a lower GDP, and therefore to a higher debt-to-GDP ratio. For internal devaluation to succeed and to offer peripheral countries a chance to start with a clean slate, it should have been accompanied by a restructuring of sovereign debt. This would have come at the expense of banks in the core countries of the euro area

---

[51] Paul Krugman, "The narrow moving band, the Dutch disease, and the competitive consequences of Mrs. Thatcher," *Journal of Development Economics*, vol. 27, issue 1–2, pp. 41–55, 1987.

but that's only deservedly so. After all, the banks should not have lent money on such a large scale at such low interest rates to the euro area's periphery in the first place.

The same does not apply to government spending in the USA. America clearly has an infrastructure deficit. Though infrastructure in some states is better than in others, in many places across the USA, it is crumbling. This phenomenon is not limited to highways, railroads, and airports like LaGuardia in New York, which Vice President Biden likened to a third-world country's airport, but is true for many other public buildings as well. The roads in New York City are full of potholes because the City has decided that it is cheaper to pay damages to anybody who gets injured than to invest in road maintenance. The Chinese who come for the first time to New York are actually surprised how rundown the place is.

For a country like the USA that chronically underinvests in public infrastructure, anytime is a good time for the government to increase infrastructure spending but especially so during an economic recession, when unemployment is high and interest rates are low. It is not obvious, though, that such a temporary fiscal stimulus will succeed in bringing about a stronger and more high-pressure economy. In a world that is characterized by unlimited supplies of labor, it may be that for every job created in a rich country's non-traded sector, a job in the traded sector will be lost due to offshoring or outsourcing. This is true even if the economy finds itself in a liquidity trap and the natural real rate of interest is below zero.[52] The transmission mechanism for such a form of crowding out is labor costs, not the interest rate. However, if the initial stock of infrastructure is of a sufficiently low quality, government spending will reinforce the traded sector as it relies in no small part on government-funded education, infrastructure, and research.

---

[52] In a neo-classical model, public spending crowds out private spending by way of higher interest rates, unless the economy finds itself in a liquidity trap (i.e., the equilibrium interest rate is negative but the official interest rate is zero). If labor is in unlimited supplies, jobs created in the non-traded sector may well crowd out jobs in the traded sector by way of higher wages, even if the economy finds itself in a liquidity trap.

CHAPTER 11

Piketty Reconsidered

RETURN ON LABOR

The part of Thomas Piketty's *Capital in the 21st Century* that has gained both most attraction as well as criticism is his proposition that the return on capital historically exceeds economic growth. On the basis of that proposition, Piketty concludes that family fortunes in the future will concentrate as they have done in the past, creating dynasties that ultimately may undermine democracy as great wealth brings great power, which is often used to reinforce the concentration of wealth. If the rate of return on capital, r, is less than the overall rate of economic growth, g, dynasties would be doomed to erode no matter how much of their fortune is devoted to wealth accumulation. But if r is greater than g, dynastic wealth can grow indefinitely, even if in practice it may not.

To get this result, Piketty postulates that the elasticity of substitution between capital and labor is more than 1, meaning that machines can smoothly replace workers in producing goods and services. A higher ratio of capital to labor results in an increase in the share of capital, so the return on capital falls less than the growth rate.[1,2] Whether r is, in fact, larger

---

[1] Mainstream economic models like Cobb-Douglas assume that the elasticity of substitution is 1.

[2] According to Larry Summers, there are no studies suggesting that the elasticity of substitution is greater than 1, and quite a few studies suggesting the contrary (Larry Summers, "The Inequality Puzzle," *Democracy Journal*, no. 33, 2014).

than g depends in his view primarily on changes in the rate of economic growth. According to Piketty, there was an exceptional period in the twentieth century—roughly from 1920 to 1980—that was characterized by rapid labor force growth and technological progress, when the rate of return on capital was less than the overall rate of economic growth.

It is more logical to focus on the decline in the rate of return on capital than the overall rate of economic growth. In the early twentieth century, the rate of return on capital declined by more than the overall rate of economic growth rose. Without the decline in the rate of return on capital, r would still have exceeded g and inequality would, therefore, have continued to surge between 1920 and 1980. A better way of describing the period from 1920 to 1980 is that during that period, the return on labor, l, exceeded economic growth, g. It is the dog, l, that wags the tail, r; not the other way around.[3] The question is why the return on labor was high compared to the period from 1920 to 1980.

Through a combination of economic and political factors, workers during the period spanning 1920 to 1980 were better able to assert themselves compared to the preceding and following years. As John Stuart Mill had already noted in 1871: "If it were possible for the working classes, by combining among themselves, (...) they would have limited power of obtaining, by combination, an increase of general wages at the expense of profits." By some measures, the pre-1914 world was more globalized than the world is today. With World War I, however, the first wave of globalization came crashing down. By undermining financial stability, free trade policies, international investment, and migration, the war undid much of the foundations of the late nineteenth-century globalization. Not until after the fall of the Berlin Wall, did the world economy truly recover from the impact of the World War I. The breakdown of globalization actually shielded Western laborers from competition with the rest of the world.

This was reinforced by the fact that during World War I, which lasted from July 1914 until November 1918, more than 9 million combatants and 6 million civilians were killed. As Western powers had already been largely urbanized before the start of the war, the labor shortage in the

---

[3] Thomas Piketty agrees that the changing bargaining power between labor and capital is the key determinant in the relation between r and g. As he points out, however, even in the perfect competition dream of neoclassical economists, there would still be powerful inequalizing forces, in particular high r-g would lead to the perpetuation of high wealth concentration.

years following World War I could not easily be solved through migration from the countryside. This strengthened the bargaining position of workers considerably. In the UK, the wage bill in 1925 was three times what it had been before the war. Another, related, factor was the Russian Revolution of 1917, which marked the beginning of the spread of communism in the twentieth century. For workers in capitalist systems, it was one more reason to assert themselves and, conversely, for capitalists and governments to meet the workers halfway to stave off a potential revolution on their own territory. In the UK in 1909, the first statutory minimum wage was enacted. In 1918, the minimum wage law was expanded considerably and supplemented with rules for collective bargaining.

The American industrialist Henry Ford offered in 1914 a $5 per day wage, which is $120 today, more than doubling the wage of most of his workers. Not only did the pay rise reduce the turnover of employees and attract the best mechanics and raise productivity, but the pay rise also ensured that workers in the Ford factories could actually afford a Model T, creating a new class of consumers. At the same time, Ford reduced the workweek to 6 days and the workday to 8 hours, forcing his competitors in Detroit to follow suit.

Massachusetts was the first American state to adopt non-compulsory minimum wages for women and children in 1912. By 1920, at least 13 States and the District of Columbia would pass minimum wage laws, which the US Supreme Court consistently struck down. The laws were considered unconstitutional for interfering with the ability of employers to negotiate freely appropriate wage contracts with employees. In 1933, President Franklin Delano Roosevelt proclaimed that "No business which depends for existence on paying less than living wages to its workers has any right to continue in this country." It would, however, take another five years before a federal minimum wage was enacted that could withstand the US Supreme Court's scrutiny.

By then, the world was in the grip of World War II and with it came not only unspeakable casualties but also labor shortages. In the USA alone, nearly 10 million men of prime working age were drafted into the military, creating a huge skills gap between the jobs that needed to be done on the home front and the remaining workforce.[4] Factories simplified production methods and housewives took to work in the US aircraft and muni-

---

[4] Christina Romer, "What do we know about the effects of fiscal policy? Separating evidence from ideology," 2011.

tions industry, heartened by the government's "We Can Do It!" campaign starring Rosie the Riveter. Between 1940 and 1945, the female percentage of the US workforce increased from 27 percent to nearly 37 percent. However, after World War II, women receded to being housewives again, giving birth to the baby boomers. By any metric, labor was in short supply during the post-war reconstruction years. Although population growth was strong during those years, it was not strong enough to keep up with economic growth.

After the war, many countries in Europe moved from a partial or selective provision of social services to a relatively comprehensive coverage of the population, providing citizens with income, health care, education, housing, and employment, which strengthened the position of labor vis-à-vis the capitalists. In particular in the UK, trade unions were at the pinnacle of power by the end of the 1970s, organizing strikes in the winter of 1978/79 in what would become the trade unions' own undoing.

The relative hegemony of workers ended much as it started, through a combination of economic and political factors. Since 1980, wage growth has trailed labor productivity growth in most years. The difference between the productivity growth and the wage growth ended up in the coffers of the capitalists, instead of in the pockets of the workers. As a result, labor's share of national income fell while profit's share increased. What caused this momentous change?

First, Thatcher and Reagan swept into office. The economic reforms that Thatcher and Reagan propagated undermined the position of labor while strengthening the position of capital. They reduced the role of government, allowed a much greater role for the markets, and broke the power of the trade unions. Membership of trade unions has since been cut in half both in the UK as well as in the USA. Organized labor can be an essential force for equality, both because it gets higher wages for ordinary workers and because it is a political counterweight to the power of organized money. Reagan and Thatcher presided over sharp cuts in marginal tax rates, which in turn, contributed to the polarization among wage earners and encouraged rent seeking. They also ushered in an era of deregulation, which may not have directly caused the global financial crisis but did well exacerbate it.

Second, by 1980, the baby boom generation was reaching prime working age, which, while contributing to economic growth, also eroded the bargaining power of workers. More critically, women were entering the labor market in droves, not only in the USA but Western Europe as well.

Between 1960 and 2000, the female labor force participation rate in virtually all OECD countries rose at least by half, if not doubled. Women's educational attainments were almost comparable to those of their male peers, but they entered the labor market at somewhat lower-ranking positions, which may explain the rise in the level of skills within industries, extending across pretty much the entire economy. The fact that women's wages in the USA grew more quickly than men's wages may serve as a contraindication. It may also mean that women, who typically entered the labor market below their skill level, got promoted more quickly to catch up with their skill level.[5]

Third, some have argued that the information technology revolution reduced the need for routine manual labor while increasing the demand for conceptual work. Although the average education level was rising, it was not rising fast enough to keep up with the increased demand for high-skilled workers. The rise of technology could thus explain that the earnings of the college-educated in the 1980s rose while the relative, and perhaps absolute, earnings for those without the right skills declined. However, wage trends in the 1990s and 2000s do not fully support the theory of skill-biased technological change, as there was no further polarization in the US labor market. The wage gap between low- and middle-wage earners remained stable instead and the growth of the college wage premium has decelerated since the early 1990s.[6] Moreover, if an information technology revolution were indeed responsible for the wage polarization, one would expect to see productivity growth accelerating instead of slowing down, which is what happened.

Fourth, rising monopoly power may have induced a shift of rents away from labor toward capital and thus explain the fact that labor's share in GDP has fallen while the share of profits has risen. The shift in rents is not only apparent between capital and labor, but also within labor, witness the increasingly skewed distribution of labor income. Piketty has pointed out that the increased income share of the top wage earners may have been the result of rent-seeking rather than increased productivity. Rent-seeking may be particularly germane in the financial sector, which is hugely over-

---

[5] It also doesn't quite explain why wage polarization occurred in the 1980s while the female labor force participation rate had been rising since 1960 and even before.

[6] John Schmitt, Heidi Shierholz, and Lawrence Mishel, "Don't Blame the Robots – Assessing the Job Polarization Explanation of Growing Wage Inequality," Economic Policy Institute, 2013.

represented in the top 1 percent wage earners in both the USA as well as the UK, i.e., 25 percent while the financial industry accounts for less than 10 percent of the overall economy.

Fifth, globalization in combination with the rise of computer technology that enabled companies to offshore and outsource not only the production of goods but of services as well, has accelerated the shift from labor to capital, lowering the return on labor while increasing the return on capital. In the USA, the share of national income going to employee compensation shows a clear break in the early 2000s, with a decline of 0.1 percentage points per year in the period from 1970 to 2000, and a decline of 0.8 percentage points in the period from 2000 to 2014.[7] The break occurred right at the time of China's accession to the World Trade Organization. As the effect of China's low labor costs spilled over to other countries as well, virtually all industrialized countries experienced a similar decline as the USA in labor's share and a slowing labor productivity growth.

Sixth, the rising prices of oil and other commodities in the 2000s eroded real wages and aided the owners of natural resources. This shift is apparent in the prosperity that resource-rich countries like Norway, Australia, the United Arab Emirates, and Canada enjoyed in the 2000s and beyond. Not until the shale energy revolution and the slowdown of China's economy, they saw their fortune reversed. In resource poor countries, capital and labor were both affected adversely by the rising commodity prices as far as workers were able (or not) to get compensation for the increased cost of living without labor productivity rising correspondingly. According to Lewis, in a world with unlimited labor supplies, a shortage of natural resources was the only fly in the ointment.

At the start of the twenty-first century, the global economy as a whole was pretty much back where it was at the beginning of the twentieth century. With labor in abundance and resources in short supply, capitalists and semi-capitalist wage earners have been able to reap excess profits, that is, the capitalist surplus. As a result, the wealth-income ratios in the USA, the UK, Germany, and France, have been rising gradually in recent decades, from about 200–300 percent in 1970 to 400–600 percent in 2010. As Piketty and Zucman have pointed out, today's ratios appear to be returning to the high values observed in eighteenth- and nineteenth-century

[7] Menzie Chinn, EconBrowser, 2013.

Europe.[8] However, it is not an intrinsic feature of capital, as Piketty argues, but the dire position of labor that causes income and wealth inequality to grow.

Labor's Future

Arthur Lewis' model predicts that, as a country transitions from an emerging economy with unlimited supplies of labor into an advanced economy where labor is in short supply, labor's share of national income will rise at the expense of capital's share. The kind of society that advanced economies have considered normal, where high incomes reflect personal achievement rather than inherited wealth, is, in fact, the normal state of an economy or the end state, instead of an aberration. But how likely is it that advanced economies will indeed return to the state in which labor is in short supply anytime soon?

Some of the factors that have boosted capital and hurt labor over the past decades, either have already run their course or are about to run their course. The shale revolution has sent the price of oil and natural gas in a tailspin. In its course, it has taken the price of many other commodities down with it. The reason is that energy is often the most costly factor in the creation or extraction of other commodities. If the price of oil goes down, the production of other commodities increases. This is even true for oil itself. Since the price of oil has gone down, the costs of getting the oil out have dropped dramatically as well. Since the demand for commodities is generally price inelastic, even a modest increase in supply will have a relatively large effect on the price.

Many economists have bemoaned the precipitous drop in commodity prices because it would signal a global economic recession, or, at the very least, a hard landing for the Chinese economy. But the fall in commodity prices is part of the solution, not the problem. Lower oil prices work like a tax cut that favors foremost lower and middle-income households without it adding to the government budget deficit. It comes, of course, at the expense of oil-exporting countries but only deservedly so. Since the oil producing nations only stash away their cash, there are few negative externalities associated with the loss of petrodollars.[9] If anything, the drop

---

[8] Thomas Piketty and Gabriel Zucman, "Capital is Back: Wealth-Income Ratios in Rich Countries 1700–2010," *The Quarterly Journal of Economics*, 2014.
[9] Environmentalist may disagree with that assessment.

in the prices of oil and other commodities disempowers authoritarian rulers in the Middle East and Africa.

Nonetheless, the drop in oil prices below $50 a barrel came with considerable turmoil in the financial markets, which seems, in part, the result of oil-exporting countries liquidating the assets of their sovereign wealth funds and, in part, because of the high leverage of the investments in oil extraction. As long as the government does not come to the rescue of the financiers at the expense of the taxpayers, this remains confined to the capitalist sector. The drop in oil prices is associated with higher consumer confidence, which may, in turn, boost business sentiment. In as far as the Federal Reserve's zero interest rate policy enabled the shale energy revolution, it may be the single most important transmission mechanism of monetary policy to the real economy. The redistribution from capital happened without any bloodshed. It did not require a war and may well have made the world a safer place since falling oil prices severely undermine the authoritarian regimes in the Middle East.

A further redistribution from capital to labor may be in the offing. The first cohort of baby boomers is already retiring. The biggest gains from women entering the labor force have already been spent. Even though the female labor participation rate is still lower than the male labor force participation rate, there seems limited room for further improvement. These secular trends will slowly but surely strengthen labor's bargaining power.

For the USA, the Congressional Budget Office projects that labor income will grow faster than other components of national income over the next decade, increasing labor's share by 1 percentage point from 2016 to 2026. The Congressional Budget Office expects the labor share to rise because employment is expected to rise and real compensation per hour is projected to grow more strongly than productivity for several years as cyclical weakness in the labor market abates. As a result, the bargaining power of workers will improve and the share of income going to corporate profits will be smaller. By the end of the projection period, however, real hourly compensation is projected to move in step with growth in labor productivity. This trend will not be enough to return labor's share to the level before 2000. The factors that have depressed labor's share since 2000 will continue during the coming decade.[10]

---

[10] "The Budget and Economic Outlook: 2016 to 2026," The Congressional Budget Committee, January 25, 2016.

Although China's working population is shrinking, it will take almost another ten years before it will reach the Lewis Turning Point and labor becomes in short supply. During those ten years, new candidates will line up to take China's place and become the world's factory. Garment production has already started to spread out of China, mostly to countries like Myanmar and Bangladesh. Advanced manufacturing, too, is starting to trickle out of China: Vietnam, Thailand, and Indonesia are picking up part of the electronics work that was previously done in China. The ten countries making up the ASEAN (Association of South-East Asian Nations) are home to 630 million people, less than half China's population. Another obvious candidate is India, the second most populous country in the world, counting almost 1.3 billion people in 2015. India's population is projected to surpass China's by 2022 and reach 1.6 billion by 2050.

For all its potential for growth, India's economy has disappointed so far. India's Prime Minister Narendra Modi wants India to grow as fast over the next 20 years as China has over the past 20, but it is not clear whether India has the institutions to pull that off. A somewhat less obvious candidate is Africa. The continent has a vast and growing population of more than 1 billion. When capital accumulation in China catches up with labor supply and wages that are rising above the subsistence wage begin to affect the capitalist surplus adversely, China may choose to export capital to places where there is still abundant labor at a subsistence wage.

In the past decade, China has already shown quite some deftness in dealing with Africa, much more so than advanced economies have. China's main goal in Africa has been to secure the natural resources that it has in short but Africa has in abundant supply. Why would China change course when it runs out of its unlimited supplies of labor? China's enormous overseas spending has already helped it displace the USA and Europe as the leading financial power in large parts of the developing world. Beijing's push to revive the Silk Road, the ancient trade routes that connect China to Eastern Africa and Western Europe, and the launch of the Asian Infrastructure Investment Bank suggest that China is not done exporting capital yet.

Without the rise of the robots, it would be safe to assume that the global economy would eventually return to the state it had between 1920 and 1980, which may be considered the end state for the economy much in the same way as Fukuyama declared the end of history for political ideology. However, Erik Brynjolfsson and Andrew McAfee, among others, have argued that information technology may be poised for exponential growth and that we are witnessing the Fourth Industrial Revolution, meaning that electronics and information technology will be used to further automate production.[11]

In this new age, machines will be thinking as well as doing, sensing as well as dissecting, adapting as well as enacting. They will thus span a much wider part of the skill distribution than ever before. The more skillful robots become, the more jobs are at risk. How many jobs? According to research by Carl Benedikt Frey and Michael Osborne, no less than 47 percent of all US jobs are at risk because of the impact of future computerization on the US labor market. However, the more skilled and better paid a job is, the smaller the probability of computerization.[12] According to the Bank of England, 80 million jobs in the USA and up to 15 million jobs in the UK could be at risk of automation.[13] Accountants have a 95 percent probability of vocational extinction; for a hairdresser, it is 33 percent; and for economists, it is only 15 percent.

These studies are reminiscent of Alan Blinder's estimates in 2007 that between 22 percent and 29 percent of all American jobs were or would be susceptible to offshoring within a decade or two.[14] Jobs that have the highest probability of being offshored are often also the jobs that are susceptible to computerization. It is not a coincidence that China is at the forefront of the robot revolution. By 2017, it will have more manufacturing robots installed than any other country.[15] Foxconn, which makes consumer electronics for Apple and other companies, already has a fully robotic factory in Chengdu and plans to automate about 70 percent of factory work in the coming years. If China is successful, it may take much longer before the world's most populous nation runs out of its surplus of labor supply.

There are also jobs that cannot be offshored but that are susceptible to computerization nonetheless. These are jobs that require proximity. An obvious example is the taxi drivers whose jobs cannot be offshored but may soon well be computerized by means of a driverless car. Or the

---

[11] Brynjolfsson and McAfee also argue that technological change instead of globalization is responsible for the decline of labor's share in GDP since the 1980s but, as discussed before, the facts do not buttress that conclusion.

[12] Carl Benedikt Frey and Michael A. Osborne, "The Future of Employment: How Susceptible Are Jobs To Computerization?," 2013.

[13] Andy Haldane, "Labor's Share," Bank of England, 2015.

[14] Alan Blinder, "How Many U.S. Jobs Might Be Offshorable?," 2007.

[15] Martin Ford, *Rise of the Robots: Technology and the Threat of a Jobless Future*, 2015.

passport control at international airports, which is rapidly being computerized because of the advent of biometrics. It is another type of job that can hardly be offshored but is indeed susceptible to computerization. The chief executive of Facebook, Mark Zuckerberg, set out to develop a robot that could help him with household chores, including watching over his newborn. Zuckerberg is less fearful than Elon Musk that rogue AI, or artificial intelligence, will one day come to haunt the human race.

The anxiety of machines taking over from humans is of all ages; it can be traced back as far as Greek mythology. It often surfaces in times of tepid economic growth. In that respect, this time is no different. However, as Brad Delong points out, the fear is that this time things really are different (as it, of course, always is).[16] That this time around the anxiety over technological change is not misguided. That this time around, the social status and living standards of the median human are really under attack. The reason for the existential angst is that, this time around, machines not only compete with our physical qualities but with our cognitive qualities as well.

What if humans become superfluous in the production process altogether, just as happened to horses after the invention of the automobile? The horse population today is much lower than it was a century ago. In 1915, a period that Brad Delong dubs "peak horse," the USA counted more than 21 million domestic horses. Today, the equine population stands at no more than 7 million. What if, in a marginal-cost pricing world, humans are no longer wanting? Will the capitalists still be willing to pay all humans the subsistence wage? Or are we now, as DeLong suggested, at "peak human"?

Arthur Lewis argued that in developing countries with a large population relative to capital, the code of ethical behavior so shapes itself that it becomes good form for each person to offer as much employment as he can. It is also a recurring meme in *Downton Abbey*, the British television series set in the early twentieth century about the aristocratic Crawley family and their little army of servants. It does not strike as entirely reassuring, though. After all, how many servants can the Chan-Zuckerberg household effectively employ if it already has butler robots and self-driving cars?

---

[16] Brad Delong, "Technological Progress Anxiety: Thinking About "Peak Horse" and the Possibility of "Peak Human"," blog, September 24, 2015.

CHAPTER 12

What Lies Ahead?

CHINA

If you look at what Deng Xiaoping set out to do with his policy of reform and opening up and the way that China has changed ever since, you can only conclude that China's leadership has followed Arthur Lewis' script for economic development with unlimited supplies of labor remarkably well. In 1986, Deng emphasized that China needed to develop "productive forces" first, which it did in no small part. Lewis did not think that an all-powerful state was necessary to create the preconditions for development and to organize most of the required directly productive activities. Instead, Lewis clearly saw the overarching need for private actors to complement government planners, just as Deng Xiaoping envisioned for China.[1]

The birdcage economy that Zhao Ziyang so abhorred has served China well. China's economic policy is still guided by Five-Year Plans, which are styled after the Five-Year Plans that Joseph Stalin introduced in the Soviet Union in 1928.[2] By ignoring much of the Washington consensus, China has been able to avoid many of the pitfalls that former Eastern Bloc and former states of the Soviet Union encountered after the fall of the Berlin

---

[1] Gustav Ranis, "Arthur Lewis' Contribution to Development Thinking and Policy," 2004.
[2] In order to reflect China's transition from a Soviet-style planned economy to a socialist market economy, the name of the 11th Five-Year Plan was changed to 'guideline.'

Wall. China did not engage in the fire sale of state assets far below the actual market value as in Russia with oligarchs hiding billions of dollars of state treasures in private Swiss bank accounts. There was no spike in the poverty rate as in many former Eastern Bloc countries. With the exception of the years leading up to the global financial crisis, when the current account surplus peaked at 10 percent of national income, the capitalist surplus was virtually in its entirety used for the formation of new capital in the Chinese economy.

Most major reform initiatives in healthcare, pension reform and education in post-Mao China were prepared and tried out using experiments before they were universalized in national regulations. Geographical units and jurisdictions were designated as experimental zones that had broad discretionary powers, for example, to streamline the economic bureaucracy or to promote foreign investment and thereby generate or test new policy approaches. The experimental approach also created fierce competition between the different regional centers. The highly successful Special Economic Zones are the best-known examples. China's political economy has proven to be highly innovative in finding policies and institutions to master the complex challenges of large-scale economic change while avoiding systemic breakdown.[3]

China's current economic state is often likened to Japan's in the first half of the 1990s, just before the bursting of the asset bubble from which Japan's economy never quite recovered.[4] Such worries about China (or rather smugness disguised as concern) are untimely. In 1995, Japan's income per capita at a formal exchange rate basis was 150 percent of income per capita in the USA, while China's income per capita in 2015 was only 15 percent of that in the USA.[5] On a purchasing power parity basis, Japan's income per capita in 1995 was 80 percent of income per capita in the USA while China's income per capita in 2015 was only 25 percent of income per capita in the USA. For all the advances China has made over the past three decades, it still has ample room for catch-up growth. Urbanization has not run its course. In the coming decades, another 300 million Chinese, that is almost the population of the USA, are expected to leave the countryside and move to the city. It will take ten cities the size of Shanghai, or 30 cities the size of New York, to house them.

---

[3] Sebastian Heilmann, Policy Experimentation in China's Economic Rise, 2007.
[4] Gavyn Davies, "Is China the new Japan? *Financial Times* blog, November 16, 2015.
[5] International Monetary Fund, WEO Database, October 2015.

Another often-heard objection to China's growth prospects is that China finds itself in the middle income trap. The idea behind it is straightforward. Rich countries boast the best technologies while poor countries offer the lowest wages. Middle income countries have neither. Common wisdom is that they must struggle to compete with countries above and below them. Poor countries still benefit from moving workers out of the subsistence sector into factories, where they are many times more productive. But most middle-income countries have run out of surplus workers, so they have to raise productivity within their factories if they are to further improve living standards.

Economic slowdowns as a result of the middle-income trap are likely to occur at income levels around $10,000–11,000 and $15,000–16,000 measured at purchasing-power parity, the latter being almost China's level in 2015.[6] Apart from the fact that the empirical evidence underlying the middle-income trap studies is tenuous at best; China is by no means a middle-income country in spite of the headline income per capita. It is better to think of China consisting of two countries, one being a high-income country and the other being a developing country. That is why China can still enjoy almost another decade of unlimited labor supplies even though it has already reached the status of a middle income country.

In this two-speed model that was ushered in with Deng Xiaoping's call to let some people and some regions get rich first, economic growth can feed on itself. Immigrants no longer flock to the cities to work in factories but to work in the burgeoning services industry instead, just as immigrants who come to the USA do. See, for example, the couriers on their electric tricycles who deliver the "Jack Ma economy" in China's mega-cities.[7] The couriers work long hours, making ¥5000 per month ($750) while they are separated from their families who continue to live in the countryside. During the Cultural Revolution service jobs were condemned, as they were considered gentrified, bourgeois, and exploitative.[8] Nowadays, home delivery in Chinese cities often consists of no more than a box of Kleenex or a pair of shoelaces.

---

[6] Barry Eichengreen, Donghyun Park, and Kwanho Shin, "Growth Slowdowns Redux: New Evidence on the Middle Income Trap, NBER Working Paper No. 18673, 2013.

[7] "China migration: Delivering the Jack Ma economy," *The Financial Times*, September 16, 2015.

[8] Schell, 1984.

Some economists object that China's debt level is unsustainably high and that, because of falling producer prices companies will not be able to pay the interest on their debt. Although private debt levels are indeed high and rising, virtually all debt is domestically financed and renminbi-denominated, so the country is not very vulnerable to capital outflows and currency fluctuations that created financial havoc in other emerging economies. Also, household debt in China is minimal. Notably, household mortgage debt is only 16 percent of GDP even though homeownership rates are very high; 9 out of 10 families in China own their home.[9]

The biggest increase in debt is tied to local government connected entities. If these entities were to default, or, preferably, if their debt were to be restructured, the burden would fall almost entirely fall on the capitalist sector, that is, corporations and capitalist-like wage earners. The Chinese government guarantees deposits up to ¥500,000 yuan ($80,550) made by businesses and individuals per bank. More than 99 percent of depositors are thus covered. An orderly default or a debt restructuring would, therefore, hardly affect the real economy and, in fact, work as a back tax.

Another grievance often leveled at present-day China concerns the widespread corruption and income inequality. More than a few Western media outlets found themselves being banned after they published stories about the riches of Chinese leaders' family members. In October 2012, the Chinese government blocked access to the English and Chinese-language websites of *The New York Times* from computers in mainland China in response to an article describing the wealth accumulated by the family of the country's then prime minister, Wen Jiabao. Two months earlier the *Bloomberg News* website had already been blocked from computers in mainland China after the news organization published details about the multi-million dollar fortunes of Xi Jinping's extended family.

Ironically enough, in November 2012, after his elevation to Secretary General of the Communist Party, Xi Jinping vowed to crack down on corruption by "powerful tigers and lowly flies", that is, high-level officials and lower-level civil servants alike. Xi followed through on that promise. Initially, the campaign's primary targets were functionaries at all levels of the party apparatus and government bureaucracy. Most of the officials investigated were removed from office and faced accusations of bribery and abuse of power, in what is by some seen as a political purge.

[9] "9 in 10 families own their homes," *Xinhuanet*, July 20, 2013.

However, private business leaders have not escaped scrutiny in Beijing's anti-corruption drive either.

The anti-corruption campaign must not distract from the fact that many of the new Chinese multi-millionaires and billionaires are truly self-made. In 2015, Modigliani's "Reclining Nude" fetched more than $170 million at Christie's in New York, making it the second-priciest artwork ever auctioned. Its buyer was Liu Yiqian, one of China's many rags-to-riches billionaires who left school as a teenager to sell handbags and worked as a Shanghai taxi driver, before making his fortune trading stocks on the Chinese exchanges. Liu and his wife Zhao Wei now collect masterpieces for their private museum in Shanghai.

Zhou Qunfei made her fortune manufacturing the cover glass that is used in laptops, tablets, and mobile phones. Zhou was born in a tiny village in the Hunan Province of central China. At age 16, she went to work in a factory, working 16 hours a day or more, making watch lenses for about $1 a day. At age 23, she started her own factory with $3000 in savings. Nowadays, her three factories in China employ more than 75,000 people, operating 24 hours a day, churning out more than a billion glass screens per year. Zhou's net worth is estimated to be more than $7 billion.

More importantly, income inequality was a prerequisite for China's economic transformation. As Arthur Lewis noted, the central problem in the theory of economic development is to understand the process by which a community that was previously saving and investing 4 or 5 percent of national income or less, converts itself into an economy where voluntary saving is running at about 12–15 percent of national income or more. According to Lewis, economic development cannot occur without rapid capital accumulation. The solution Lewis saw to this problem is that the distribution of incomes is altered in favor of the saving class, that is, the elite.

Western media tend to focus on the darker aspects of China, which is, in part, natural as it is the task of the press to expose abuses everywhere. In the case of China, the role of foreign media is all the more essential as the Chinese media is heavily censored. However, over the past decade, Western media reports have bordered on China-bashing, either depicting China as an ominous giant that has not been playing by the rules, stealing jobs, and threatening Western prosperity, or, more often, painting China as a paper tiger that is on the verge of imminent collapse.

The reporting in Western media reached peak hysteria in the summer of 2015 when the Chinese stock market crashed. While stock markets all over the world had made significant gains since 2009, China's indexes had remained flat. That is, until October 2014 when the Chinese government announced the liberalization of the financial markets. As of November 2014, foreign investors were allowed to invest directly in the shares of companies listed in mainland China, albeit subject to restrictions. This led to the influx of foreign capital. More importantly, the rising share prices lured Chinese investors back to the stock market, who had been staying on the sidelines ever since the stock market collapse in 2008.

The rising stock prices thus became a self-fulfilling prophecy, attracting more and more investors in line with the greater-fool-theory: it is not irrational to buy overpriced stocks if you expect to find a greater fool willing to pay an even higher price. China's economy is prone to bubbles because of the income divide and the limited spending opportunities. The nerves of Western investors seemed even more frayed than those of the Chinese leaders who haphazardly and in vain tried to stem the stock market route. On August 24, 2015, the Dow Jones Industrial Average lost 1000 points right after the opening bell. Tim Cook, the chief executive of Apple, had to step in to calm Western investors, assuring Jim Cramer on CNBC News that Apple's sales numbers in China in July and August were coming in above expectation.[10]

It is not surprising that the stock market crash did not cause a ripple in the real economy. The vast majority (94 percent) of Chinese households own no stock at all.[11] Of the households that do own stocks, 21 percent held less than ¥10,000 ($1600) worth of stock at the end of June 2015, while 69 percent held less than ¥100,000. This implies that more than two-thirds of investors owned less than 5 percent of the total market value. At the other end of the spectrum, just 0.1 percent of all investors held between ¥10 million and ¥100 million, and about 0.06 percent of all investors held more than ¥100 million.[12] In short, a few big players, whose spending does not depend on capital gains, dominate the Chinese stock market.

---

[10] After Apple CFO Luca Maestri assured investors in a conference call on July 21, 2015, that looking at the macro conditions in China, they couldn't be more positive, Apple shares lost 10 percent of their market value.

[11] In the USA, 55 percent of households are invested in the stock market according to a Gallup poll in April 2015.

[12] "Myth of China's retail investors understates large players' role," *The Financial Times*, July 13, 2015.

When, back in 1983, Orville Schell arrived in Beijing after an absence of less than two years, he found the streets markedly transformed, as if he was walking back in on a film that had mysteriously speeded up in his absence.[13] China is growing so quickly that the change is still palpable after an absence of a few years or even a few months. Notably, the rapid growth of the services industry, not only in the nation's capital but in other cities as well, has changed the makeup of the country.[14] In 2015, services accounted for 51 percent of GDP, up from 44 percent in 2011, with the biggest growth in sectors like entertainment, healthcare, and education.[15]

If anything is holding back the growth of the services sector in China, it is the lack of supply instead of the lack of demand. While the upper middle class in Beijing may financially be somewhat comparable to the upper middle class in Manhattan, Beijing is home to more billionaires than New York, it has far fewer options when it comes to leisurely activities. The Chinese coastline is hardly developed. There are no Hamptons or Jersey Shore to sojourn in the weekends and summers. While cities have arduously built museums and music halls in the past decades, they do not have full programs on offer yet. Beijing counts beautiful parks and impressive historical sights, but you can only visit those so often and they are not easy to spend money on. The best option available often is to go to the cinema, which the Chinese do in droves even though movie tickets are relatively expensive, or to go to one of the numerous malls and bide your time.[16] In China, there is an undersupply of other services such as education and health care as well due to a lack of homegrown capital. As the income level has been rising so quickly, these sectors, which typically need considerable homegrown capital, have difficulty keeping up.

The transition of the Chinese economy away from heavy industry toward services is of little solace to countries that have come to depend on China for the export of commodities. China's services sector is relatively closed and relies only modestly on imports. It will, however, help the Chinese government confront what is perhaps its biggest challenge—the

---

[13] Schell, 1984.

[14] In 2014, after an absence of 18 months, I told Louis Kuijs that it felt as if the Chinese had taken over Beijing, meaning they were much frequenting places where normally mostly foreigners would go. He agreed that the Chinese spend much more money on services, and hence, were much more visible.

[15] China National Bureau of Statistics.

[16] China's box office receipts jumped nearly 50 percent between 2014 and 2015.

air pollution. China's main strategy is to close the outdated capacity of the industrial sectors like iron, steel, aluminum, and cement and increase nuclear capacity and other non-fossil fuel energy. It also includes an intention to stop approving new power plants and to cut coal consumption in industrial areas.

China's perceived economic woes have led many a Western intellectual to speculate on an impending revolt. In May 2015, the historian Timothy Garton Ash, in literary cafe The Bookworm in Beijing, suggested that if economic growth in China would slow any further, the people would finally rise up against the regime. It is the typical Western way of (wishful) thinking. But the Chinese middle class does not quite expect incomes to rise year after year by 10 percent anymore. In fact, they do not even wish for it. As one of my Chinese research assistants sighed: "My life is changing way too fast." My hairdresser in Beijing said exactly the same when I lived there in the summer of 2015.[17]

The promise that is embedded in Deng Xiaoping's "let some people get rich first," is, of course, that the others will follow. That is also how Arthur Lewis framed the economic development of emerging economies. In 2014, rural incomes increased 9.2 percent on average, while urban incomes rose 6.8 percent. The gap between urban and rural incomes, which peaked at a ratio of 3.3-to-1 in 2009, fell to about 2.9 in 2014. This should not be upsetting the urban middle class for the average Chinese with a city registration knows all too well that the distinction being made between Chinese born in the city and Chinese born in the countryside is quite problematic.

Advanced Economies

The decline in labor's share in GDP in advanced economies is, in part, due to policies that flow directly from the Thatcher/Reagan revolution and the rise of the Washington consensus, such as the undoing of the trade unions, lower marginal tax rates, and deregulation. It is also due to social changes such as women entering the labor market and the increase in immigration. Most importantly, the fall in labor's share is due to the rise of China, as can be deduced from the fact that the pace of the decline in

---

[17] There is a lot of anxiety, though, among the Chinese upper middle class that they may lose it all. This is not surprising in light of China's recent history.

labor's share in GDP rose eightfold since 2001, just when China accessed the World Trade Organization.[18]

The rise of the robots narrative cannot easily be reconciled with the slowing labor productivity growth that advanced economies have witnessed in the past decade. However, the advent of the robots may still be upon us. Robert Gordon points out that the rise of "big data" is mostly a zero-sum game, that is, it does not raise total factor productivity but merely shifts consumers from one merchant to another. Also, information technology does not only help but also hurts productivity by cluttering our minds and mailboxes. On the other hand, it is hard to conceive that the world will have no more major inventions.

We may soon indeed be seeing flying cars. The first passenger drone, presented by Guangzhou-based Ehang Inc. at the CES 2016, suggests so. From the perspective of a worker, it does not matter whether you lose your job to workers in China or to robots in China. Even more profound may be inventions that allow people to live longer and healthier than they currently do, which will directly affect the supply of labor. Scientists say that soon they will be able to extend life well beyond 120, which would come down to a doubling of the working life.[19] Whether due to robots or longer longevity, there will be a shift from labor to capital. The capitalist surplus will rise as labor—due to the loss of bargaining power—will not be able to monetize its own productivity. It is for this reason that Marx regarded the capitalist surplus as robbery of the workers.

In emerging economies like China, the decline of labor's share in GDP is a sign of progress as the capitalist surplus is for the most part used for capital formation, which in turn, draws more and more workers out of the subsistence sector into the capitalist sector. That is why we see in the chart that plots global income growth from 1988 to 2008 (Fig. 4.2) that incomes in emerging markets (mainly China) rise the most. They do so at the expense of rich countries' middle class who see their income stagnate or fall. As the global elite reaps the benefits of low labor costs, they enjoy significant income gains as well between 1988 and 2008.

---

[18] In the second half of the nineties, labor's share of GDP did stage a notable, albeit short-lived, comeback in spite of the policy changes and the rise in the female labor participation rate.

[19] "Live for ever: Scientists say they'll soon extend life 'well beyond 120,'" *The Guardian*, January 11, 2015.

In advanced economies, the capitalist surplus works like a tax on labor that shifts the demand curve inward. In a sufficiently dynamic economy, the supply curve would shift outward as the lower costs of production would be handed back to consumers, leaving the equilibrium quantity, real wages, and corporate profits unchanged. This is not what actually happened. Instead of returning the capitalist surplus by way of lower prices, the capitalists (corporations, China, and oil-exporting countries alike) let households *borrow* the money so the latter could increase spending, shifting the demand curve back outward again.

As the global financial crisis has demonstrated, this is not a sustainable—and even a self-defeating—solution. Credit booms undermine productivity growth by drawing labor out of the traded sector into the non-traded sector. The temporarily bloated construction sector in many advanced economies may serve as an example. It affects other non-traded sectors as well. Because technological progress is higher in the traded sector compared to the non-traded sector, credit booms structurally harm a country's long-term productivity growth and reduce potential output. As the Bank for International Settlements has pointed out, the impact of the labor reallocations that occur during a credit boom is much larger if a financial crisis follows.[20]

If the government borrows money to prop up demand in workers' stead after the credit bubble has gone bust, it may have similar labor reallocation effects that undermine the traded sector. A better way is for the government to obtain the capitalist surplus by means of taxation and use the proceeds to prop up the traded sector by investing in infrastructure, education, research and development, energy, tax reform, and expanding international trade.[21] According to Paul Krugman, such long-termism is destructive. In his view, if the problem is inadequate demand, then the government should implement policies to solve that problem, even if such a solution takes the form of a new credit bubble.[22,23]

---

[20] Claudio Borio, Enisse Kharroubi, Christian Upper and Fabrizio Zampolli, "Labor reallocation and productivity dynamics: financial causes, real consequences," BIS Working Papers No 534, 2015.

[21] Obtaining the capitalist surplus of foreign, resource-rich nations will no doubt run into insurmountable diplomatic obstacles.

[22] Paul Krugman, "Destructive Long-Termism," *The New York Times* blog, December 28, 2015.

[23] Paul Krugman, "Bubbles, Regulation, and Secular Stagnation," *The New York Times* blog, September 25, 2013.

This kind of short-termism, however, ignores the fact that credit bubbles affect potential output. While the secular stagnation hypothesis emphasizes that the lack of demand creates the lack of potential supply, the perpetual bubble hypothesis highlights the fact that artificial demand creates the lack of potential supply.[24] This is all the more pertinent because advanced economies will continue to face competition from China and other emerging economies. While trade with China has followed economic orthodoxy so far, with technology in China improving mostly in sectors that the USA imports, thus improving the terms of trade, there is no guarantee that this will be the case in the future as well.

The Chinese government is already investing heavily in research and development, and it is also luring academic talent back to China. In case China, or India for that matter, can close the innovation gap, it has the potential to overtake the USA in sectors that the latter exports, yielding net losses for the USA. Jagdish Bhagwati and others have argued that such an assessment of China and India's capabilities almost borders on the ludicrous. According to Bhagwati, the fact that a country has a lot of people does not mean they are qualified.[25]

However, to close the innovation gap, you do not need to raise the general attainment level; you only need to raise it at the top. It is by the same logic that China can win Olympic gold in the category 100 meters freestyle even though most Chinese still depend on floatation devices if they take a swim. It is not a coincidence that China and the USA often compete during the Olympics as to who brings home most medals. The same may soon apply just as much to the skills and innovation gap.

Those who think that it will not come to that may want to think twice. Fifteen years ago, Western politicians worried about the job losses in China if it would be exposed to the competition of Western companies. That is not quite how it turned out. Instead, China went through the industrial revolution in a time it takes to change a light bulb. Why would it stop now? Why would not China master the Fourth Industrial Revolution just as quickly? Actually, there are already plenty of signs that it will. During the annual Mobile World Congress in Barcelona and the Consumer Electronica Show in Las Vegas, Chinese manufacturers often offer the most disruptive technologies.

---

[24] The drop in the labor force participation rate may be an indication of that.
[25] "An Elder Challenges Outsourcing's Orthodoxy," *The New York Times*, September 9, 2004

Another way for governments to reduce the capitalist surplus is by strengthening the labor protection laws. Some cities and states in the USA have already moved to raise the minimum wage to $10 per hour, and they are eyeing further minimum wage hikes up to $15 or even $20 per hour while the federal minimum wage is $7.25 per hour. Other states have introduced legislation that compels employers to continue to pay salaries and wages during maternity leave or sick leave.[26] Employers, however, may be able to avoid this kind of charges by simply cutting the number of workers, avoiding hiring at-risk employees, or replacing workers with robots altogether.

At the current low level of minimum wage, there may be little to no negative effect of raising the minimum wage on employment at the lower ranks of the labor market. However, with minimum wages at $15 per hour, that is bound to change. In that case, a better course of action is to raise taxes, not only on corporates but on high-earners as well. The proceeds should be used to invest in education, introduce universal healthcare, raise the Earned Income Tax Credit that benefits low-wage workers, and set up a federal fund to pay for items like maternity leave, sick leave, and a guaranteed minimum income.

If the corporate sector runs a structural surplus of savings over investment, other sectors must run offsetting structural deficits, inducing credit bubbles that are detrimental to the economy. For that reason, Martin Wolf favors a higher corporate taxation on retained earnings.[27] That way, corporations that reap the highest capitalist surplus pay the most tax while they can avoid higher taxation altogether by investing more. As we have seen, corporations that are best able to reap the capitalist surplus may also be most apt to avoid taxation. As a result of corporate tax avoidance, US firms are able to save $130 billion annually, contributing to a decline in the effective corporate tax rate from 30 percent in the late 1990s to about 20 percent today.[28]

In *Capital in the Twenty-First Century*, Piketty calls for a global wealth tax and an increase in the inheritance tax. Given the wealth that has already been accumulated since the eighties by corporations and the elite without

---

[26] To most Europeans, these kinds of measures seem obvious, but in the USA, there is no federal paid maternity leave or sick leave. European countries may use the taxes collected from corporations and high-earners to lower the tax burden on labor.

[27] Martin Wolf, "Corporate surpluses are contributing to the savings glut," *The Financial Times*, November 17, 2015.

[28] Gabriel Zucman, "Taxing across Borders: Tracking Personal Wealth and Corporate Profits," *Journal of Economic Perspectives*, Volume 28, Number 4, Pages 121–148, 2014.

properly being taxed, these taxes are an important complement to higher taxes on corporate income, top earners, and capital gains, as these latter will only affect the current returns on capital. However, capital has become increasingly mobile and countries have been competing for new investments by offering favorable tax treatments and secrecy. That is an important reason why corporations and wealthy individuals have been able to avoid taxation in the first place. It is not a given that countries will give up their sovereignty on tax matters either. It is, therefore, easy to overestimate the amount of tax that can be collected from corporations and wealthy individuals in liberal democracies.[29]

Gabriel Zucman suggests a world financial registry that would enable countries to assess how the actual distribution of revenues compares to the benchmark allocation. The registry would include information on the residence and nationality of corporate shareholders, thus making it possible for countries to check whether the total taxes they levy on corporate profits—at both the corporate and shareholder level—are in line with the corporate profits that indeed accrue to resident taxpayers. It is a transparent way to enforce a fairer distribution of corporate tax revenue globally. In addition to corporate tax evasion, Zucman estimates that wealthy individuals hide about 8 percent of the world's wealth, or $7.6 trillion, in tax havens. In the USA, the annual tax loss is estimated to be $35 billion; in Europe, it is $78 billion. In African nations, it is $14 billion. Just as with corporate tax evasion, the automatic exchange of information from banks to tax authorities is prerequisite to solving the problem.

Piketty emphasizes that we are in the early stages of returning to a society dominated by great dynastic fortunes because dynastic wealth can grow to enormous size if the return on capital, r, is greater than the rate of growth, g. As Piketty points out, even if labor's share in national income would be constant instead of falling as it has been over the past decades, r might still exceed g because even in the perfect-competition dream of neoclassical economists, there would still be powerful inequalizing forces, such as the concentration of income in the hands of the top 1 percent and 0.1 percent of wage-earners. However, the correlation between earned income and capital income has substantially increased in recent decades in the USA, suggesting that if profit's share in GDP

---

[29] The rollback of the Bush tax cuts, which raised the top income tax rate from 35 to 39 percent, was sufficient reason for some Americans to rescind their US passport.

falls, the top 1 and 0.1 percent of income earners will see their income decline as well.[30]

Rather than a scenario of the infinite perpetuation of high wealth concentrated in the hands of a few dynastic families, however, the world appears to teeter on the brink of revolt or even a new world war for that matter. Both Europe, America, and the Middle East are experiencing episodes of considerable social and political upheaval, illustrated by the electoral success of populist politicians and the meteoric rise of radical parties on the right and the left of the political spectrum. The losers of globalization rise up against the ruling elite, either by supporting anti-immigrant politicians or radical left wing politicians. Anti-immigrant politicians promise to rollback globalization altogether while left wing politicians vow to redistribute the spoils of globalization more evenly. There is often a time lag between the onset of an economic disaster, i.e., the global financial crisis, and the accumulation of social fury. The inflow of over a million refugees in Europe, the British vote in favor of Brexit, or yet another terrorist attack, may just prove the tipping point.

So far, most economists have treated the fallout of the global financial crisis as a cyclical shortfall of demand for which Keynesian remedies, such as a monetary stimulus and debt-financed government spending, will suffice to restore full employment. However, replacing one asset bubble with the other, which is what monetary policy mainly does, or replacing a private credit boom with a public credit boom, is merely treating symptoms instead of providing a cure. The lackluster economic growth in the aftermath of the global financial crisis may not be sufficient to bring back workers to the labor market that suffered most from the global financial crisis. For that, a stronger, high-pressure economy is needed, which disproportionately benefits those who are last to be hired. Such a high-pressure economy can only be attained by a redistribution of the capitalist surplus to labor. It is quite close to the old Marxist idea that if profits grow much faster than wages, there is not enough consumption, and capitalism is going to self-deconstruct.

China's accession to the World Trade Organization and the introduction of the euro are both the fruit of the fall of the Berlin Wall. Both ventures were undertaken with no small amount of idealism and a cer-

---

[30] Alvaredo, Facundo, Anthony B. Atkinson, Thomas Piketty, and Emmanuel Saez, "The Top 1 Percent in International and Historical Perspective," *Journal of Economic Perspectives*, 27(3): 3–20, 2013.

tain degree of triumphalism. They did not quite bring about "The End of History" (= liberal democracy) as Fukuyama had suggested. Instead, China's entry into the global economy and the introduction of the euro almost became the USA' and the European Union's undoing as they still might. Arguably, the disruption of the global economy would have been less extensive had both not been realized at virtually the same time. For all the economic pain inflicted as a result of the crisis in the euro area, the rise of China will continue to pose the biggest challenge to advanced economies' well-being.[31]

---

[31] The interest rate convergence associated with the introduction of the euro, which sparked the housing bubbles in the euro area's periphery, is in principle a one-time event.

Index

A
absorption constraints, 111–14
According to the Bank of England, 172
AIG, 64, 65
Apple, xiii, 27, 86, 129, 172, 180, 180n10
Asian financial crisis, 104, 117
Asian Infrastructure Investment Bank, 171
austerity, 48, 49n32, 52, 70, 72, 74, 81, 157
Autor, Dorn, and Hanson, 137

B
bailout, 31, 42, 59, 64, 65–7, 70–4, 75, 80
Bank of England, 35, 36, 44n21, 124, 129, 151, 152, 172n13
Bank of Japan, 35, 36
bear stearns, 58–62, 64
beggar-thy-neighbor, 155

Berlin Wall, xi, xvi, 6, 15–16, 18, 133, 164, 175, 188
Bernanke, Ben, 37–40, 45n22, 59, 115–18, 120, 121, 125, 152
Bhagwati, Jagdish, 185
Blanchard, Olivier, 149n36, xiv
Brandt, Loren, 3n5, 7n17, 19n19, 90n1, 100n5
Branstetter, Lee, 19n19, 20
Brazil, 28, 100, 101, 105, 116
Brynjolfsson, Erik, 139n11, 171, 172n11
Buiter, Willem. H., 12n2, 31n25, 59, 59n11, 118n5, 60, 72
Bulgaria, 6, 8, 16
Bush tax cuts, 34, 34n1

C
capital, xiii, xiv, 13, 14, 16, 28, 29, 31, 34, 37, 38, 47, 49, 67, 68, 72, 84, 86, 87, 90–2, 94–7, 100, 103–5, 112–16, 121–3, 125, 126,

Note: Page numbers followed by *n* denote footnotes.

126n17, 127, 128, 130, 131, 135, 137–41, 144–6, 148, 149, 151, 154, 155, 163, 164, 164n3, 166–71, 173, 176, 178–81, 183, 187
capital inflows, 121–3
Capital in the 21st Century, 47, 186, 188
capitalist sector, xiii, xv, 92, 93, 95, 131, 138, 144, 145, 170, 178, 183
capitalist surplus, xiii, xvi, 93, 95, 96, 133, 138, 141, 143–6, 171, 176, 183, 184, 186, 188
capitalist wage, 92, 93, 138, 168
causality, 43, 121–3
Chimerica, 38, 38n11
China Investment Corporation (CIC), 29–31
CIC. *See* China Investment Corporation (CIC)
Citigroup, 31, 61, 65, 66n16, 76
Clinton, Bill, xi, 18, 19, 33, 34
commodities, xv, 56, 89, 95, 97, 102, 146, 168, 169, 181
Communist Party, 2, 4, 5, 16, 30
corporate cash, xiv, 115–31
corporate income tax, xv, 12, 141–3
corporate profits, xii, xiv, 85, 128, 131, 133, 142, 170, 184, 187
Cramer, Jim, 31, 180
currency exchange regime, 20
current account, 28, 29, 37, 38, 106, 114, 115–19, 121–3, 126, 127, 146, 176
Czech Republic, 6

D
Deaton, Angus, 50
decentralization, 4, 9
Delong, Brad, 173, 173n16
democracy, xi, xii, xv, 6, 18, 18n14, 140, 163, 189
Deng Xiaoping, xv, 1, 2, 4, 5, 7–9, 22, 27, 175, 177, 182
Deng, Xiaoping, 90, 113
disguised unemployment, 90
dot-com bubble, 35, 39, 85, 147
Draghi, Mario, 73, 73n23, 79, 153
dual price system, 3, 9, 102, 109
Dutch disease, 112n27, 158n50, 161n51

E
Eastern Bloc, 6, 8, 175
economic orthodoxy, 140–1, 185
The Economist, 27n14, 29n19, 35, 148, 157, 158
Eichengreen, Barry, 81, 81n7
Elsby, Hobijn, and Şahin, 137
The End of History, 189
The End of History, 16–18, 23
euro area, 34, 34n5, 36, 38, 39, 48, 49, 52, 52n37, 61, 67, 69–74, 76–9, 79n3, 80, 80n5, 81, 83, 85, 105, 120, 122, 151, 157, 161, 189, 189n31, 449n32
European Central Bank, 28n18, 34–6, 34n4, 44n21, 45n24, 56, 61, 70–4, 73n23, 79, 124, 151, 153
European Financial Stability Facility, 71
European Union, 34, 44n21, 51, 52, 70–4, 78–80, 80n5, 83, 101, 142, 150, 189
exchange rates, 13, 23, 37, 155, 158
experimentation, 8

F
Fannie, Mae, 29, 41, 42, 62, 63, 120
Federal Open Market Committee, 35, 39, 124, 153

Federal Reserve, 33, 35, 35n7, 35n8, 36, 39, 42, 42n17, 45n22, 45n23, 56, 57, 57n5, 57n6, 59, 60, 64, 65, 67, 67n18, 67n19, 76, 85, 120, 122, 124–9, 147, 151, 154, 170
Financial Times, 31n25, 38, 59n11, 177n7, 180n12, 186n27
The Financial Times, 100n4, 118n5
Finland, 39, 41, 42
fiscal multiplier, 155–7
Five-Year Plan, 175n2
Ford, Henry, 18, 165
Ford, Martin, 172n15
foreclosure, 44, 58, 77
foreign direct investment, 13, 14, 20, 26, 27, 29, 102, 109, 110
foreign exchange reserves, xvi, 28–30, 32, 116, 120, 128, 146
Fourth Industrial Revolution, 172, 185
Foxconn, xiii, 27, 27n14, 172
Freddie, Mac, 29, 42, 62, 63, 120
Friedman, Milton, 15, 25, 108
Friedman, Tom, 53, 53n38
fu-erdai, 145
Fukuyama, Francis, xii, 14, 16, 17, 17n11, 23, 189

G
Gang of Four, 1, 2
Geithner, Timothy, 59
Germany, xiii, 12, 16, 36, 39, 43, 48, 68, 76, 79, 107, 112, 124, 129, 134, 135, 143, 161, 168
Glaeser, Ed, 25, 26
global elite, 46, 133, 183
global financial crisis, xiv, xvi, 13, 29, 51, 55–74, 82, 105, 125, 147, 148, 150, 151, 156, 166, 184, 188

global imbalances, xvi, 38, 48, 115–31
globalization, xiii, 7, 14, 46, 50, 52, 53, 129, 130, 136–41, 164, 168, 172n11, 188
Gorbachev, Mikhail, 15, 15n7
Gordon, Robert, 87, 87n23, 183
gradualism, 6–8
Great Leap Forward, 90
Great Recession, 40n13, 41, 78n2, 82, 83
Greece, 34, 39, 48, 52, 69–74, 79, 80, 123
Greenspan, Alan, 33–7, 35n9, 57n6, 85, 124, 125

H
Hansen, Alvin, 84, 84n19
hot money, 28
household debt, xvi, 40–3, 44, 45, 55, 81, 122, 151, 178
household responsibility system, 3, 8, 101
housing bubbles, xiv, xvi, 33–53, 78, 122, 157, 189n31
Huawei, 31, 31n24
Hulshof, Michiel, 24
Hungary, 15
Hu Yaobang, 2, 4, 9
hysteresis, 84

I
Iceland, 62, 68
IMF. *See* International Monetary Fund (IMF)
income inequality, xvi, 34, 41, 42, 45–51, 107, 108, 152, 178, 179
India, xii, xiii, xiv, 2, 28, 89, 96, 100, 101, 105, 116, 133, 135–7, 171, 185
innovation gap, xv, 185

interest rates, xiv, xvi, 13, 36–9, 42, 43, 56, 61, 62, 76, 84, 86, 100, 110, 115, 122–6, 128–31, 147, 148, 151, 153–5, 158, 162

International Monetary Fund (IMF), xv, 7, 8, 11, 12, 20, 38, 53, 68, 70, 72, 176n5, 82n11, 82n12, 83, 83n17, 99, 99n1, 100, 102, 103n10, 105n13, 106n15, 112, 112n26, 114, 118, 118n3, 118n6, 126n18, 133, 133n1, 145, 146, 147n31, 148n35, 149n37, 152n41, 155n47, 156, 157n49

Ireland, 36, 39, 40, 70, 72, 73, 78–80, 122, 123

iron rice bowl, 107, 110

J

Japan, xiii, 22, 29, 35, 39, 75, 82, 86, 107, 120, 133, 135, 144, 146, 152, 161, 176, 176n4

Jiang Zemin, xi, 5, 18, 18n14, 18n15, 19

K

Karabarbounis and Neiman, 136, 137, 139

Keynes, 89, 149–51, 155

Keynes, Keynesian, 15, 188

Krugman, Paul, 15n6, 35n6, 38, 85n20, 122n11, 153, 157, 158, 161n51, 184, 184n22, 184n23

Kynge, James, 24, 112

L

labor, xiii, xiv, xv, xvi, 5, 7, 8, 11, 15, 23, 25, 36, 38, 47, 49, 78, 79, 85–7, 89–97, 100, 101, 103, 104, 110, 119, 123, 130, 131, 133–41, 143–5, 148, 150, 158, 162–4, 164n3, 165–7, 167n5, 168–72, 172n11, 177, 182, 183, 183n1, 184, 185n24, 186, 186n26, 187, 188

labor productivity, xiii, 7, 8, 25, 87, 92, 100, 101, 104, 135, 137–9, 168, 170, 183

labor's share, xiii, xiv, 167–70, 182, 183, 187

labor's share, 95, 131, 133, 135–8, 148

Lardy, Nick, 19n19, 20

Lehman Brothers, 56, 63, 64, 64n15 65, 69, 75, 78, 82, 84, 151

let some people get rich first, 4

Lewis, Arthur, xiii, xvi, 7, 89–91, 94–7, 135, 138, 145, 150, 168, 169, 171, 173, 175, 179, 182

Lewis, Michael, 40, 602n13

Lewis Turning Point, 171

liberalization, 4–6, 13, 16, 19, 20, 102, 180

Li, Keqiang, 100

liquidity trap, 156, 162, 162n52

long-term interest rates, xiv, 36, 39

looting, 16, 176

M

Malthus, 95, 146

Mao Zedong, xii, 1, 2, 5, 8, 101, 176

market economy, 1, 6, 9, 14, 15, 102

Marx, Karl, 95, 183, 188

McAfee, Andrew, 139n11, 171

McCulley, Paul, 85

Mees, Heleen, 120n8, 128n23

Mexico, 28, 100, 101, 105, 116, 137

Mian, Atif, 40, 40n13

middle income trap, 177

Middle Kingdom, xv

Milanoviæ, Branko, 45, 46, 49, 49n33
Mill, John Stuart, 140, 140n12, 164
minimum wage, 145, 165, 186

N
National Bureau of Economic Research, 83
Netherlands, 48, 51, 68, 123, 142
The New York Times, 5, 17n11, 31n26, 61n12, 64, 64n15, 81n7, 82n13, 85n20, 122n11, 142n19, 178, 184n22, 184n23, 185n25
Norway, 32, 39, 41, 41n16, 42, 44, 168

O
OECD. *See* Organization for Economic Cooperation and Development (OECD)
oil-exporting countries, xiv, 30, 116, 119, 146–9, 169, 170, 184
oil prices, 31, 118, 169, 170
1 billion people market, 20, 22
Organization for Economic Cooperation and Development (OECD), 24, 24n8, 25, 38, 39, 41, 43, 44n19, 142n18, 142n20, 143n2, 143n21, 167

P
Paulson, Henry, 58n10, 59, 63–6
People's Bank of China (PBoC), 29, 81, 120, 152
perestroika, 7, 15
personal income tax, 143
Philips, 21
Piketty, Thomas, xvi, 47, 47n28, 49, 49n34, 58n29, 143n23, 143n24, 163–173, 186, 187, 188n30

Poland, 2, 6, 7, 15
Polman, Paul, xiv
populism, 50–3
poverty, xv, 5, 8, 14, 23, 45, 46, 176
Prince, Charles. O., 61, 62

R
Rajan, Raghuram, 38, 41
rating agencies, 69–71, 73
Rawski, Thomas. G., 3n5, 3n6, 7n17, 9n22, 19n19, 90n1, 100n5
Reagan, Ronald, 11–15, 136, 166, 182
reform and opening up, 1–6, 9, 27, 101, 175
renminbi, 20, 28, 104, 117–19, 178
return on capital, 47, 163, 164, 168, 187
Ricardo, David, 20n21, 86n21
Roaring aughties, 55
robots, xvi, 136, 139, 171–3, 183, 186
Roggeveen, Daan, 24
Rogoff, Kenneth, 153
Russia, 6, 14, 16, 28, 63, 75, 116, 119, 176, 188
Russian Revolution, xvi, 165

S
Saez, Emmanuel, 48, 48n30, 49, 49n35, 143n23, 188n30
SAFE. *See* State Administration of Foreign Exchange (SAFE)
Samuelson, Paul, 140
Sandridge lecture, 37, 40, 115, 118, 121, 125
savings rate, 28, 37, 105, 106, 106n15, 107–9, 111, 114, 114n28, 115, 122, 126, 127, 150, 150n40, 152

Say's Law, xiv, 149–51
Schell, 177n16, 181, 181n13
Schell, Orville, 2n2, 3n4, 23n4, 101, 181
secular stagnation, xv, 84–7, 87n22, 87n23, 185
securitization, 44, 44n2, 45n24
Shepard, Wade, 25
Shirk, Susan. L., 7n16, 8n20
shock therapy, 6–8
60 Minutes, 2, 4
Skidelsky, Robert, 38
Southern Tour, 4
South Korea, 22, 116, 119, 144
sovereign wealth funds, 30–2, 117, 126, 127, 170
Spain, 36, 39, 40, 44, 44n19, 45n24, 48, 52, 69, 70, 72, 79, 80, 122, 123, 161
Special Economic Zones, 1, 24, 26, 102, 176
State Administration of Foreign Exchange (SAFE), 28n17, 29
state-owned enterprises, 2, 4, 5, 5n11, 30, 103, 105, 107–10, 144
Stiglitz, Joseph, 7n15, 14, 53
subsistence wage, xiii, 92, 96, 119, 138, 171, 173
Sufi, Amir, 40, 40n13
Summers, Larry, xiv, xv, 30n21, 84, 149n38

T
Taylor, John, 35n8
TED-spread, 61, 65
Thatcher, Margaret, xv, 11–15, 136, 161n51, 166, 182
Tiananmen Square, xii, 1, 4, 17, 20
Tibet, 18

top 1 percent, 34, 46, 47, 49–51, 133, 134, 143, 168, 187
trade unions, 11, 13, 123, 166, 182
Troubled Asset Relief Program, 65–7

U
UK. *See* United Kingdom (UK)
unemployment rate, 35, 78, 79, 79n3, 81, 157
Unilever, 149, xiv
United Kingdom (UK), xiii, 11, 13, 15, 39, 40, 47–9, 52, 62, 68, 83, 83n16, 124, 129, 141, 143, 165
United Nations, 24, 25n9, 91n2
unlimited supplies of labor, xiii, xvi, 7, 89–97, 109, 119, 133, 145, 162, 169, 171, 175
urbanization, 24–6, 113, 144, 176
U.S. Treasuries, xiv, xvi, 29, 63, 77, 117, 120, 121, 125–9, 152

W
Wallace, Mike, 2
Wal-Mart, 22, 22n2
Washington consensus, 11, 11n1, 12, 14, 16, 142, 143, 175, 182
Wen Jiabao, 178
Whitney, Meredith, 61, 62
Wolf Martin, 38
Wolf, Martin, 186
World Bank, 7, 8, 11–14, 21, 23, 45, 53, 100
World Trade Center, xi, 50, 53
World Trade Organization, xi, xii, xvi, 18–21, 27, 50–3, 55, 56, 89, 104, 105, 110, 122, 123, 140, 168, 183, 188
World War I, xvi, 164
World War II, xvi, 165

X
Xi Jinping, xii, 178

Y
Yellen, Janet, 154

Z
Zhao Ziyang, 1, 2, 4, 9, 175
Zhu Rongji, 5
Zuckerberg, Mark, 173
Zucman, Gabriel, 16n9, 48, 48n30, 49, 49n35, 168, 169n8, 186n28, 187

GPSR Compliance

The European Union's (EU) General Product Safety Regulation (GPSR) is a set of rules that requires consumer products to be safe and our obligations to ensure this.

If you have any concerns about our products, you can contact us on

ProductSafety@springernature.com

In case Publisher is established outside the EU, the EU authorized representative is:

Springer Nature Customer Service Center GmbH
Europaplatz 3
69115 Heidelberg, Germany

www.ingramcontent.com/pod-product-compliance
Lightning Source LLC
La Vergne TN
LVHW020345260326
834688LV00045B/1539